D1416035

PUBLIC SPEAKING

SECOND EDITION

PUBLIC SPEAKING

a rhetorical perspective

JANE BLANKENSHIP

The University of Massachusetts

PRENTICE-HALL, INC., Englewood Cliffs, New Jersey

ISBN: 0-13-738906-X

Library of Congress Catalog Card No.: 72-161463

10 9 8 7 6 5 4 3 2 1

Printed in the United States of America.

Prentice-Hall International, Inc., *London*
Prentice-Hall of Australia, Pty. Ltd., *Sydney*
Prentice-Hall of Canada, Ltd., *Toronto*
Prentice-Hall of India Private Limited, *New Delhi*
Prentice-Hall of Japan, Inc., *Tokyo*

ACKNOWLEDGMENTS

The epigraph to Chapter 1 is reprinted by permission of the author, Karl R. Wallace.

The epigraph to Chapter 2 is from Bess Sondel, *The Humanity of Words* (New York: The World Publishing Co., 1958), p. 20. Reprinted by permission of the publisher.

The epigraph to Chapter 4 is from Allan Nevins, *The Gateway to History* (Lexington, Mass.: D. C. Heath and Company, 1938). Reprinted by permission of the publisher.

The epigraph to Chapter 5 is from Kenneth E. Boulding, *The Image* (Ann Arbor, Mich.: The University of Michigan Press, 1956). Reprinted by permission of the publisher.

The epigraph to Chapter 6 is from Richard Ohmann, *Shaw: The Style and the Man* (Middletown, Conn.: Wesleyan University Press, 1962), pp. xii–xiii. Reprinted by permission of the publisher.

The epigraph to Chapter 7 is from Alfred North Whitehead, *The Aims of Education and Other Essays* (New York: The Macmillan Company, 1967). Reprinted by permission of the publisher.

In speech-making, as in life,
not failure, but low aim, is crime.

WAYLAND MAXFIELD PARRISH

CONTENTS

II
PRINCIPLES AND APPLICATIONS

III
ANALYSIS AND CRITICISM

APPENDIX

PREFACE
TO THE
SECOND EDITION

To discover that anyone at all has read what one writes is a pleasure; that enough people have read it to warrant a second edition is gratifying, indeed. The second edition of *Public Speaking: A Rhetorical Perspective* is different from the first in a number of ways. The most substantial difference occurs in the two chapters on Invention; e.g., there is an expanded discussion of audience awareness and of the substance of speeches. Further, the discussion of the constituents of the rhetorical act has been expanded mainly on the very basic assumption that speeches ought to be viewed as part of a rhetorical act—an act which is made up of more than a speech text. Thus, more emphasis is placed on how the other constituents of that act help to shape the speech text and on how together they work to shape the rhetorical event.

The book still reflects the same essential rationale, hopefully better defined and supported by additional years of teaching public speaking and a lecture course, Modern Public Discourse. And, of course, it reflects the comments of those who have used the book— for that is the best test of whatever worth a text may have.

The central function of rhetorical theory is to provide an understanding of the factors contributing to free and enlightened choices by those responding to persuasion—to answer the questions: "*Why* is one speaker more effective than another? *Why* may a suggested procedure secure a desired response?" This book will, in a limited way, answer the question "Why?" Whenever possible, theory is integrated with illustrations from great speeches of the past and from speeches given in the classroom. The assumption is that the relationships between theory and skills are many and varied and that principles are useful mainly as they find practical application in speeches.

The purpose of this book is to provide the student with both principles and applications which he can use in his own speaking. Part One offers a brief discussion of communication in general and of the rhetorical act in particular. Part Two discusses each of the canons of rhetoric and considers some central ideas of both classical and modern theory which provide the student with an approach to public speaking and which will help him develop "a rhetorical perspective." And, since a beginning student will probably hear more speeches than he will give, Part Three discusses speech criticism and offers a commentary on brief samples of student speeches. Appendix A provides texts on which the student can try his own critical abilities.

The book includes collateral reading lists for additional reading by interested students. Since it is useful, even for the beginning student, to be exposed to as wide a range of materials as possible, I have included references to journals as well as books. My own students have enjoyed hearing about recent experimental studies which related to what they are studying. From time to time we have duplicated an experiment, or part of it, in the classroom. This variety of activity provides additional information with a real sense of immediacy. The more the student reflects carefully about *why* his speeches or the speeches he hears are effective or not, the more his speaking becomes a truly conscious art.

The rationale and subject matter of the book reflect a heavy debt to rhetoricians of the past who have conceived and taught a rhetoric in the tradition of humane studies. The speakers of the past who have so often eloquently pleaded "the cause of human dignity and the rights of free men" have contributed to no less an extent. Whatever part of this book is worthwhile is due to their good counsel. But, the most complete philosophical debt I owe is to Professor Karl R. Wallace, formerly a patient but demanding teacher, now, a patient but demanding colleague.

Many of my own students have participated very directly in the preparation of this book. A number of them have read it in whole or in part and have discussed it, sometimes vigorously, with me. I would especially like to thank those whose outlines and speeches are included in the text. Students have also been helpful in suggesting materials for inclusion in the text; e.g., the topoi of values on pp. 8–9 was suggested by Elizabeth Corea, now at the University of Maryland.

Other colleagues have helped. The section on attitudes and attitude change was written by Professor Vernon Cronen; the section concerning creative ideation reflects discussions with Professor Ronald F. Reid; and, the section concerning the anatomy of proof reflects discussions with Miss Nancy Mihevc. All three are at the University of Massachusetts. My thanks would not be complete without including my efficient and helpful typist, Mrs. Barbara Loveland, my production editor, Sandra Messik, and my proofreader, Joanne Gurry.

Jane Blankenship
University of Massachusetts, Amherst

PUBLIC SPEAKING

I

BASIC ASSUMPTIONS
AND
DEFINITIONS

If rhetoric teaches nothing else, she requires that her
student make up his mind, that he take decision only
after search and full inquiry, that he speak from his
convictions with all the skill he can acquire.

Karl R. Wallace

1

THE NATURE

OF

RHETORIC

Ours is a rhetorical world. We are virtually surrounded by talk; we
are talking or listening a large part of our day. We may be discussing
last weekend's football scores over coffee or debating the role of the
federal government in higher education or listening to a professor
discuss the "Tragic Vision in Contemporary Literature." The Congress may be holding open committee hearings on Vietnam, environmental pollution, and drug abuse in the United States, or spokesmen
for many nations may be meeting to discuss disarmament agreements.

How we cope with our problems through talk determines
whether or not we can fulfill our aspirations. How each man participates in this "great conversation" of trying to solve our common
problems determines, in the end, the overall quality of the human
condition in a free society. The beginning speaker would do well to
remember the words of Isocrates in the fourth century B.C.:

. . . in the other powers which we possess, we are in no respect
superior to other living creatures; nay we are inferior to many in
swiftness and in strength and in other resources; but, because there
has been implanted in us the power to persuade each other and to
make clear to each other whatever we desire, not only have we
escaped the life of wild beasts, but we have come together and
founded cities and made laws and invented arts; and, generally
speaking, there is no institution devised by man which the power
of speech has not helped us to establish. For this it is which has
laid down laws concerning things just and unjust, and things hon-
ourable and base; and if it were not for these ordinances we should
not be able to live with one another. It is by this that we confute
the bad and extol the good. Through this we educate the ignorant
and appraise the wise; for the power to speak well is taken as the
surest index of a sound understanding. . . . With this faculty we both
contend against others on matters which are open to dispute and
seek light for ourselves on things which are unknown. . . . [W]e
shall find that none of the things which are done with intelligence
take place without the help of speech, but that in all our actions
as well as in all our thoughts speech is our guide, and is most employed by those who have the most wisdom.[1]

This book is concerned mainly with one kind of speech—public
speaking, not in the sense of discussion or debate (or discontinuous
discourse), but in the sense of giving *a speech* (with continuous
discourse). The art of rhetoric has existed since the fifth century B.C.
The ancients, the eighteenth and nineteenth century theorists, and
our contemporaries have all attempted to interpret the term "rhetoric" in order to determine its proper use. Through the centuries
it has been called a synonym for bombast; sophistry; elocution;
style, especially as exemplified by the "purple passage"; the theory
of spoken and written discourse; Freshman English; "empty" words,
especially in political discourse; and recently "the study of misunderstanding and its remedies." Since there is so much confusion
about the term, let us first determine what we are studying, and
then its relation to other disciplines.

[1]Isocrates, *Antidosis*, trans. George Norlin, The Loeb Classical Library
(London: William Heinemann Ltd., 1929), pp 253–57.

a definition of rhetoric

Aristotle defined rhetoric as "the faculty of observing in any given case the available means of persuasion."[2] This definition has useful implications for today's beginning speaker. Rhetoric is, according to this definition, a *faculty*, an ability. We often hear about "the natural born speaker," but it is doubtful that such a creature exists. Skill in speechmaking usually results from a rigorous study program rather than some happy accident or native faculty. Most distinguished speakers have either systematically studied the principles of effective speechmaking, or have deduced these principles through constant practice and careful analysis of their own failures and successes. Skill in speechmaking has always been sought by young men and women working to make their ideas known.

Rhetoric is a particular kind of faculty—it is the faculty of observing in any given case the available means of persuasion. Aristotle suggests that the faculty of rhetoric is the faculty for observing. In other words, the speaker should consider the widest possible variety of materials on his topic for inclusion in his speech.

The speaker, however, does not determine the materials for his speech only according to his topic. He must also consider the specific audience and specific occasion. He surveys each speech situation to decide which materials will be most appropriate and most impressive.

Finally, the Aristotelian definition of rhetoric suggests that the speaker must have a thorough grasp of "all the available means of persuasion." A description of the means of persuasion forms the major substance of this book. The arguments, the organization, the style of the speech, and the manner of delivery are all included as means of persuasion. They help the speaker accomplish his specific purpose.

2Aristotle, *Rhetoric*, trans. W. Rhys Roberts (New York: Random House, Inc., 1954), 1355b, pp. 26–27.

the nature and scope of rhetoric

There is now much vigorous discussion over the scope of rhetoric. In this text we focus on beginning points—that is, with oral discourse and with the intentional coding of messages. Still, the beginning speaker may well want to think further about: What may the discipline of rhetoric include? Can the term "rhetorical" describe only those events in which discursive means are used? Or may nondiscursive events (such as picketing, sit-ins and boycotting) also be said to contain rhetorical elements? Shall the label "rhetorical" be applicable only to the intentional coding of messages designed to influence particular audiences? Or may sometime unintentional, yet persuasive means such as clothing, hair style, and so on, also contain rhetorical elements? Furthermore, shall only speeches be labelled "rhetorical?" Or, shall all of the symbolic efforts of man—novel, drama, painting, poetry, and so forth, be said to be rhetorical?

Rhetoric is used quite practically to direct men's thoughts and actions toward the realization of a particular course: to present a plan which will provide medical care for the aged, to encourage interest in student government organizations, to offer support to the Organization of American States. Thus, rhetoric operates as an instrument of social facilitation.

One writer on the subject of oral communication asserts that there is a twofold approach to it, the rhetorical and the evaluative. He notes: "Through a study of rhetorical principles the student learns to organize and present his thoughts according to acceptable standards of composition. Through the evaluative approach he learns to weigh carefully the validity and accuracy of his statements. He learns to talk sense, not nonsense."[3] By suggesting the rhetorical and the evaluative as two separate approaches to the study of oral communication, this writer is almost suggesting that rhetoric may teach nonsense as long as it is well-composed nonsense. He forgets that evaluation is part of the rhetorical act.

We have already emphasized the role of the speaker as *selector*.

[3]Glenn Capp, *How To Communicate Orally* (Englewood Cliffs, N.J.: Prentice-Hall, Inc., 1961), p. ix.

At each stage in the rhetorical process he selects from many alternatives: one subject out of many, one set of opinions instead of others, one structure of arguments. Implied in his choice is evaluation. Each of the speaker's statements is based on an assumption he makes about values. Consider the commitments in these statements:

1. John Marshall in 1788 stood before the Virginia Convention to urge the ratification of the new national constitution and affirmed that the underlying principles of good government were "[a] strict observance of justice and public faith, and a steady adherence to virtue."[4]

2. Daniel Webster, not quite half a century later, at the early signs of discord between North and South, stood before the Senate to plead not for "liberty first, and union afterwards" but "liberty and union, now and forever, one and inseparable."[5]

3. Clarence Darrow, speaking in 1926 on housing segregation, said: ". . . the last analysis is, what has man done?—and not what has the law done?"[6]

These statements were prompted by the necessity for confronting decisions from which speaker and audience could not turn away. Rhetoric, as the study of purposive speech about the human condition, requires intense feeling, powerful intellect, and direct, responsible judgment. The search for arguments, evaluation and decisions about which are good and which bad, and the framing of those arguments in the best possible language all share equally in the domain of rhetoric.

With what kinds of topics does the speaker concern himself? With what class of subjects is rhetoric properly concerned? Aristotle, in his *Rhetoric*, says:

Every other art can instruct or persuade about its own particular subject-matter; for instance, medicine about what is healthy and unhealthy, geometry about the properties of magnitudes, arithmetic about numbers, and the same is true of the other arts and sciences. But rhetoric we look upon as the power of observing the means of

[4]Lewis Copeland and Lawrence Lamm, eds., *The World's Great Speeches* (2nd rev. ed.; New York: Dover Publications, Inc., 1958), p. 240.

[5]*Ibid.*, p. 278.

[6]Arthur Weinberg, ed., *Attorney for the Damned* (New York: Simon and Schuster, Inc., 1957), p. 233.

persuasion on almost any subject presented to us; and that is why we say that, in its technical character, it is not concerned with any special or definite class of subjects.[7]

What are the proper topics for speeches? The examples from speeches of the past indicate that they were statements about courses of action, or evaluation of those actions, or basic assumptions underlying those courses of action. Thus, the speaker is concerned with judgments about the conduct of human affairs, judgments which enable man to adjust to his environment and, perhaps more importantly, allow him to change it.

To inquire into the substance of rhetoric, perhaps one would do well to recall why rhetorical communication happens in the first place. We have already noted that rhetoric comes into existence as a response to a situation. Not only is rhetoric situational in character, but it is also largely pragmatic. As Lloyd Bitzer has commented, rhetoric "comes into existence for the sake of something beyond itself; it functions ultimately to produce action or change in the world . . . ."[8] Thus, rhetoric may take many forms, the public speech only one among them. But whatever the form, rhetoric is advisory in nature, and so the substance of rhetorical discourse very largely consists of *topoi*, or lines of argument consistent with the giving of advice. They involve: (1) Reasons for acting; (2) Reasons for acting in a particular way; (3) Reasons evaluating the actions we have taken.

From a speech by Senator Edward Brooke to a university audience, a former student evolved the following topoi—a set of "reasons" Senator Brooke provided as a rationale for working within the system to effect political change:[9]

    I. Certain character traits are desirable. One ought to be:
       A. Actively concerned
       B. Prudent
          1. Moderate

[7]*Rhetoric*, pp. 28–36.

[8]Lloyd F. Bitzer, "The Rhetorical Situation," *Philosophy and Rhetoric*, I, No. 1 (January 1968), 3–4.

[9]Speech given by Sen. Brooke, "The Political Dynamics of Protest," at Boston University, May 19, 1968.

    2. Foresighted
    3. Reasonable
  C. Open-minded
    1. Questioning
    2. Adaptive
    3. Tolerant
  D. Industrious
  E. Candid
  F. Moral
  G. Intelligent
  H. Just
  I. Optimistic

II. A certain life style results from these traits.
  A. The pragmatic
    1. Prudent
    2. Practical
    3. Relevant
    4. Effective
    5. Progressive
    6. Adaptive
    7. Purposive, etc.
  B. The established
    1. Maintaining the status quo
    2. Obeying the law
    3. Keeping a sense of continuity
  C. The peaceful
    1. Noncoercive
    2. Nonviolent
    3. Cooperative
  D. The industrious

III. These characteristics and this life style are conducive to achieving the following goals:
  A. General goals
    1. Perpetuation of institutions as an ideal
    2. Freedom of the individual
    3. Obtainment of a sense of community
    4. Mastery of environment
    5. Security
    6. Prosperity
  B. Specific goals
    1. Eliminating of poverty
    2. Equality of the races
    3. Peace

This is not to suggest that these particular topoi underlie all speeches, but rather that the substance of rhetorical discourse is, as Karl R. Wallace has suggested, good reasons.[10] Most speakers will suggest why the audience ought to accept their view of the world, and many times they will be called upon to support their claims that their reasons are good ones. Thus, the substance of rhetorical discourse consists of reasons and support for those reasons, that is, reasons and proofs that the modes of action suggested by the speaker are "good," "valuable," and so on.

A value statement is defined as a statement which expresses either explicitly or implicitly the relative worth of an event, idea, or object, and so influences the speaker's selection of available means and ends of action. This definition points to the interesting characteristic that value statements are not just for giving information. For example, to label something as "good," "valuable," "worthwhile," "desirable," or "groovy" is to imply a quality of magnetism. One would suppose that anyone who labels something as "desirable" would tend to act preferentially toward it. Thus, values are both *revealed by and tend to influence one's choices of means and ends.*

One writer has commented that rhetoric is the "organizing and animating principle of all subject matters which have a relevant bearing on [public] decision."[11] To this extent, rhetoric is bound to all other subject matters. Whenever human affairs are directed toward a predetermined end in any area, such as ethics or politics, the situation is rhetorical. As rhetoric works toward a particular intent, as it provides a basis for public decision, ultimately it determines the very structure of men's thoughts and actions as they operate to mold the entire pattern of society. Thus, rhetoric is concerned with the principles of persuasion, and the essence of persuasion lies in the content of the subject under discussion.

Although we have stressed the persuasive intent, not all speeches are governed by it. Some speeches are designed primarily to give information: to describe a process, a place, a person, or an event; to tell about personal experiences; or to clarify concepts, materials, or ideas. In these cases, the speaker's main purpose is not to arouse his listeners to action or to change their attitudes and

[10]Karl R. Wallace, "The Substance of Rhetoric: Good Reasons," *The Quarterly Journal of Speech* Vol. XLIX, No. 3 (October 1963), 239–49.

[11]Donald C. Bryant, "Rhetoric: Its Function and Its Scope," *Quarterly Journal of Speech* Vol. XXIX, No. 4 (December 1953), 408.

opinions, but to give them new knowledge (which may eventually move them to action). But even in speeches of exposition and narration the speaker is, at a very basic level, trying to get the audience to accept him as a good source of information. The speaker wants the audience to accept the method he is describing as effective, to accept the materials of his speech as accurate. Thus, to a certain extent the persuasive intent is present by the very nature of the speech act: stimulus seeking to elicit a predetermined response.

rhetoric as participation

To let only a few lead, or only a few speak is to have too narrow a view of public speaking and of the function of men in our contemporary democratic society. Thomas Jefferson wrote in a letter to John Tyler: "No experiment can be more interesting than that we are now trying, and which we trust will end in establishing the fact, that man may be governed by reason and truth . . . ."[12] This experiment is still going on today. The speaker, in a sense, is the catalyst in this experiment. The basic difference between the rationale of liberal democracy and the rationale of totalitarian forms of government is that a democracy holds to the belief that men of good will and intelligence can, through general communication, reach understanding and agreement. A liberal democracy actively facilitates an environment in which men can function together as they work to secure the common good.

The speaker, as a participator in a liberal democracy, should not be misled by the contention that rhetoric is solely a technique, and as such has no inherent morality. It is vitally concerned with the end to which it subscribes as well as with the means to that end. Rhetoric demands responsible commitment. Central to it is the power of ideas as manifested by the conceptions, choices, and value judgments of the speaker. So the speaker needs to raise very early and very seriously these questions: "What values should I apply when choosing ends?" "What values should I choose when considering the means to those ends?"

12As cited in Adlai E. Stevenson, *Major Campaign Speeches of 1952* (New York: Random House, Inc., 1953), pp. xxx-xxxi.

There is no generally adopted code of ethics. Four central responsibilities of the speaker, however, are clear:

1. Duty of search and inquiry.
2. Allegiance to accuracy and fairness.
3. Revelation of individual motives.
4. Tolerance of dissent.[13]

In the final analysis, ethics and persuasion cannot be separated. At the basic level, man's ageless enemies must be conquered if he is to fulfill his potential for growth and development. Disease must be overcome, poverty alleviated, illiteracy wiped out. Survival must be assured in an atmosphere conducive to free, creative enterprise, rather than in the shadow of nuclear war and environmental pollution conducive only to the disintegration of human values. These goals can only be met through the vigorous and free exchange of ideas, through verbal agreements and persuasions. Ethical rhetoric thus has the potential of creating the kind of communication which helps man to be the best he can become. The responsibility of the public speaker is challenging, and the study of rhetoric is not an easy task; but it is essential to public and private decision-making.

rhetoric as identification

Too much emphasis may have been placed in the past on rhetoric as *manipulative*. Communication, or communion, is reached when the speaker and his audience find identification with one another. Persuasion is the means through which identification occurs. The task of the speaker is not to manipulate the audience, but to evoke in them "a sense of collaboration."[14]

Perhaps a useful starting point is rhetoric's chief tool, language. Kenneth Burke suggests that we begin by viewing language as symbolic action, a view that requires us to differentiate between

---

[13]Karl R. Wallace, "An Ethical Basis of Communication," *Speech Teacher*, Vol. IV, No. 1 (January 1955), 9.

[14]Hugh Duncan, *Communication and Social Order* (New York: Oxford University Press, Inc., 1968), p. 170.

motion and action, for although machines are capable of motion, only humans are capable of action.

Our approach to inanimate things is different from our approach to other human beings. We do not reason with machines, or send petitions to them, or persuade them to act; we move them physically. We switch on a light, turn an ignition key, or throw a baseball. We do this because we have some implicit understanding that men have free will and machines do not, and it is the capacity to make choices that is the essential difference between men and the machines they operate. Burke puts it succinctly. "If one cannot make a choice, one is not acting, one is being moved, like a billiard ball tapped with a cue and behaving mechanically in conformity with the resistances it encounters."[15] Thus, action is the essence of our behavior.[16] In order for us to act we must choose, and it is this ability to choose that makes us self-moving beings.

To understand fully this difference between motion and action, let us consider Patrick Henry's speech, "Liberty or Death," delivered March 23, 1775 (included in the Appendix). He suggests that, in their struggle with Great Britain, the colonists had, at one time, many alternatives, many ways of choosing to act. They could "remonstrate," "petition," "supplicate," or even "prostrate" themselves before the ministry and Parliament. But, he says, these alternatives have been exhausted. Their

> petitions have been slighted,
> remonstrances have produced additional violence and insult,
> supplications have been disregarded,

and they

> have been spurned, with contempt, from the foot of the throne.

Therefore, he suggests that only one alternative is left: "We must fight." But notice that Patrick Henry's audience retained the option of acting on two alternatives: they could accept his analysis and take up arms, or they could reject it and refuse to arm themselves. Thus, although Patrick Henry could harangue the audience, it was self-

[15]Kenneth Burke, *Rhetoric of Religion* (Boston: Beacon Press, 1961), p. 188.

[16]See Kenneth Burke, *Language as Symbolic Action* (Berkeley, Calif: University of California Press, 1966).

moving. Had he shot an arrow, it would have moved because an arrow cannot act of itself. But he could only try to persuade his audience to accept his suggestion as the best or only alternative. An arrow has no choice—it has to move. But the audience makes a decision to act.

As a result of some mental action man causes himself to do A rather than B, and because he himself makes this choice, he is responsible for its results. The purpose in making choices is to act. Since action is based on purpose, since there must be a reason for choosing A instead of B, action is not merely a means of doing, but rather a way of being. If action were only a means to an end, it would be called instrumental; because it is also the end itself, it is termed substantial.[17]

To illustrate this, again consider Patrick Henry's speech and continue our analogy of the arrow. The colonists had a reason for adopting Patrick Henry's resolution, whereas an arrow would have no reason for moving or not moving. An arrow has to move in a certain direction, at a certain rate of speed, and its course and rate are therefore said to be determined by instrumental means. On the other hand, the course of action and rate at which the colonists moved to implement Patrick Henry's resolution are called substantial. The distinction is that the arrow's motive force comes from outside itself—from the motion of the archer's wrist and arm— whereas the colonists' motive force came primarily from inside themselves. Patrick Henry apparently understood this, for he pointed to the nature of that motivating force:

> If we wish to be free—if we mean to preserve inviolate those inestimable privileges for which we have been so long contending—if we mean not basely to abandon the noble struggle in which we have been so long engaged, and which we have pledged ourselves never to abandon until the glorious object of our contest shall be obtained, we must fight!

Because man has reasons for making choices, his action is *purposive*. What moves a man to act helps shape the nature of his action; for example, according to Patrick Henry, *because the colonists*

---

[17]This treatment of Patrick Henry's speech follows, in part, the one originally proposed in Jane Blankenship, *A Sense of Style* (Belmont, Calif: Dickenson Publishing Co., 1968), pp. 14–17.

wish to remain free they must strike off the fetters of British tyranny. There would be no reason for taking up arms if they did not wish to remain free. Just as purpose shapes action, motive shapes purpose. Man has not only a reason but also a need for acting, which may be termed his *motivation*. Certain needs such as the physiological needs, safety, love, esteem and self-fulfillment are shared by all people, and as each need is fulfilled others emerge. (A fuller schematization of needs appears on pp. 156–69.) Note how Patrick Henry appealed to at least three of them here.

safety

"Ask yourselves how this gracious reception of our petition comports with those war-like preparations which cover our waters and darken our land."

"Are fleets and armies necessary to a work of love and reconciliation? Have we shown ourselves so unwilling to be reconciled, that force must be called in to win back our love? . . . These are the implements of war and subjugation."

"They are sent over to bind and rivet upon us those chains which the British ministry have been so long forging."

"Our chains are forged! Their clanking may be heard on the plains of Boston!"

esteem

"Our brethren are already in the field!"

"The battle . . . is not to the strong alone; it is to the vigilant, the active, the brave."

self-fulfillment

"Is life so dear, or peace so sweet, as to be purchased at the price of chains and slavery?"

". . . give me liberty or give me death!"

It is clear that man feels obliged to socialize his world view because he does consider, explain, and justify the reasons for his choices. Patrick Henry explains why he feels compelled to speak, though others may call him a traitor for doing so:

Should I keep back my opinions at such a time, through fear of giving offense, I should consider myself as guilty of treason toward my country, and of an act of disloyalty toward the Majesty of Heaven which I revere above all earthly kings.

Socialization is, as Marie Hochmuth Nichols suggests, an individual's appeal to his group through language.[18] Consider how Henry displays conduct that his audience probably deemed admirable. There are at least five dominant character traits manifested. Henry appears:

1. conciliatory
2. reasonable
3. understanding
4. reassuring
5. courageous

Although we cannot discuss this fully here, we can indicate some of the ways this means of identification appears to be working.

1. The opening of the speech is *conciliatory*. The debate which preceded it was heated and passionate, and Henry's audience clearly was divided. One of his tasks was to bring them together as best he could. Even though they do not all agree with him, he does not doubt their patriotism or their abilities.

2. Henry takes great care to appear *reasonable*. He tells them why he should be allowed to speak as he will; he urges that they consider the lessons of experience, and that they ask themselves the real meaning of "those war-like preparations which cover our waters and darken our land"; he asks further questions ("Are fleets and armies necessary to a work of love and reconciliation?"), letting the audience arrive at answers; he continues to question, suggesting that they have done everything they could ("petitioned," "remonstrated," "supplicated," "prostrated ourselves before the throne," "implored its interposition to arrest the tyrannical hands of the ministry and Parliament"); he posits a chain of "ifs." Only after this does he state explicitly his position that the war has already started, and that the Colonists would therefore be reacting to aggression rather than starting a war.

[18]Marie Hochmuth Nichols, *Rhetoric and Criticism* (Baton Rouge: Louisiana State University Press, 1963), pp. 82–83.

3. In this trying and inflammatory situation, Henry appears to be *understanding*. He realizes why the audience has not acted before, suggesting that it is "natural" to indulge in "the illusions of hope." He is concerned for their safety and for their esteem.

4. Henry is as *reassuring* as he can be in so tense a situation. "The battle," he suggests, "is not to the strong alone; it is to the vigilant, the active, the brave." Moreover, their fight for liberty is a "holy cause." God is on their side.

5. Even if his audience does not agree with him, there is *courage* in both his final appeal and his personal decision. He asks: "Is life so dear or peace so sweet as to be purchased at the price of chains and slavery?" Here his appeal is to man's fulfillment, not his mere existence. In any event, his personal choice is clear: "I know not what course others may take; but as for me, give me liberty or give me death!"

His interests are clearly joined with those of his audience. They all have a "responsibility" to God and country. They may all be forced into "submission"; they may all wear the chains that Great Britain has sent her armies to "bind and rivet" upon them. They would all be subject to the "next gale that sweeps from the north." Thus, they are interested in the same values and they will, largely, share the same fate.

The speaker aligns himself with what he takes to be recurrent patterns in the experience of his audience:

a. Men of debate rather than violence, they are aware that different men (of equal ability and patriotism) often see the same subject in different lights.

b. Most would acknowledge that in proportion to the magnitude of the subject ought to be the freedom of the debate.

c. Most desire peace; few will rush gleefully into the war. That, after all, is *why* the petitions, remonstrances, and the like.

He "talks their language" largely by the manner in which he conducts himself, sharing their interests in safety, esteem, and self-fulfillment, and by virtue of the fact that he and his audience have shared experiences.

This analysis of how one speaker attempted to socialize his view of the world is by no means exhaustive. You may wish to explore further the question of how Patrick Henry appealed to his particular audience.

Now let us ask where the initial motivation for any action comes from? Burke would say from the nature of man himself; that is, generically, man is a biological organism, an animal with need for property—for food and shelter. But he also uses symbols, and therein lies a trait that distinguishes him from other animals. Man not only uses symbols, he invents them.[19] As symbol-inventing, symbol-using animals, we are concerned not only with survival but with other motives as well; for example, we worry about security. We want the freedom to exist without anxiety and doubt; we worry about the quality of our survival.

As animals, we want to exist; as symbol-users, we want to exist as human beings. We attempt to overcome our generic separateness by communication, for, as Nichols puts it, "communication is compensatory to division."[20] Language promotes socialization and thereby facilitates social cohesion. Without socialization and the sense of order it brings, we would face chaos. As philosopher Suzanne Langer has observed, one "can adapt himself somehow to anything his imagination can cope with; but he cannot deal with chaos."[21]

Because we can identify with others, we are able to transcend our separateness. Our identification (explored more fully in Chapter 3) with one another or with a group does not eliminate our separateness or difference—rather, it resolves them, allowing us to be joined and separate. Each of us remains unique, yet capable of acting with others, as we seek ways of acting together. Identification and communication demand sharing, participation by both speaker and audience.

Thus, language has its origin in the very essence of human behavior. It is a species of action that depends on choice, purpose, and motive, and that translates man's biological needs into symbols which form an orientation in which we can function as human beings. Socialization provides this orientation. Through language and persuasion, we are able to resolve the generic differences among us, and to cooperate in promoting "the good life."[22]

[19]Burke, *Rhetoric of Religion*, p. 42n.

[20]Nichols, *Rhetoric and Criticism*, p. 82.

[21]Suzanne K. Langer, *Philosophy in a New Key* (Cambridge, Mass.: Harvard University Press, 1942), p. 241.

[22]Nichols, *Rhetoric and Criticism*, p. 91.

the relationship of rhetoric
to other subjects

Rhetoric is inextricably bound to other disciplines, as indeed they are to it. Let us explore these relationships a bit more thoroughly.[23]

HISTORY

The study of history attempts to recover the past, and to make the present more intelligible through interpretation of the past. Since a speech grows out of a need, it occurs in time (referring in its largest sense to time in the life of problems). The speaker must understand the background relevant to the speech. He may discuss either the chronological life of a problem, its history, or one aspect of its history. Furthermore, the time at which a speech occurs may be called the environment of that speech, the environment of a problem or a solution. Time may be reflected in the choice of topic, materials included, values expressed, and policies advocated.

Speakers have been catalysts in history. The United States without Samuel Adams, James Otis, Patrick Henry, Henry Clay, John C. Calhoun, Daniel Webster, the abolitionist orators, and Abraham Lincoln would be much different, as would Britain without Sir Winston Churchill, William Pitt, and Edmund Burke. It is hard to envision Greece without Demosthenes or Rome without Cicero. All these men, speaking out in their times, have helped to shape the destinies of their nations. As Landor has Pericles say:

Show me how great projects were executed, great advantages gained, and great calamities averted. Show me the generals and the statesmen who stood foremost, that I may bend to them in reverence; tell me

23The author is heavily indebted to Professor Karl R. Wallace for this treatment of the relationship between rhetoric and other disciplines.

their names, that I may repeat them to my children . . . place History
on her rightful throne, and, at the sides of her, Eloquence and war.[24]

The impact of Churchill, speaking to the House of Commons,
and indeed to all of Great Britain, in the "gathering storm" of
World War II, cannot be overemphasized. Recall his words:

> The whole fury and might of the enemy must very soon be turned
> upon us. Hitler knows he will have to break us in this island or lose
> the war.
> If we can stand up to him all Europe may be freed and the life
> of the world may move forward into broad sunlit uplands; but if we
> fail, the whole world, including the United States and all that we
> have known and cared for, will sink into the abyss of a new dark
> age made more sinister and perhaps more prolonged by the lights
> of a perverted science.
> Let us therefore brace ourselves to our duty and so bear ourselves
> that if the British Commonwealth and Empire last for a thousand
> years, men will say "This was their finest hour."[25]

POLITICAL SCIENCE

The end of political science is to understand political ways of
life and the processes which provide effective political power. The
speaker on a political subject needs at least a basic knowledge of
political behavior and the ways of influencing it. To influence, he
must possess some understanding of the relations among mass attitudes, communications, political institutions, and formation of public policy.

The speaker may be a politician, appealing directly via television or face-to-face with an audience. Both persons in office and
those seeking office manifest concern about effective communication.

The political scientist can often use the tools of audience
analysis developed by rhetorical theorists. He can gain insight into
specific strategies and the effects of those strategies on different kinds
of audiences. Lasswell, for example, has pointed out that "one of the

---

[24]Sidney Colvin, ed., *Selections from the Writings of Walter Savage Landor*
(London: Macmillan & Co. Ltd., 1882), p. 277.

[25]Copeland and Lamm, *The World's Great Speeches*, p. 446.

principal problems of political science is the study of the factors making for the restriction or diffusion of political doctrine and formulas. . . ."[26] Political scientists, Leiserson says, should not overlook "the value of communications studies for their own work in political-party and pressure-group publicity, communications between representatives and constituents in policy-making, administrative public relations and . . . revolutionary and war propaganda."[27] In a still larger sense, Godkin has pointed out that in the United States, England, and France, "the work of bringing the popular will to bear in filling the offices of government, and in performing any act of government . . . needs almost constant attention."[28] Political processes in a democratic society are carried out by rhetorical means.

PSYCHOLOGY AND
PSYCHOLINGUISTICS

The intention of psychology is largely to understand sensory and motor experience in their physiological and neurological setting in the human organism. Thus it shares with rhetoric a need for knowledge of such basic mechanisms as those involved in organically-centered motivations and desires and those entailed in emotion; knowledge of such compensatory mechanisms as rationalization and identification; knowledge of the character of perception, belief, motivation, conviction, opinion, and attitude; and knowledge of the conditions of learning, retention, recall, and so on.

The discipline of psycholinguistics is concerned with messages and the characteristics of the people who send and receive them. It deals, in short, with the processes of encoding and decoding as they relate the states of communicators to the states of messages. Both psycholinguistics and rhetoric are concerned with human language and verbal behavior. They are therefore concerned

[26]Harold D. Lasswell, Nathan Leites, *et al.*, *Language of Politics* (New York: G.W. Stewart, 1949), p. 14.

[27]Avery Leiserson, "Problems of Methodology in Political Research," *Political Science Quarterly* (December 1953), 576.

[28]E.L. Godkin, *Problems of Modern Democracy* (New York: Charles Scribner's Sons, 1898), p. 287.

with the nature and function of language, and with various approaches to language such as linguistics, learning theory, and information theory.

SOCIOLOGY AND
SOCIAL PSYCHOLOGY

Sociology attempts to understand the behavior patterns of large groups, while social psychology pertains to the behavior of small groups and the interaction of the group and the individual. They share with rhetoric the need for knowledge of the institutional character of audiences, institutional motivations, and values; knowledge of the ways in which the individual is affected by the presence of others; and a concern with social interaction and influence, group structure, role theories, decision-making, and so on.

The interest of a sociologist such as Hugh Duncan in communication and social order, in the ways symbols arise and come to work in society, has provided stimulating insights for those interested in communication and human behavior, whatever their disciplinary home may be.[29]

PHILOSOPHY

The journal *Philosophy and Rhetoric* is an auspicious contemporary sign of the relationship between these two disciplines. That relationship is very old and very close. We need only list a few of the philosophers who have written treatises on rhetoric: Plato devoted not one but several of his works to it, Aristotle wrote perhaps the soundest rhetoric ever conceived, and the list continues through St. Augustine to the present day. The whole of the educational system in ancient Greece was built around the study of Politics-Ethics-Rhetoric. In the medieval trivium plan of education, it was Rhetoric-Logic-Grammar.

There is an especially close relationship between rhetoric and

---

[29]Hugh Duncan, *Symbols in Society* (New York: Oxford University Press, Inc., 1968), and *Communication and Social Order, op. cit.*

two branches of philosophy, ethics and logic. The end of ethics is to discover ways of evaluating conduct on a scale labeled good–bad, to provide individuals with methods of making acceptable choices among values. The speaker's selection of topics and arguments reveals his character. On the other hand, values are animated and disseminated by the speaker.

We have mentioned that the chief tool of rhetoric is logical proof. In turn, rhetoric offers a practical method for utilizing the forms of logic. Both studies share a common vocabulary (argument, probability, validity, induction, premise, and so on). Moreover, philosophers such as Chaim Perelman and logicians such as Stephen Toulmin have contributed recently to argumentation theory. Philosophers and rhetoricians also share an interest in language. The work of J.L. Austin, P.F. Strawson, and John Searle with kinds of speech acts has been a particularly fruitful line of inquiry.[30] Others have asked such questions as: How do words relate to things? What is the difference between a string of meaningless words and a meaningful one? How is it possible for a speaker to emit sounds that mean something? How do they come to mean something to a listener?

FINE ARTS

One may secure a deeper appreciation of the art of public speaking when it is seen as one of many arts. The artist brings into being an object which stimulates others to respond. The relation of rhetoric to literature especially needs to be mentioned. The speech may be literature if the language and form have lasting value: (1) The speeches within a piece of literature, e.g., the famous "Friends, Romans, countrymen" speech in Julius Caesar; (2) The speeches within a history, e.g., Pericles' oration for the dead Athenian soldiers as recorded by Thucydides; (3) The speech as a speech, e.g., Cicero is included in studies of Latin literature, and Edmund Burke in many studies of English literature. Many of Emerson's

[30]J.L. Austin, *How to Do Things With Words* (Oxford: Oxford University Press, 1962); P.F. Strawson, "Intention and Convention in Speech Acts," *Philosophical Review*, Vol. IV, No. 408 (October 1964), 439–460; John R. Searle, *Speech Acts: An Essay in the Philosophy of Language* (Cambridge: Cambridge University Press, 1969).

"essays" were speeches delivered orally before they were printed. Faulkner's "Nobel Prize Acceptance Speech" is included in numerous volumes of collected essays. Not long ago, Winston Churchill was awarded a Nobel Prize for Literature, in part for material that first appeared as speeches.

A number of writers have differentiated between rhetoric and poetic in terms of the ends toward which they are directed. Ong says, for example: "Works of rhetoric have their finality only in terms of that action toward which they are directed."[31] Poetic, on the other hand, "produces works ordered to contemplation and to no other direct end. . . . Such works are produced simply to be enjoyed by the one contemplating them."[32] Often, however, pieces of literature are rhetorical or contain rhetorical aspects. Novels and plays serve not only as articulators of ideas and emotions, but often urge sociopolitical action. For examples, turn to some of the plays of George Bernard Shaw, the "agitprop" plays of the thirties by Clifford Odets and others, and certain plays of Arthur Miller or of the contemporary Black playwright, Leroi Jones.

Another point of contact between rhetoric and poetic lies in one of the functions of those who criticize either or both. Oscar Brockett has put the matter concisely: "Every piece of criticism is an implied argument for the validity of the questions raised and of the evidence adduced just as much as it is for the answers reached, and if the reader doubts either the questions or the evidence he usually finds the answers unacceptable."[33] Thus, the critic often finds himself in the role of the persuader.

summary

As students of rhetoric, we are examining what people say when they want to have an effect upon others. The key word is effect, for speech is purposive. It is a response to needs which have

[31]Walter J. Ong, "The Province of Rhetoric and Poetic," in *The Province of Rhetoric*, ed. Joseph Schwartz and John A. Rycenga (New York: The Ronald Press Company, 1965), p. 50.

[32]*Ibid.*

[33]Oscar G. Brockett, "Poetry as Instrument," in Donald C. Bryant, ed., *Rhetoric and Poetic* (Iowa City: University of Iowa Press, 1965), p. 15.

grown out of a time, a place, and a subject. Men give speeches when they are trying to decide whether to act, when to act, how to act, and when they are evaluating actions. The conversation Adlai Stevenson records with Albert Schweitzer points to the main task for speakers:

> . . . he told me that he considered this the most dangerous period in history. I said, "In contemporary history?" "No," he said, "in all human history." "Why?" "Because," he said, "heretofore nature has controlled man in the last analysis, but now man has learned to control elemental forces of nature—before he has learned to control himself."[34]

As communication facilitates social control, it makes adjustment and conciliation possible.

rhetorical exercises

1. Give a five minute informative speech in which you describe a process, place, person, or event; or give a five minute speech about one of the related fields of rhetoric.

2. Nichols points to the essential confusion concerning the meaning of the term "rhetoric" when she contrasts two comments concerning Lincoln. Parrington remarks: "Matter he judged to be of greater significance than manner. Few men who have risen to enduring eloquence have been so little indebted to rhetoric. Very likely his plainness of style was the result of deliberate restraint, in keeping with the simplicity of his nature." Basler, on the other hand, writes: "It would be difficult to find in all history a precise instance in which rhetoric played a more important role in human destiny than it did in Lincoln's speeches of 1858."[35] Parrington uses the word "rhetoric" to mean style. Basler uses it to mean much more. Note the various ways in which the word "rhetoric" is used by contemporary writers. How many different uses could you find?

[34]Adlai E. Stevenson, *Putting First Things First* (New York: Random House, Inc., 1960), p. 29.

[35]Nichols, *Rhetoric and Criticism*, p. 69.

3. Discuss the place of rhetoric in our contemporary society. Can you find direct support for the statement that ours is a rhetorical world?

4. Think of the various codes of ethics of many professions. Suggest a code of ethics for a public speaker. Discuss your code with other members of the class.

collateral readings

Arnold, Carroll C., "Oral Rhetoric, Rhetoric, and Literature," *Philosophy and Rhetoric*, Vol. I No. 4 (Fall 1968), 191–210.

Auer, J. Jeffrey, ed., *The Rhetoric of Our Times*. New York: Appleton-Century-Crofts, 1969. See especially Leland M. Griffin, "The Rhetorical Structure of the 'New Left' Movement"; Parke Burgess, "The Rhetoric of Black Power: A Moral Demand?"; Franklyn S. Haiman, "The Rhetoric of the Streets: Some Legal and Ethical Considerations"; and Barnet Baskerville, "The Cross and the Flag: Evangelists of the Far Right."

Burke, Kenneth, *The Philosophy of Literary Form*. Baton Rouge: Louisiana State University Press, 1941. See especially "The Rhetoric of Hitler's 'Battle.'"

Eubanks, Ralph T., and Virgil L. Baker, "Toward an Axiology of Rhetoric," *Quarterly Journal of Speech*, Vol. xlviii, No. 2 (April 1962), 157–68.

Haiman, Franklyn S., *Freedom of Speech: Issues and Cases*. New York: Random House, Inc., 1965.

Johannesen, Richard, ed., *Ethics and Persuasion*. New York: Random House, Inc., 1967.

Lomas, Charles, *The Agitator in American Society*. Englewood Cliffs, N.J.: Prentice-Hall, Inc., 1968.

Nichols, Marie Hochmuth, *Rhetoric and Criticism*. Baton Rouge: Louisiana State University Press, 1963. See especially "Rhetoric and Public Address as Humane Study."

O'Neil, Robert, *Free Speech: Responsible Communication Under Law*. Indianapolis: The Bobbs-Merrill Co., Inc., 1966.

*We are born into an environment of words just as
surely as we are born into an environment of weather.*

Bess Sondel

2

THE NATURE
OF
THE RHETORICAL ACT

"To understand is to be affected by." When one person communicates with another, he is attempting to share information, an opinion, a "feeling," because communication means sharing. This implies that the speaker has something to share, to say; that he knows how to make it clear to the listener; that he can say it effectively enough to gain, at the very least, the listener's attention and perhaps even assent; and that the listener is a cooperative agent in the communicative act. If there is no sharing, then the speaker may be addressing himself inwardly but he is not participating in *public dialogue*. Thus, communication is active, requiring participation by all who would engage in a truly communicative event.

The person who participates in dialogue as speaker and listener is seeking to understand a concept, a value, another person, a group, and so on. In taking this step toward understanding he is to some extent acknowledging his willingness to be "affected by" what he learns. He may not undergo an opinion change, but he is a "new" person by virtue of the communicative event—he has new information at his disposal, he has been exposed to a different perspective, or he has had his own value system reinforced. As Heraclitus observed centuries ago, no man can step into the same river twice, so a man leaves each communicative event somehow different from when he entered it.

The communicative man views the world as being "in process" —that is, he views events and their relationships as dynamic, constantly changing. Such a "process view of the world" perceives all the ingredients of a communicative act as interacting, each affecting all the others. The speaker-listener is thus a participant in the very *dynamics* of change.

When individuals are unable to communicate with each other, and groups are unable to communicate with other groups, frustration is apparent, as in angry talk of a "generation gap," a "credibility gap," or a "trust bust" between political leaders and the general public. Perhaps nowhere is the lack of communication, the sense of alienation, more dramatically apparent than in our ghettos and rural slum areas. The alternative behavior patterns there often appear to be looting and burning or sullen silence. In either case, there is little dialogue.

As sociologist Hugh Duncan suggests, voices are everywhere wanting "to be heard, *and to be heard in dialogue.*"[1] If they are not heard, the frustrations that can only continue to mount will be heard either in dialogue or destruction. There is a double danger for communities that do not participate in verbal sharing. Duncan again phrases the matter succinctly: "When our world falls apart we cannot communicate because we do not know how to communicate."[2]

Because we live in a liberal democracy as free men making free choices, the public speaker contributes to the number of decisions that society is capable of making, and to the quality of those decisions. His is a difficult task. As anthropologist Alfred Smith has suggested, at "the very least, all communication is between sub-

[1] Hugh Duncan, *Symbols in Society* (New York: Oxford University Press, 1968), p. 248.
[2] *Ibid.*, p. 160.

cultures. It crosses the borders between different traditions, between different systems of artifacts and mentifacts."[3] Professor Smith illustrates: "When I talk with women I talk with people of a different sub-culture. When I talk with teen-agers, with nonanthropologists, with Black Americans—just as when I talk with Chinese in Singapore—I am engaged in inter-cultural communication. The ways of one group are different from the ways of another group—sometimes more different and sometimes less. But even small differences can make all the difference in the world."[4] That is why he observes: "*Inter-cultural* communication is more the rule than the exception."[5]

The study of communication is in large measure the study of identification, for in identification lies "the source of co-operation."[6] It is identification that permits us to retain our unique identity and yet understand others. Kenneth Burke has explained this concept: "A is not identical with his colleague, B. But insofar as their interests are joined, A is *identified* with B. Or he may *identify himself* with B even when their interests are not joined, if he assumes that they are, or is persuaded to believe so. . . . In being identified with B, A is 'substantially one' with a person other than himself. Yet at the same time he remains unique, an individual locus of motives. Thus, he is both joined and separate, at once a distinct substance and con-substantial with another."[7]

The mass media have made the possibilities for varying levels and directions of identification far-reaching and complex. When we switch on a television set, we "have found a new self, a *public* role, far greater than the self limited to family, neighborhood, workshop, or classroom."[8] We now "participate" in wars, riots, the plight of the Biafrans, and ghetto life. We have the potential to understand and thereby be "affected by" a far greater portion of our world than ever before; identification thus becomes more complex and, at the

---

[3]Alfred G. Smith, "Communication and Inter-Cultural Conflict," in *Perspectives on Communication*, eds. Carl E. Larson and Frank E.X. Dance (Milwaukee: Speech Communication Center, University of Wisconsin, 1968), p. 166.

[4]*Ibid.*, p. 167.

[5]*Ibid.* Italics added.

[6]W.C. Blum, cited in Kenneth Burke, *The Rhetoric of Motives* (Englewood Cliffs, N.J.: Prentice-Hall, Inc., 1950), p. xiv.

[7]Burke, *The Rhetoric of Motives*, pp. 20–21.

[8]Duncan, *Symbols in Society*, p. 237.

same time, more necessary. It is through communication that we seek identification.

As students of public speaking, you are about to explore not only one of the most essential but also one of the oldest studies in the history of Western education. Since about 450 B.C. in Sicily, when Corax wrote the first known treatise on rhetoric, every generation has devoted much time and effort to exploring the theory and the practice of public speaking. Writers on rhetoric include Plato, Isocrates, Aristotle, Cicero, Quintilian, St. Augustine, and Francis Bacon, as well as many distinguished contemporary figures. Studies indicate that we currently spend approximately 60 to 70 percent of our waking time in talking or listening.

In this chapter, rather than review the tradition of rhetoric and public speaking, we shall consider two questions: (1) What does it mean to say we are "communicating" with one another? and (2) What are the elements of the rhetorical situation?

the process of communication

The word "communication" comes from the Latin *communis* —common. When we communicate with someone we are attempting to share information, ideas, or attitudes. Communication is the process of sending and receiving ideas by means of verbal symbols. Communication is viewed here as a process through which human beings relate to each other. In class you may well want to discuss nonverbal communication in its various and rich forms, but we will restrict our discussion in this text to *speech communication*, that is to the process of sending and receiving ideas largely by means of verbal symbols.

The basic pattern of communication is stimulus-response:

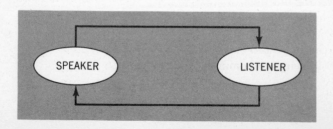

The simplicity of this diagram is deceptive. Whenever there is more than one listener, members of the audience tend to control their reactions according to those of others in the situation. Thus the diagram must include not only interstimulation between speaker and listener, but also the additional interstimulation among other listeners.

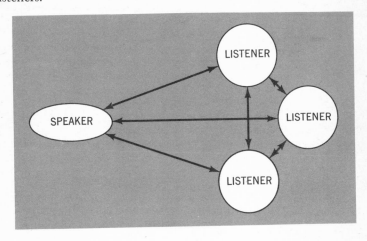

This return process can be termed *feedback*. Feedback tells us how our message is being interpreted. The hearer may say, "That's right, I agree." He may frown, look puzzled, smile, look as if he were losing interest, or nod in agreement. As the speaker is speaking, he also listens to the sound of his own voice and to what he is saying. He himself may say, "What I meant to say was . . . ," in which case he is responding to his own message. James A. Winans tells the story of nineteenth century lawyer Rufus Choate, who reiterated the arguments and pleas in one of his jury addresses for hours after eleven men were won, until he saw the frowning face of the twelfth juror relax in sympathy. He comments: "Many a passage of good oratorical prose can be turned into a dialogue by writing out the questions and objections that lie plainly between the lines. The . . . speaker can do no better for himself than to fix firmly in mind that *a speech is a dialogue* and emphasize constantly the part of the audience, anticipating and watching for its response."[9]

Viewing the communicative event in more detail, we see that it

[9] James A. Winans, *Speech-Making* (New York: Appleton-Century-Crofts, 1938), pp. 13–14.

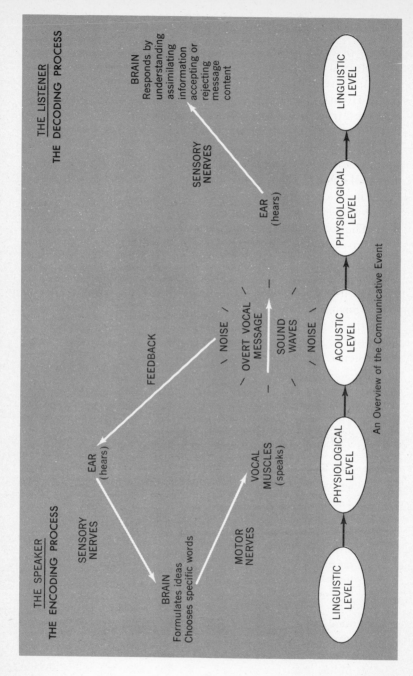

An Overview of the Communicative Event

THE SPEAKER
THE ENCODING PROCESS

THE LISTENER
THE DECODING PROCESS

SENSORY NERVES

BRAIN
Formulates ideas
Chooses specific words

MOTOR NERVES

EAR (hears)

VOCAL MUSCLES (speaks)

FEEDBACK

NOISE

OVERT VOCAL MESSAGE

SOUND WAVES

NOISE

EAR (hears)

SENSORY NERVES

BRAIN
Responds by understanding assimilating information accepting or rejecting message content

LINGUISTIC LEVEL

PHYSIOLOGICAL LEVEL

ACOUSTIC LEVEL

PHYSIOLOGICAL LEVEL

LINGUISTIC LEVEL

consists of three different levels: (1) the linguistic level; (2) the physiological level: and (3) the acoustic level. (See page 32.) At the linguistic level the speaker chooses to express one of the ideas in his mind. He makes specific language choices and "says" them aloud. Suppose Mr. Z is walking down the street and sees a friend. He could mention the weather, talk about a committee meeting they had both attended the evening before, or mention some news item he just heard or the baseball scores he read in the morning paper. From all available subjects, he chooses the weather. He could say, "Isn't it a beautiful day?" or "Nice weather we're having" or select one of a dozen other ways of saying essentially the same thing.

The saying aloud, the physiological level of speech, is a special problem in itself. When we speak, sound waves are actually the *primary message*. This primary message conveys information on a variety of levels. It gives the listener words to decode, emphasizing some words and not others. It presents words in a pattern of timing and intonation which helps to communicate the final meaning. Even the quality of voice—loud, soft, rasping, light, deep, shrill, high—carries information about the speaker and what he is saying. The listener hears the sounds, arrives at a meaning, and responds in some way to what has been said. If there is no response at all, there has been no communication.

All the steps in the communicative process must be taken with a relatively high degree of efficiency if communication is to be successful. Communication can fail at any one of many points:

1. The idea may be "fuzzy"; that is, the speaker may not have adequate, clear information.
2. The message may not be expressed in accurate, effective, transmittable words.
3. Noise (any interference with transmission) may obscure all, most, or some of the message, so that the speaker's message may not be the one received by the decoder. The speaker may speak too softly to be heard. Someone in the audience may cough. A plane may pass overhead. Noise may also be thought of in a nonmechanical sense. It can be any type of distortion by the speaker, such as poor word choice or excessive "slanting" of materials. The message may be heard accurately, but may not mean the same thing to the listener as to the speaker.
4. At the receiver's end, noise can be misinterpretation resulting from the listener's biases and emotions, or his lack of information.

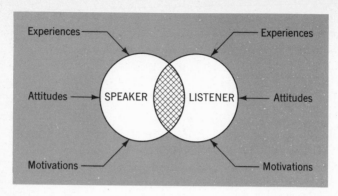

The circles represent the accumulated experiences, emotions, and motivations of two people trying to communicate. The source (speaker) can encode and the destination (listener) can decode *only* in terms of his experience. If we have never learned any German we can neither encode nor decode in that language. If a South African tribesman has neither seen nor heard of television, he can only decode the sight of a television set in terms of whatever experience he has had. If the circles do not meet, if there is no common experience, then communication is impossible. If the circles have only a small area in common, then it will be very difficult for the speaker to convey his intended meaning to the audience.

the rhetorical event

Now let us view the rhetorical act by considering the elements of the communicative situation and discussing eight of them: speaker, audience, time, place, purpose, content, style, and delivery.[10]

THE SPEAKER

In every oral communication, from the simple "Let's go get a cup of coffee" to a complex speech before the General Assembly of

[10]This treatment follows one suggested by Marie Hochmuth Nichols, "The Criticism of Rhetoric," in *A History and Criticism of American Public Address*, ed. Marie K. Hochmuth (New York: Longmans, Green & Co., Inc., 1955), Vol. III, pp. 1–23.

the United Nations, someone, some "I," is doing the speaking. He brings to the speech, as we have already seen, the sum total of his environment; he has a certain character and personality, and a certain image of the world. As Boulding explains, the individual "locates" himself in space, in time, in a field of personal relations, in a world of how things operate, and "in the midst of a world of subtle intimations and emotions."[11] It is largely this image of the world and his place in it that governs the individual's behavior. Thus, the speaker's behavior depends to a large extent on this image built up as a result of all his past experience.

In the most elementary way, the audience may or may not "know" the speaker and his image of the world. The ramifications of this apparently simple statement are manifold. For example, the 1952 campaign for the presidency of the United States was waged by a relatively unknown candidate (Adlai E. Stevenson) against a "household word" (Dwight D. Eisenhower). Because Stevenson was practically unknown to the American public, his initial problem was not to get the people to agree with him, but rather to get them to turn on the radio or television to *listen* to him.

A speaker may be known in a variety of ways; that is, his *ethos* may vary among listeners in his audience. When former Soviet Premier Khrushchev spoke to the United Nations, the ways in which he was known, the ways he was listened to because of his identity, were diverse. Each one of you may be known in a different way, hence listened to in a different way, by each person in your audience.

When Daniel Webster spoke, he was called, not altogether admiringly, the "Great Expounder." One group knew him as the "great champion of the Constitution" whose views were of "the most enlarged and liberal description," derived from feelings "of the purest patriotism." To another he was a "cordial and undeviating hater of democracy," the "champion of localities," whose views were "the opposite extreme of a liberal" and were lacking in "ardor and sympathy."[12] Some knew him as a mixture of the two descriptions, and some probably moved from one view to the other as issues and times changed.

[11]Kenneth Boulding, *The Image* (Ann Arbor: University of Michigan Press, 1968), p. 5.

[12]Wilbur Samuel Howell and Hoyt Hopewell Hudson, "Daniel Webster," in *A History and Criticism of American Public Address*, ed. William Norwood Brigance (New York: McGraw-Hill Book Company, 1943), Vol. II, pp. 665–733.

There are two ways in which a speaker may make himself known. The first is what he brings with him to the speech: his character, personality, reputation, image, ethos, and charisma (or lack of it). The second is what he says in the speech: the topics he chooses to discuss, the evidence he offers to support his point of view, the lines of argument he takes, and the values he expresses—how he views the great concerns of the day. The first way may be called by a convenient label, *extrinsic ethos*; the second may be called *intrinsic ethos*. Ethos may be defined as the attitude toward or perception of the speaker held at any given time by the audience. Ethos is not static; it is subject to change as a result of the listeners' experiences with a speaker. In fact, a speaker's ethos may even change during the course of a single rhetorical event.

Although we have been talking of *a* speaker, the actual source of a message is not always a single person. It may be a group, an organization, a government agency, or even a country. The press secretary to a President, for example, *represents* the President. What the secretary says or writes is presumed to be the view of the President, and not necessarily his own. The U.S. representative at the United Nations presumably represents the policies of his government. Obviously, when his personal views differ from the stated position of the message source (in this instance government policy), then a crisis of sorts arises. Still, the question of ethos or *source credibility* remains a primary concern of the speaker. The dimensions of ethos are discussed at length on pp. 140–41.

The message source and/or speaker faces a series of choices. Primarily he is a selector. He selects:

1. A reason for speaking; that is, his specific purpose.
2. The parts of his resources, such as materials, ideas, and meanings, which serve his purpose in a speech of any given length.
3. The most persuasive way to compose and arrange the patterns of his ideas.
4. The details, the means of supporting his ideas, and the ways of polishing them for final presentation.

To a great extent, the speaker's selections are related to his speculations about his audience—how they view him, what they know, what their attitudes are about his topic.

Speakers themselves respond differently to different topics, audiences, or occasions. They are not simply "the same man" on all occasions; in addition, sometimes the speaker wants to project a different image of himself. Often his natural tendency to respond differently to different occasions and his deliberately planned change of image combine. Note how these two dynamics work in three somewhat different Franklin D. Roosevelts talking to three somewhat different audiences.[13] First, he is humorous and satirical in an avowedly political speech:

> These Republican leaders have not been content with attacks on me or on my wife or on my sons. No, not content with that they now include my little dog Fala. [laughter, applause] Well, of course, I don't resent attacks and my family don't resent attacks. But Fala does resent them. [laughter, applause] You know, you know Fala's Scotch [laughter] and being a Scottie as soon as he learned that the Republican fiction writers—in Congress and out— had concocted a story that I'd left him behind on an Aleutian island and had sent a destroyer back to find him at a cost to the taxpayers of two or three or eight or twenty million dollars—his Scotch soul was furious. [laughter, applause] He has not been the same dog since. [laughter] I am accustomed to hearing malicious falsehoods about myself—such as that old worm-eaten chestnut that I have represented myself as indispensable. But I think I have a right to resent—to object—to libelous statements about my dog.

Second, he is solemn, firm, and formal, representing the whole nation to the world:

> It will be recorded that the distance of Hawaii from Japan makes it obvious that the attack was deliberately planned many days or even weeks ago. During the intervening time the Japanese government had deliberately sought to deceive the United States by false statements and expressions of hope for continued peace.
>
> The attack yesterday on the Hawaiian Islands has caused severe damage to American naval and military forces. Very many American lives have been lost. In addition American ships have been reported torpedoed on the high seas between San Francisco and Honolulu.
>
> Yesterday the Japanese government also launched an attack against Malaya.

13Transcribed from F.D.R. Speaks: Authorized Edition of Speeches, 1933–1944, "The Teamster's Union Address," "War Message," "Fireside Chat." Washington Records, 2243.

Last night Japanese forces attacked Hong Kong.
Last night Japanese forces attacked Guam.
Last night Japanese forces attacked the Philippine Islands.
Last night the Japanese attacked Wake Island.
This morning the Japanese attacked Midway Island.

Japan has, therefore, undertaken a surprise offensive extending throughout the Pacific area. The facts of yesterday speak for themselves. The people of the United States have already formed their opinions and well understand the implications to the very life and safety of our nation.

Last, he is a somewhat more colloquial speaker, but nevertheless the President:

My fellow Americans, over a year and a half ago I said this to the Congress: "The militarists in Berlin, Rome, Tokyo started this war but the massed angered forces of common humanity will finish it." Today that prophecy is in the process of being fulfilled. The massed angered forces of common humanity are on the march. They're going forward from the Russian front, in the vast Pacific area, and in through Europe—converging upon their ultimate objectives, Berlin and Tokyo. I think the first crack in the Axis has come. The criminal, corrupt Fascist regime in Italy is going to pieces.

THE AUDIENCE

Listening is not a passive activity. Even the most relaxed and effortless sort of listening, for example, listening to music or light after dinner talk involves doing something. Even in the formal public speaking situation it is incorrect to say that a speaker "gives" a speech to an audience. The speaker's message is heard and responded to in the context of the audience's own perceptual screen of "the way things are and ought to be." The audience does not merely "soak up" what the speaker says; his ideas, very generally, depend on the audience's reinventing the communication for itself. Thus, they too are involved in the process of generating or regenerating themselves, their beliefs, or their action stances. Communication is thus viewed as a dynamic process of interactions between speakers, messages, audiences and goals.

What each person does as a listener grows out of the same

habits, values, beliefs, and motives that serve as references for his behavior in all other settings. The implication of this point is clear —regardless of what the speaker actually *says*, the auditor interprets an incoming message within the framework of his prior experiences. The result of these experiences may be called the auditor's image of the world,[14] upon which all behavior depends. Thus, the speaker has to be concerned not only with his own view of things, but also with the varying views of his audience; he has to analyze his audience. If he fails at this task, his message has very little chance of success.

On every occasion, the *particular* audience present has an already established system of values which conditions the way in which listening occurs, or whether or not it does occur. Value systems tend to differ with educational level, age, sex, economic and social group, political heritage, special interests, and ambitions. Moreover, these values are not random, but arranged in a hierarchy. Philosopher Chaim Perelman comments: ". . . it is not so much the values to which they adhere as the manner in which they arrange the values in a hierarchy, which makes it possible to describe a particular audience."[15]

Sometimes speakers address more than one "audience" at a time, which makes their task especially difficult. Consider the example of Richard Nixon's "Veto Message."[16] Since he begins "My fellow Americans," and delivered the speech over the national television, one would observe that the audience was "the American public." But there are other "publics" as well; for example:

1. Breadwinners—"From 1960 to 1970 the cost of living went up 25 percent in this country. Now for the average family of four in America that meant an increase of 2400 dollars a year in the items that go into your cost of living, your grocery bill, your housing, your transportation, your medical costs."

2. Concerned parents—"You can be sure that no school will be closed, no school child will be denied an education. . . ."

3. Congressmen, Senators and "the education lobby"—"I realize that

---

[14]See Boulding, *The Image*, for further development of this point.

[15]Chaim Perelman, *The Idea of Justice and the Problem of Argument*, trans. John Petrie (New York: Humanities Press, Inc., 1963), p. 170.

[16]Transcribed from a tape of the speech delivered over national television on January 26, 1970. Speech included in Appendix.

a number of Congressmen and Senators as well as many of the members of what is called 'the education lobby' disagree with the views I have expressed tonight. I respect their point of view."

4. Teachers and students, patients—"I deeply share the concerns of those who want more funds for education and for health . . . but it is my duty to act on behalf of millions of Americans including teachers and students as well as patients in our hospitals. . . ."

Audiences respond to more than messages; they respond to their image of the speaker and their feeling about what is appropriate to the occasion. Furthermore, they are in varied states of perceptual readiness. The student who has had two classes in a row may not be ready for a third one. An audience of PTA members which has come from discussing a variety of subjects may not be "keyed up" to listen to a speech concerning funds for planting shrubbery around the local high school. A speaker who says "Beautiful day, isn't it?" may not find his "audience" receptive to that question if they have had a particularly bad day at the office.

Theodore Roosevelt, speaking to an outdoor audience in 1910, used the occasion to give some advice on improving farms. The audience, which expected a rousing political speech, grew restless and started to leave. Realizing what was happening, Roosevelt ad-libbed colorfully and rearoused its interest. As soon as the audience had settled back on the grass, its expectations fulfilled, he continued with his prepared speech.[17]

Thus, audiences influence both the speaker's preparation and his presentation. As Holtzman puts it: "The effective speaker's primary goal in analysis of the occasion is to understand the expectations of the listeners. The purpose of such analysis is not simply to *meet* those expectancies but to *make use* of them."[18]

Another factor that influences audience behavior is their image of the speaker. Is he friendly? What has he said to (or about) the audience in the past? Is he an authority? Is he trustworthy? Is he a man of ability? What are his motives, his intentions with regard to the audience? Does the speaker have or attempt to establish any

[17]Richard Murphy, "Theodore Roosevelt," in Hochmuth, *A History and Criticism of American Public Address*, Vol. III, pp. 313–64.

[18]Paul D. Holtzman, *The Psychology of Speakers' Audiences* (Glenview, Ill.: Scott, Foresman & Company, 1970), p. 68.

common ground with his audience? Does the audience identify with speaker? On what levels or in what ways do they identify with him? The answers to these questions may well determine whether and in what ways the audience responds.

Speakers are often asked about their "audience image." On the same Sunday afternoon two prominent political speakers were asked about it on television.[19] First, consider the remarks of Vice-President Spiro Agnew:

> *Reporter A*: Are you pleased with the image—your image—as it's emerged [since assuming the Vice-Presidency]?
>
> *Spiro Agnew*: Well, I'd have to be pretty devious if I didn't say that I thought my image had been improved over what it was at the end of the campaign. I don't regard these things with a great deal of permanency. Images change from day to day and the public generally adjusts its conception of a man based on what he's doing and what it sees of him. I would hope that what I do in the coming months and what I say will enable me to increase my acceptability among all Americans.

Now let us turn to the remarks of Senator Edmund Muskie:

> *Reporter B*: As you are aware, some people have suggested that you shy away from political battles—that you are not assertive enough. . . .
>
> *Edmund Muskie*: Well, I can't recall a candidate for the Presidency in either party in my lifetime who announced three and one-half years in advance, so I'm in good company.
>
> *Reporter B*: Well, nonetheless, this criticism is voiced of you by some Democrats and as evidence they point to the fact that you have not sought a leadership position in the Senate. What is your response to that criticism?
>
> *Edmund Muskie*: Well, I might say two things: One, without going into the gruesome details, I don't think it's an accurate assessment of my past in this respect; but secondly, I can think of only one majority leader in my lifetime who became President.

[19]Transcribed from tapes of nationally televised discussion programs, February 1, 1970. The Agnew statement was made on "Face the Nation," the Muskie statement on "Meet the Press."

Although we have so far stressed the differences among audience members and audience responses to different rhetorical situations, the speaker does have some increasingly sophisticated tools of analysis that will help him understand and use audience needs and expectations. We will discuss audience analysis in Chapter 3, but even at this early point in our discussion of the rhetorical act, the speaker will want to begin inquiring into some scheme of human motivation. He might consider the schema of Abraham Maslow,[20] who tells us that certain needs which are shared by all people may be arranged in a hierarchy of importance. As each basic need is fulfilled, others emerge. They are:

1. Physiological needs (food, water, sex, and so forth).
2. Safety needs (tangible measures of well-being; these may range from the mother's support of a child to insurance of various kinds —medical, unemployment).
3. Love and belongingness needs.
4. Esteem needs.
5. Self-actualization, self-fulfillment needs.

A speaker using this mode for analyzing human behavior can gain insights into the nature of his particular audience. For example, the Goodyear Tire and Rubber Co. published for national circulation an article called "Selling Appeals." Their advice was to make people want to buy by appealing to the instinct for self-preservation; by appealing to self-interest—for example, "Use your pencil to show the truck owner how your retreads give him lower cost per mile"; and by appealing to interest in family—for example, "Your children will thank you for the rest of their lives for having safe tires on your car." This kind of appeal is not very different from the days of the elixir sellers, the medicine men, the hucksters: "Buy Dr. Hower's Magic Tonic and cure your aches and pains, live ten years longer, grow two inches more hair, fill yourself with pep and vitality, all for the price of one dollar." In both cases, the speaker appeals directly to the needs of his audience.

[20]This treatment is based on an analysis by Abraham H. Maslow, *Motivation and Personality* (New York: Harper & Row, Publishers, 1954).

THE TIME

The time at which a speech is given represents more than four o'clock in the afternoon; it represents a stage in the life of problems. Time is reflected in the choice of topic and in the way it is handled. Note the changes in what speakers have been saying about "the Cuban problem" from 1959 to the present.

Observe how changes in time are reflected by the events about which the speaker speaks. The speeches of Adlai E. Stevenson during a four month period in 1952 are an example.[21] On July 21, in his welcoming address to the Democratic Convention, he said:

> As Governor of the host state to the 1952 Democratic Convention, I have the honor of welcoming you to Illinois.

On July 26, in his speech accepting the presidential nomination, he said:

> I accept your nomination—and your program. . . . I have not sought the honor you have done me. I *could* not seek it because I aspired to another office, which was the full measure of my ambition. One does not treat the highest office within the gift of the people of Illinois as an alternative or as a consolation prize.

On August 14 at the Illinois State Fair shortly before beginning his campaign for the presidency, he said:

> I am about to leave you on a long journey, and the route, by the way, won't be a military or a political secret. I intend to cover as much ground as time and strength and our resources permit.

On October 23, in Cleveland, Ohio, as the campaign drew to a close, he said:

21From *Major Campaign Speeches by Adlai E. Stevenson, 1952.* Copyright 1953 by Random House, Inc. Reprinted by permission.

The hour is growing late in this autumn of our political decision. But I find it necessary to talk here tonight of things which are more fundamental than the immediate political questions before us.

On November 1, in Chicago, a few days before the election, he said:

Tonight, we have come to the end of the campaign, and a long, long journey—and I have come home to old friends and to familiar surroundings. . . . There have been times when I have wondered whether you, my friends here in Illinois, couldn't have found some easier way of getting rid of me.

On November 5, from his campaign headquarters in Springfield, Illinois, he conceded defeat on radio and television:

I have sent the following telegram to General Eisenhower. . . . "The people have made their choice and I congratulate you. That you may be the servant and guardian of peace and make the vale of trouble a door of hope is my earnest prayer. . . ." Someone asked me, as I came in, down on the street, how I felt, and I was reminded of a story that a fellow-townsman of ours used to tell—Abraham Lincoln. They asked him how he felt once after an unsuccessful election. He said he felt like a little boy who had stubbed his toe in the dark. He said that he was too old to cry, but it hurt too much to laugh.

Now observe the way in which one speaker responds to changes in a specific policy. William Pitt (Lord Chatham), twice Prime Minister of Great Britain, spoke frequently on British policy concerning the American Colonies between 1766 and 1778.[22] On January 14, 1766, after news of the colonies' resistance to the Stamp Act, he spoke on the subject of taxing the American colonies:

There is an idea in some that the colonies are *virtually* represented in the House. I would fain to know by whom an American is represented here.

.   .   .

[22]Chauncey A. Goodrich, *Select British Eloquence* (Indianapolis: The Bobbs-Merrill Co., Inc., 1963), pp. 103–42. Reprinted by permission of The Bobbs-Merrill Co., Inc.

Upon the whole, I will beg leave to tell the House what is my opinion. It is, that the Stamp Act be repealed absolutely, totally, and immediately. That the reason for the repeal be assigned . . . because it was founded on an erroneous principle. At the same time, let the sovereign authority of this country over the colonies be asserted in as strong terms as can be devised, and be made to extend to every point of legislation whatsoever; that we may bind their trade, confine their manufactures, and exercise every power whatsoever, except that of taking their money out of their pockets without their consent.

On May 27, 1774, in ill health, but deeply troubled by British desire to quarter troops in the homes of the colonists, he said:

The Americans had almost forgot, in their excess of gratitude for the repeal of the Stamp Act, any interest but that of the mother country. . . .

.　　.　　.

But, my Lords, from the complexion of the whole of the proceedings, I think that administration has purposely irritated them into those late violent acts, for which they now so severely smart, purposely to be revenged on them for the victory they gained by the repeal of the Stamp Act. . . .

.　　.　　.

This, my Lords, though no new doctrine, has always been my received and unalterable opinion, and I will carry it to my grave, *that this country had no right under heaven to tax America*. It is contrary to all the principles of justice and civil polity, which neither the exigencies of the state, nor even an acquiescence in the taxes, could justify upon any occasion whatever.

On January 20, 1775, he spoke again, this time to urge the immediate removal of troops from Boston homes:

When I urge this measure of recalling the troops from Boston, I urge it on this pressing principle, that it is necessarily preparatory to the restoration of your peace and the establishment of your prosperity.

.　　.　　.

[I]f the ministers thus persevere in misadvising and misleading the King, I will not say that they can alienate the affections of his subjects from his crown, but I will affirm *that they will make the crown not worth his wearing*. I will not say that the King is betrayed, but I will pronounce *that the kingdom is undone*.

On May 30, 1777, in one last effort to end the contest with America, Pitt said:

> My Lords, this is a flying moment; perhaps but six weeks left to arrest the dangers that surround us. The gathering storm may break; it has already opened, and in part burst. It is difficult for government, after all that has passed, to shake hands with defiers of the King, defiers of the Parliament, defiers of the people. . . . They are rebels; but for what? Surely not for defending their unquestionable rights!
>
> .   .   .
>
> You have been the aggressors from the beginning. . . . You have made descents upon their coasts; you have burned their towns, plundered their country, made war upon the inhabitants, confiscated their property, proscribed and imprisoned their persons. . . . A repeal of those laws, of which they complain, will be the first step to that redress.

On November 18, 1777, he protested allowing mercenaries to attack the colonists:

> My Lords, no man wishes for the due dependence of America on this country more than I do. To preserve it, and not confirm that state of independence into which *your measures* hitherto have *driven them*, is the object which we ought to unite in attaining. The Americans, contending for their rights against arbitrary exactions, I love and admire. It is the struggle of free and virtuous patriots. But, contending for independency and total disconnection from England, as an Englishman, I cannot wish them success. . . .
>
> .   .   .
>
> Spain armed herself with blood-hounds to extirpate the wretched natives of America, and we improve on the inhuman example even of Spanish cruelty; we turn loose these savage hell-hounds against our brethren and countrymen in America, of the same language, laws, liberties, and religion, endeared to us by every tie that should sanctify humanity.

On December 11, 1777, he spoke of his fears about the outcome of the war:

> I tremble for this country. I am almost led to despair that we shall ever be able to extricate ourselves. At any rate, the day of retribution is at hand, when the vengeance of a much-injured and afflicted people will, I trust, fall heavily on the authors of their ruin. . . .

On April 7, 1778, little more than a month before his death, Chatham urged the Parliament:

> In God's name, if it is absolutely necessary to declare either for peace or war, and the former can not be preserved with honor, why is not the latter commenced without delay? . . . Let us at least make one effort, and, if we must fall, let us fall like men!

THE PLACE

The speaker and his audience meet in a place, and place helps determine both what the speaker says and how an audience will react. For example, people do not react in a crowded, smoke-filled convention hall the way they do in the more dignified atmosphere of the Senate gallery, although the day on the Senate floor in 1857 when Preston Brooks struck Charles Sumner on the head with a cane may be an exception.

Washington's farewell to his troops on a battlefield contrasted with his inaugural address in the Senate chambers; and it was only because he was delivering a speech in Faneuil Hall, Boston, that Wendell Phillips in 1837, protesting against the death of Elijah Lovejoy, an abolitionist editor, said:

> Sir, when I heard the gentleman lay down principles which place the murderers of Alton side by side with Otis and Hancock, with Quincy and Adams, I thought those pictured lips [pointing to the portaits in the hall] would have broken into voice to rebuke the recreant American—the slanderer of the dead.
>
> . . .
>
> James Otis thundered in this hall when the King did but touch his pocket. Imagine, if you can, his indignant eloquence had England offered to put a gag upon his lips.[23]

It was the place, the cemetery at Gettysburg, which allowed Lincoln to say:

> We are met on a great battlefield of that war. We have come to dedicate a portion of that field as a final resting place for those who

[23]From *The World's Great Speeches*, ed. Lewis Copeland and Lawrence Lamm (2nd rev. ed.; New York: Dover Publications, Inc., 1958), p. 281.

here gave their lives that that nation might live. It is altogether
fitting and proper that we should do this.

But, in a larger sense, we cannot dedicate—we cannot consecrate—
we cannot hallow—this ground. The brave men, living and dead,
who struggled here, have consecrated it, far above our poor power
to add or to detract.[24]

One of the clearest examples of the influence of place on the
speaker's message is John F. Kennedy's "Ich bin ein Berliner" speech
delivered in June, 1963:

I am proud to come to this city as the guest of your distinguished
Mayor, who has symbolized throughout the world the fighting spirit
of West Berlin, and I am proud to visit the Federal Republic with
your distinguished Chancellor who, for so many years, has committed
Germany to democracy and freedom and progress, and to come here
in the company of my fellow American, General Clay, who has been
in this city during its great moments of crisis and will come again
if ever needed.

Two thousand years ago the proudest boast was "Civitas Romanus
sum." Today, in the world of freedom, the proudest boast is "Ich bin
ein Berliner." (I appreciate my interpreter translating my German.)

There are many people in the world who really don't understand,
or say they don't, what is the great issue between the free world and
the Communist world. Let them come to Berlin. There are some
who say that Communism is the wave of the future. Let them come
to Berlin. And there are some who say in Europe and elsewhere we
can work with the Communists. Let them come to Berlin. And there
are even a few who say that it is true that Communism is an evil
system, but it permits us to make economic progress. "Lasst sie nach
Berlin kommen."

Freedom has many difficulties and democracy is not perfect, but
we have never had to put a wall up to keep our people in, to prevent
them from leaving us. I want to say, on behalf of my countrymen,
who live many miles away on the other side of the Atlantic, who are
far distant from you, that they take the greatest pride that they have
been able to share with you, even from a distance, the story of the
last eighteen years. I know of no town, no city, that has been besieged
for eighteen years that still lives with the vitality and the force, and
the hope and the determination of the city of West Berlin. While
the wall is the most obvious and vivid demonstration of the failures

[24]*Ibid.*, p. 315.

of the Communist system, for all the world to see, we take no satisfaction in it, for it is an offense not only against history but an
offense against humanity, separating families, dividing husbands
and wives and brothers and sisters, and dividing a people who wish
to be joined together.

What is true of this city is true of Germany—real, lasting peace
in Europe can never be assured as long as one German out of four
is denied the elementary right of free men, and that is to make a
free choice. In eighteen years of peace and good faith, this generation of Germans has earned the right to be free, including the right
to unite their families and their nation in lasting peace with good
will to all people. You live in a defended island of freedom, but your
life is part of the main. So let me ask you, as I close, to lift your eyes
beyond the dangers of today to the hopes of tomorrow, beyond the
freedom merely of this city of Berlin, or your country of Germany,
to the advance of freedom everywhere, beyond the wall to the day of
peace with justice, beyond yourselves and ourselves to all mankind.
Freedom is indivisible, and when one man is enslaved, all are not
free. When all are free, then we can look forward to that day when
this city will be joined as one—and this country, and this great
continent of Europe—in a peaceful and hopeful glow. When that day
finally comes, as it will, the people of West Berlin can take sober
satisfaction in the fact that they were in the front lines for almost
two decades.

All free men, wherever they may live, are citizens of Berlin, and,
therefore, as a free man, I take pride in the words "Ich bin ein
Berliner."[25]

Here the place, West Berlin, becomes the symbol of "the great issue
between the free world and the Communist world"; it is "a reminder
that freedom is indivisible." West Berlin becomes the symbolic home
of all free men and, therefore, of the American President. Thus he
is "consubstantial" with his audience of West Berliners; they *share*
the same "substance"—the same home, the same ideas, the same
fortitude and pride—and can both make the same proud boast, "Ich
bin ein Berliner."

[25]Transcribed from a tape of the speech. For text and other remarks at
the same occasion see: "Remarks in the Rudolphe Wilde Platz," June 26,
1963, in *Public Papers of the Presidents of the U.S.: John F. Kennedy:
Containing the Public Messages, Speeches, and Statements of the President:
January 1 to November 22, 1963* (Washington, D.C.: U.S. Government
Printing Office, 1964), pp. 525–52.

The physical aspects of place also played an important part in this rhetorical act. The people were standing outside crowded close together, not seated in neat, separated rows of chairs in an air conditioned building. Thus, it was easier for the crowd members to respond to each other, and in turn to respond more emotionally to the speaker. Arthur Schlesinger, Jr., described the crowd in this way:

> . . . three-fifths of the population of West Berlin streaming into the streets, clapping, waving, cheering, as if it were the second coming. . . . the seething crowd in the Rudolf Wilde Platz [was] compressed into a single excited, impassioned mass. . . . The crowd shook itself and rose and roared like an animal. . . . The hysteria spread visibly through the square.[26]

As Schlesinger describes him, Kennedy was "first exhilarated, then disturbed; he felt, as he remarked on his return, that if he had said, 'March to the wall—tear it down,' his listeners would have marched."[27]

The physical and metaphysical aspects of place generally are inextricably associated. An election eve speech of Senator Muskie was delivered in a room occupied only by the apparently solitary figure of the Senator, while the opening and closing television shots showed the calm ocean off Cape Ann, Maine. Presented in close juxtaposition to a cluttered, crowded, and noisy speech delivered by President Nixon, the contrast in place was not accidental. Moreover, the state where the speech was delivered became more than that. Note the Senator's words:

> Today the air of my native Maine was touched with winter and hunters filled the woods. I have spent my life in this state which is both part of our oldest traditions and a place of wild and almost untouched forests. It is rugged country, cold in the winter but a good place to live. There are friends and there are also places to be alone, places where a man can walk all day and see nothing but woods and water. We in Maine share many of the problems of America and I am sure others are coming to us. But we've had no riots, no bombings, and speakers are not kept from talking. This is not

---

[26]Arthur Schlesinger, Jr., *A Thousand Days* (Boston: Houghton Mifflin Company, 1965), pp. 737–38.
[27]*Ibid.*, p. 738.

because I am Senator or because the Governor is a Democrat. Partly, of course, it is because we are a small state with no huge cities and partly it is because the people here have a sense of place. They are part of a community with common concerns and problems and hopes for the future. We cannot make America smaller but we can work to restore a sense of shared purpose and of great enterprise. We can bring back the belief, not only in a better and more noble future but in our own power to make it so.[28]

THE PURPOSE

The fifth constituent of the rhetorical act is purpose. Presumably the speaker has a reason for speaking. Speeches can be viewed as responses to given social, political, and economic needs within a community. You might want at this time to examine three speeches included in the Appendix: William Faulkner's "Nobel Prize Acceptance Speech," John F. Kennedy's "Cuban Missile Crisis Speech," and Richard Nixon's "Veto Message."

Faulkner is clearly responding to several needs. First, he had been given an enormously important award and was invited to accept it orally. Second, his purpose as a creative artist, was considerably broader and perhaps more important. It was to use that moment to speak to other creative people—as he states it in the speech, to be "listened to by the young men and women already dedicated to the same anguish and travail" that he was. Further, he states his purpose to consider the "problems of the human heart in conflict with itself." You may discover other purposes. Perhaps he ultimately wanted to convey his vision of the future: "I believe that man will not merely endure: he will prevail." Thus, the speaker conceived of his purpose as more than to say simply, "Thank you."

President Kennedy's decision to blockade Cuba could have been made without a speech, but one of his purposes in the speech was clearly to alert the whole nation to the danger of offensive missiles off the coast of Florida, and to inform the American public that measures were being taken to meet that threat. Moreover, he wanted to convince his audience that the measures his administra-

[28]From a transcript of a tape recording of the speech televised nationally on November 2, 1970.

tion was taking were the best among the several alternatives publicly suggested by prominent men, ranging from "Do nothing" to "Bomb the missile sites."

Consider Richard Nixon's "Veto Message," delivered on January 26, 1970, over national television. He could have chosen to sign the veto of a key Health, Education, and Welfare bill in his office without the presence of the television networks. In part, the purpose of the speech was informational, in effect to say "I am vetoing this bill because . . ." Still, even in the message itself the President recognized that its timing also lent it a political cast. ("Now, why in an election year particularly would a President hesitate for one moment to sign a bill providing for such politically popular causes as this one?") The political implications of the speech were so clear that CBS, ABC, and NBC all agreed to abide by the "equal time" rule and ran a message of equivalent length sponsored by the Democratic Party.

The speaker's specific purpose is to speak with persuasive effect toward the end that he has in mind. He has a reason for speaking, and everything he says must be directed to fulfilling that purpose. Ultimately the speaker must confront the question: "Have I fulfilled my purposes?" Before we discuss monitoring effects, it might be well for us to recall four basic points about all messages and their possible effects. Theodore Clevenger, Jr., explains in this way:

1. Messages, even those we are inclined to dismiss as relatively trivial and insignificant, have effects.
2. The same message may have different effects upon different auditors, or on the same auditor at different times.
3. Even a short message is likely to have more than a single effect upon any given auditor.
4. Some of the effects of a message are unlikely to have been anticipated by the message source.[29]

The speaker's task is to control effects as much as he possibly can. A careful answer to the questions: "What is (are) my purpose(s) in this speech? What do I hope to accomplish by my speech?" will help the speaker to answer more effectively the next crucial question: "How can I accomplish my purpose?" A consideration of pur-

[29]Theodore Clevenger, Jr., *Audience Analysis* (Indianapolis: The Bobbs-Merrill Co., Inc., 1966), p. 40.

pose can suggest a potential problem. Is a speech which does not prompt immediate response successful? Perhaps fulfillment of specific purpose is not the only test of success. For example, although the members of an audience may not act in precisely the way a speaker intends, they may be considering new problems and different solutions to old problems, their predispositions may be changed, and their minds alerted.

THE CONTENT

The substance of the speech calls for particular attention. Speeches may be made on any subject, but some subjects are more likely to prompt speeches than others. For example, a man may write a lyric poem extolling the beauty of moonlight shining on a lake, but he is rarely moved to give a speech about it. People generally give speeches in three situations: (1) when they are deciding whether or not to act; (2) when they are trying to determine the way in which they ought to act; and (3) when they are trying to evaluate their methods of action. To recognize something as a problem, to determine that some courses of action are better solutions than others, and to decide if a solution has actually alleviated the problem call for value judgments by the speaker. He perceives what things constitute a threat to his welfare, his institutions, his progress toward achieving his goals. Because he values some goals more than others, he decides which problems should be dealt with first. Because he views some courses of action as more satisfactory than others, he determines what alternative solutions are possible. Thus, the speaker is concerned with: (1) those forces, events, and ideas which prompt men to act; (2) alternative ways of acting; and (3) evaluating actions which have taken place.

The materials of speeches are generally facts, interpretations, values, and policies. Facts can be verified independently of the speaker; for example, "In 1948, the steel and chemical town of Donora, Pennsylvania, was visited by a fog and a temperature inversion which left 20 dead." One could check the fact in many different sources and then label it true or false.

Sometimes it is more difficult to check the facts, and the audience becomes increasingly dependent on the speaker (as a source with recourse to more materials) to provide them; for example, President Kennedy said in his Cuban Missile Crisis speech that several of the missile sites included "medium-range ballistic missiles capable of carrying a nuclear warhead for a distance of more than 1000 nautical miles." The audience depended upon the source credibility of the speaker and the surveillance photos and interpretations of the photos presented over national television and in the newspapers. Of course, the President's next sentence could be checked by any listener who referred to a map: "Each of these missiles, in short, is capable of striking Washington, D.C., the Panama Canal, Cape Canaveral, Mexico City, or any other city in the southeastern part of the United States, in Central America, or in the Caribbean area." Often speakers themselves worry about their use of the facts and how this relates to their ethos. Irish reformer Bernadette Devlin once commented:

> My biggest fault—which I would personally consider—is a certain amount of arrogance which makes me say something which is my own opinion as if it were a recognized statement of fact which the whole world was prepared to admit, with the exception of a few idiots. And this simply isn't true. It's the way I say it. And this arrogance is coupled with a certain amount of, indeed too much, emotionalism. And when I do state facts leads to people taking what I say as being a veiled threat.[30]

The speaker may well move beyond the facts to interpretations or inferences. While inferences are based on statements of fact, they themselves go beyond the facts. Recall a major inference of the Cuban Missile speech:

> But this secret, swift, and extraordinary build-up of Communist missiles—in an area well known to have a special and historical relationship to the United States and the nations of the Western Hemisphere, in violation of Soviet assurances, and in defiance of American and hemisphere policy—*this sudden, clandestine decision to station strategic weapons for the first time outside of Soviet soil— is a deliberately provocative and unjustified change in the status quo which cannot be accepted by this country* if our courage and our commitments are ever to be trusted again by either friend or foe [italics added].

[30]Transcribed from a tape of a newscast.

To a great extent, the facts one selects (out of all the available ones) and the inferences one draws (out of all the possible ones) reflect the speaker's values; for example, Stewart Udall, former Secretary of the Interior, comments:

> We spend as much for chewing gum as for the model cities program. The ladies spend as much for hair dye as we are spending for urban mass transportation systems. We are spending more for pet food than on food stamps for the poor. . . . The point I am trying to make is that if we are really concerned about doing the things that must be done across the board to make the cities more livable, to tackle pollution head on, to do the conservation work that we must do, we are going to have to have a significant upgrading of these activities in terms of our national priorities.[31]

Or consider the value hierarchy implicit in Senator Henry Jackson's speech on the subject of environmental quality:

> Dealing with the issues posed requires more than a nation-wide beauty contest or an anti-litter campaign or even the policing of pollution. The task is far more fundamental than that. We must be concerned with survival—for the very lives of all men are threatened.
>
> For more than two decades we have had to contend with the fact that man has invented weapons capable of destroying mankind. Now we must also be conscious of the fact that man has unwittingly set some environmental time bombs which could be equally capable of rendering mankind extinct. We have been using up or poisoning the very substances on which life depends. That is the threat we must contend with—a threat which is just as deadly as the threat of war.
>
> When I introduced "The National Environmental Policy Act" and when it was passed by the Senate it provided that Congress recognizes that each person has a fundamental and inalienable right to a healthful environment and that each person has a responsibility to contribute to the preservation of the environment.
>
> We lost that strong language in subsequent Congressional action on the measure. Opponents felt it would allow people to assert and protect their right to a "healthful environment" in the courts and

[31]Stewart Udall testifying during Hearings before the Committee on Interior and Insular Affairs, U.S. Senate, 91st Congress, First Session, April 16, 1969, *National Environmental Policy.*

in administrative proceedings. I plan to introduce legislation in the next few weeks to restore this language and to affirm this right by law.[32]

Last, consider the value hierarchy implicit in these words of Robert F. Kennedy:

> Some believe there is nothing one man or one woman can do against the enormous array of the world's ills. Yet many of the world's great movements of thought and action have flowed from the work of a single man.
>
> A young monk began the Protestant Reformation. A young general extended an empire from Macedonia to the borders of the earth. A young woman reclaimed the territory of France, and it was a young Italian explorer who discovered the New World, and the 32-year-old Thomas Jefferson who explained that all men are created equal.
>
> These men moved the world, and so can we all. Few will have the greatness to bend history itself, but each of us can work to change a small portion of events, and in the total of all those acts will be written the history of this generation.
>
> Each time a man stands for an ideal, or acts to improve the lot of others, or strikes out against injustice, he sends forth a tiny ripple of hope.
>
> And crossing each other from a million different centers of energy and daring, those ripples build a current that can sweep down the mightiest walls of oppression and resistance. Few are willing to brave the disapproval of their fellows, the censure of their colleagues, the wrath of their society. Moral courage is a rarer commodity than bravery in battle or great intelligence. Yet it is the one essential vital quality for those who seek to change a world that yields most painfully to change.[33]

Value judgments may be stated explicitly by the speaker, for example: "This is a good movie," but more often they may be inferred by the listener. A value statement may be defined as a statement which expresses, either explicitly or implicitly, the relative worth

---

[32]From a speech, "Environmental Quality in the Decades of the Seventies," delivered to the National Wildlife Federation, Chicago, Illinois, March 21, 1970.

[33]As cited in a speech by Senator Edward Kennedy delivered in New York, November 7, 1968. Transcribed from a tape of the speech.

of an event, idea, or object, and so influences the individual's selection of available means and ends of actions. Thus, value statements indicate the kinds of judgments or attitudes the speaker holds toward his topic and, often, toward the audience as well. They are, perhaps, "the real sources of attention and interest. . . ."[34]

Based upon the facts of the matter, certain inferences drawn from the facts, and a priority of values, speakers often suggest policies for their audiences to consider (e.g., Kennedy in the Cuban Missile Crisis and Nixon in the Veto Message).

Another basic way of viewing the content of speeches is to say that speeches consist of statements and support of those statements. Thus, the speaker needs to consider the concept of proof. Proof may be defined as *"the process of securing belief in one statement by relating it to another statement already believed."*[35] Stephen Toulmin has given us a useful vocabulary with which to talk about proof: Proof may be defined as securing belief in *claims* by relating them through warrants to the evidence already accepted.[36] In the course of a formal speech, as well as in casual conversation, we persistently make claims based on empirical evidence (statistics, examples, analogies, and so on), the credibility of the speaker, and the motives and emotions of the audience. Thus the speaker deals with three types of proof—substantive, authoritative, and motivational proof. One point should be clear by this time. The speaker selects the materials of the speech not only on the basis of availability, but also from a consideration of whether or not those materials are likely to be meaningful and persuasive to his audience.

Whatever his topic, the speaker is responsible for each statement he makes, for the facts he selects, and for the inferences he draws from those facts. Each public statement is a commitment. Observe how the statements below imply certain commitments:

The future towards which we are marching, across bloody fields and frightful manifestations of destruction, must surely be based upon the broad and simple virtues and upon the nobility of mankind.

[34] Karl R. Wallace, *Understanding Discourse: The Speech Act and Rhetorical Action* (Baton Rouge: Louisiana State University Press, 1970), p. 80.
[35] Douglas Ehninger and Wayne Brockriede, *Decision by Debate* (New York: Dodd, Mead & Co., 1963), p. 99.
[36] Stephen Toulmin, *The Uses of Argument* (Cambridge, England: Cambridge University Press, 1958).

It must be based upon a reign of law which upholds the principles of justice and fair play, and protects the weak against the strong if the weak have justice on their side [Winston Churchill, speaking to the House of Commons in 1944].[37]

I believe that man will not merely endure: he will prevail. He is immortal, not because he alone among creatures has an inexhaustible voice, but because he has a soul, a spirit capable of compassion and sacrifice and endurance. The poet's, the writer's, duty is to write about these things. It is his privilege to help man endure by lifting his heart, by reminding him of the courage and honor and hope and pride and compassion and pity and sacrifice which have been the glory of his past [William Faulkner, accepting the 1949 Nobel Prize in Stockholm, Sweden].[38]

THE STYLE

The style of a speech must also be considered. Style in the narrow meaning is the effective use of language, but in a broad sense it is an overt manifestation of the speaker's general outlook on life. Whether you define it as "the man himself"[39] or "proper words in proper places,"[40] style is a means of persuasion, a way of identifying the speaker's attitudes, ideas, and so on, with those of his audience. Consequently, the speaker first determines what effect he wants to achieve, and selects the words and structures which will best achieve it. Lincoln, for example, in his "First Inaugural Address," was seeking unity. When one of his assistants suggested the phrase "passion has strained," Lincoln changed it to "passion may have strained," in order to temper his words. Because he wanted to appear direct and friendly, he said "we are not enemies, but friends" rather than "we are not, we must not be aliens or enemies but fellow

[37]F.B. Czarnomski, ed., *The Eloquence of Winston Churchill* (New York: The New American Library of World Literature, Inc., 1957), p. 178.

[38]Copeland and Lamm, *The World's Great Speeches*, p. 638. The whole of this speech is reprinted in the Appendix.

[39]Buffon, "Discourse on Style," in *The Art of the Writer*, ed. Lane Cooper (Ithaca, N.Y.: Cornell University Press, 1952).

[40]Jonathan Swift, "A Letter to a Young Clergyman," in Cooper, *The Art of the Writer*.

countrymen and brethren."[41] The first is simple and kind; the second is less positive, less personal.

Listen to the speeches, the conversations around you and consider these questions: (1) What did the speaker hope to achieve? (2) By what linguistic strategies did he try to achieve his purpose? (3) How else could it have been done? (4) Which of the alternative suggestions are better? (5) Why are they better? Frances Perkins tells of the time she suggested this sentence to Franklin Roosevelt during a speechwriting effort: "We are trying to construct a more inclusive society."[42] President Roosevelt simplified and clarified that statement when he changed it to: "We are going to make a country in which no one is left out." Why? Because he was working to attain directness and clarity.

Almost every participant in a recent high school oratory contest quoted President John F. Kennedy's statement, "Ask not what your country can do for you—ask what you can do for your country."[43] The same thought has been expressed thousands of times, by many writers and speakers, but a distinctive use of language added vitality to the thought.

THE DELIVERY

Communication cannot occur if the speaker talks too softly to be heard, or mumbles so the audience can only guess at what he is saying. The most brilliant idea, the most effective style are lost if the speech is not heard. If the audience is conscious of delivery itself—whether good or bad—it is not paying complete attention to the message of the speaker. Cicero criticizes the delivery of one of his contemporaries because of "ridiculous gestures." He ridicules another because, in shifting his weight from side to side, he looked

[41]See Marie Hochmuth, "Lincoln's First Inaugural," in *American Speeches*, ed. Wayland Maxfield Parrish and Marie Hochmuth (New York: Longmans, Green & Co., Inc., 1954), pp. 21–71.

[42]Frances Perkins, *The Roosevelt I Knew* (New York: The Viking Press, Inc., 1946), p. 113.

[43]Ernest J. Wrage and Barnet Baskerville, eds., *Contemporary Forum: American Speeches on Twentieth-Century Issues* (New York: Harper & Row, Publishers, 1962), p. 320.

as if he were "speaking from a boat." On the other hand, he praises a third because his actions corresponded to the meaning of every sentence.[44]

The more natural the delivery, the more likely it is to be effective as a means of persuasion, in the sense that it does not call attention to itself. It was commonly said of Wendell Phillips, the great nineteenth century abolitionist orator, that his voice "had the effect of 'finding' its auditor . . . as if it were speaking to each one as an unknown friend,"[45] that it was as if he simply repeated in a slightly louder tone what he had just been saying to a friend at his elbow.

Audiences respond to more than the words of a speaker, they also respond to how he says them. In a very important way, delivery is a part of what the speaker says. It tells us something about the speaker, his relationship to his message, and his relation to the audience.

Delivery reveals the workings of the speaker's mind. For example, Theodore Roosevelt's voice and manner have been described as "consistent with the rough-and-ready vigor of his personality." He had a "strong, direct voice, slightly strained and rasping, but not unpleasant in quality." His "whole manner was vigorous, suggestive of his moods."[46] Critics recall that William Pitt had "[s]uch . . . power of his eye, that he very often cowed down an antagonist in the midst of his speech, and threw him into utter confusion, by a single glance of scorn or contempt."[47]

Delivery also gives the listener cues as to what is important in the message. Comments about Lincoln's "First Inaugural Address" include: He had "firm tones of voice" and spoke with "great deliberation and precision of emphasis."[48] A writer in the *Chicago Daily Tribune* noted that "With great solemnity of emphasis, using his gestures to add significance to his words," Lincoln remarked: "*You* have no oath registered in Heaven to destroy this Government,

[44]Cicero, *Brutus*, trans. G.L. Hendrickson, The Loeb Classical Library (London: William Heinemann Ltd., 1939), LXIII, LX, XXXVIII.

[45]As cited by Willard Hayes Yeager, "Wendell Phillips," in *A History and Criticism of American Public Address*, ed. William N. Brigance, Vol. I, p. 359.

[46]Murphy, "Theodore Roosevelt," pp. 355, 358.

[47]Goodrich, *Select British Eloquence*, p. 71.

[48]Hochmuth, "Lincoln's First Inaugural," pp. 44–45.

while I shall have the most solemn one to preserve, protect, and defend it." Emphatic delivery made prominent Lincoln's main point—that his duty was to keep the Union whole.

A speaker not only gives cues to his audience about what is significant in the speech, but his delivery also tells something about his relationship with his audience. One who speaks in an informal and conversational manner to his audience usually shares a different relationship than a formal speaker who reads from a manuscript.

summary

The communicative situation is not simple. Each speech reflects, both directly and indirectly, a particular speaker, speaking to a particular audience, at a particular time, in a particular place, for a particular purpose, and in a particular manner. How well or poorly a speaker succeeds is often a result of how he analyzes his unique communicative situation, and how he responds to the challenge of his analysis.

Clearly, the speeches of some speakers are not time-bound. They address universal or nearly universal values in audiences regardless of time. When a speaker addresses several audiences at one time or throughout time, the task of analysis becomes intrinsically complex, and the communicative situation much broader in meaning.

rhetorical exercises

1. Give a three to five minute speech in which you give your political, social attitude toward something. During the speech employ all three kinds of proof—substantive, authoritative, and motivational.

2. Attend a speech on or off campus and write a description of it in terms of the eight elements in the communicative situation. Read your descriptions aloud in class and compare notes on the kinds of things observed. Consider these questions:

a. *About the speaker*: Was the speaker known or unknown? How did this affect the way in which people listened to him? What did he say in the speech to reveal his character, personality, and general outlook?

b. *About the audience*: Did the audience share certain characteristics: Age? Sex? Educational development? Economic class? Social strata? Political heritage? Special interests? Do you think the audience had certain expectations about the speaker and his topic? Do you think they were fulfilled?

c. *About the purpose*: What was the speaker's specific purpose? Was it explicitly stated or implied? Do you think he fulfilled his purpose?

d. *About the time*: At what time was the speech given? How was time likely to affect the audience? Was time reflected in how the speaker handled his subject? In what he said?

e. *About the place*: Where was the speech given? Did it condition the audience's reactions?

f. *About the content*: What were the speaker's main points? How did he support them? Was the content adequate? Varied? Appropriate to the audience? Interesting?

g. *About the style*: Was the speaker's style clear? Was it appropriate to the occasion and to the audience? Was it impressive?

h. *About the delivery*: Was the speaker direct? Fluent? Was he animated and communicative?

3. Analyze any one of the speeches in the back of this text. From studying the speech text itself, what could you discover about the speaker, audience, time, place, and purpose(s).

4. Analyze any one of the speeches in the back of the text, asking: "In this speech is the speaker dealing largely with facts, values, interpretations? On what types of proof(s) does the speaker rely most heavily—substantive, authoritative, or motivational?"

collateral readings

Barnlund, Dean C., "Communication: The Context of Change," in *Perspectives on Communications*, ed. Carl E. Larson and Frank E. X. Dance. Milwaukee: Speech Communication Center, University of Wisconsin, 1968.

Berlo, David K., *The Process of Communication*. New York: Holt, Rinehart and Winston, Inc., 1960. See especially "A Model of the Communication Process" and "The Fidelity of Communication: Determinants of Effect."

Bettinghaus, Erwin P., *Message Preparation: The Nature of Proof*. Indianapolis: The Bobbs-Merrill Co., Inc., 1966.

Blankenship, Jane, *A Sense of Style*. Belmont, Calif.: Dickenson Publishing Co., Inc., 1968. See Chapter One, "Toward a Definition of Style."

Boulding, Kenneth, *The Image*. Ann Arbor: University of Michigan Press, 1956.

Clevenger, Theodore, Jr., *Audience Analysis*. Indianapolis: The Bobbs-Merrill Co., Inc., 1966.

Holtzman, Paul D., *The Psychology of Speakers' Audiences*. Glenwood, Ill.: Scott, Foresman & Company, 1970.

[Nichols], Marie K. Hochmuth, ed., *A History and Critcism of American Public Address*. Vol. III. New York: Longmans, Green & Co., Inc., 1955. See "The Criticism of Rhetoric."

Nilsen, Thomas R., *Ethics of Speech Communication*. Indianapolis: The Bobbs-Merrill Co., Inc., 1966. See Chapter Three, "On Significant Choice."

II

PRINCIPLES
AND
APPLICATIONS

*When the speaker understands what persons are
persuaded by what arguments, and sees the person
about whom he was speaking in the abstract actually
before him, he can say to himself, "This is the man
. . . who ought to have a certain argument applied to
him in order to convince him of a certain opinion. . . ."*

Plato

3

RHETORICAL INVENTION: PRELIMINARY PLANNING

A person doesn't become a speaker when he stands up to speak, but
long before, when he begins to select a topic to talk about. In this
chapter we will discuss some of the preliminary problems involved
in planning a speech. The speaker must first consider what he knows
about attitudes in general, and what he knows about the attitudes
and beliefs of his audience in particular. On the basis of what he
wants to accomplish in his speech and what he thinks he can accomplish because of the nature of his audience, he decides on the lines
of argument to advance and the strategies of identification to pursue.

The first steps in preliminary planning are crucial to the overall effectiveness of the speech. They form the foundation for all decisions the speaker will have to make as he decides what to say and
the most effective ways of saying it.

audience attitudes and beliefs[1]

Pogo Opossum has observed, "Human bein's make the best folks." He has also noted: "The trouble with people is people." Whether we see man as a potentially perfectable creature "created in God's image," or as a bundle of irrational drives behind a thin veneer of civilization, as speakers we must face Pogo's dilemma. We must deal with people. Whatever their frailties, people must come together to arrive at decisions. If we are to act as responsible advisers in real social situations, we must attend to the behavior of the human respondents we intend to influence. In Bryant's well-known phrase, rhetoric involves the adjustment of "ideas to *people* and *people* to ideas."[2]

If our goal is to influence the attitudes of people, it is important to examine the nature of the construct *attitude*. We must attempt to understand the role of attitudes within the cognitive processes that determine response to verbal communication.

AN OVERVIEW

Our discussion of the cognitive processes operating in the respondent is predicated upon a view of man and man's relationship to his environment. Gordon Allport classifies modern psychological theories according to two "broadly contrasting approaches"[3] which he labels the Lockean and Leibnitzian traditions. According to Allport, the Lockean tradition views man's mind as essentially passive, while the Leibnitzian tradition views the intellect as active.[4] He says:

[1]The section "Audience Attitudes and Beliefs," was written by Vernon E. Cronen, Assistant Professor of Speech, University of Massachusetts. Prepared especially for this volume.

[2]Donald Bryant, "Rhetoric: Its Function and Scope," *Quarterly Journal of Speech*, Vol. XXXIX, No. 4 (December 1953), 407.

[3]Gordon Allport, *Becoming* (New Haven: Yale University Press, 1955), pp. 5–7.

[4]*Ibid.*

> John Locke, we all recall, assumed the mind of the individual to be
> a *tabula rasa* at birth. And the intellect itself was a passive thing
> acquiring content and structure only through the impact of sensa-
> tion and the crisscross of associations. . . . Locke insisted that there
> can be nothing *(nihil est in intellectu quod non fuerit in sensu)*.
> To this formula Leibnitz added a challenging supplement: noth-
> ing save the intellect itself *(excipe: nisi ipse intellectus)*. To Leibnitz
> the intellect was essentially active in its own right. . . .[5]

The view that we offer in this chapter may be roughly classed
in the tradition of such men as Leibnitz, Dewey, and Bruner, as
opposed to the tradition represented by Locke, Pavlov, and Skinner.
This does not mean that we ignore the insights of classical conditioning or the import of external events for attitude formation and
change, nor does it mean that we hold a largely rational model of
man as a logical problem solver. Rather, this classification simply
suggests that we place emphasis on the internal mediating responses
that go on within the listener. Some of these internal processes are
conscious choices, others occur below the threshold of awareness.[6]
Some may fit the syllogistic model of rationality, other processes
may violate that model. What is crucial is the view that understanding attitude change in rhetorical situations necessarily entails an
understanding of the distinctive human cognitive processes that
occur during verbal communication. *We view our listeners as active
processors of messages, not as passive receivers.*

The distinctive function of human language places man in an
active role with respect to the stimuli provided by the environment.
Through the categorizing function of language we attempt to order
and thus make sense out of the infinite variety of sense impressions.
This sorting activity makes it possible for us to bring order into
what William James called the "blooming, buzzing confusion" that
is the world of the newborn child. Scheidel argues persuasively
against the view that man is simply a passive receiver of sense data.
He says "human behavior is much more than adaptive. Man also
adjusts the world to fit himself; he imposes order on nature. This

[5]*Ibid.*, pp. 7–8.

[6]The student interested in the problem of processes below the threshold
of awareness may be interested in a provocative series of essays edited by
Charles W. Eriksen, *Behavior and Awareness* (Durham, N.C.: Duke University Press, 1962).

is accomplished largely by means of categories or constructs and with the assistance of language."[7] Note that Scheidel stresses the imposition of order on nature, not the observation of order in nature. Bruner, Goodnow, and Austin also stress the importance of categorizing activity for human behavior. They argue that:

> . . . were we to utilize fully our capacity for registering the differences in things and to respond to each event encountered as unique, we would soon be overwhelmed by the complexity of our environment. Consider only the linguistic task of acquiring a vocabulary fully adequate to cope with the world of color differences! The resolution of this seeming paradox—the existence of discrimination capacities which if fully used, would make us slaves to the particular —is achieved by man's capacity to categorize.[8]

Imagine attempting to determine a name for each of the seven million discriminable colors that men can perceive! Categorizing activity allows us to simplify in a great many ways. For example, a child might form a category of red vehicles and label them all "fire engines." Our only objection to this means of classification would be that of its utility. When the child sees a bright red XK-E Jaguar and asks where the fire is, he will get responses that reveal the unsatisfactory nature of his classification system. Eventually, the child will break up his category of red vehicles. Only those with a distinguishing characteristic, such as ladders on the sides, will bear the label "fire engine." All other red vehicles will be absorbed into the category "cars." The restructured classification labeled "fire engine" will prove much more useful. Expectations associated with it (noise, excitement) are much more likely to be fulfilled. This simple illustration illuminates three practical principles regarding the listeners who comprise our audience: (1) Each of our listeners will come to us with his own more or less successful ways of categorizing and labeling phenomena. The system of labeled categories may or may not be similar to our own in essential respects. (2) The listener's expectations about the world around him are framed in light of his own category system. Thus, if he categorizes all long-

[7]Thomas M. Scheidel, *Persuasive Speaking* (Glenwood, Ill.: Scott, Foresman & Company, 1967), p. 32.

[8]Jerome Bruner, Jacqueline Goodnow, and George Austin, *A Study of Thinking* (New York: John Wiley & Sons, Inc., 1956), p. 1.

haired college age people as "radical terrorists," he will expect terrorism from long-haired college age people whether they are members of the Young Democrats or the Weathermen. (3) The way in which the listener will make sense out of the speech being presented will be influenced in part by the world view that he brings with him into the rhetorical situation.

The following discussion proceeds from a view that conceives of the listener's role in the rhetorical transaction as active rather than passive. We view the listener as a "peculiar critter" whose contact with reality is not direct, but rather mediated through the processes of categorizing and labeling. The listener comes with the problem of making some useful sense out of the environment. We will pursue an understanding of how listeners function to cope with this problem in rhetorical situations.

THE CONCEPT OF COGNITIVE STRUCTURE

Many researchers in the field of attitude change take the view that our beliefs are patterned in sets. Milton Rokeach, for example, warns against focusing on "single beliefs and attitudes rather than on belief systems and attitude systems."[9] Bruner, Goodnow, and Austin also stress the concept of cognitive structure. We have already taken note of their view that the individual reduces the complexity of his environment through categorizing. The idea of categorized perceptions implies a patterned system with a hierarchical organization. Bruner and his associates provide the following illustration:

[An] achievement of categorizing is the opportunity it permits for ordering and relating classes of events. For we operate as noted before, with category systems—classes of events that are related to each other in various kinds of superordinate systems. We map and give meaning to our world by relating classes of events rather than by relating individual events. "Matches," the child learns, will "cause" a set of events called "fires." The meaning of each class of things placed in quotation marks—matches, causes, and fires—is given by the imbeddedness of each class in such relationship maps. The

[9]Milton Rokeach, *The Open and Closed Mind* (New York: Basic Books, Inc., Publishers, 1960), p. 18.

moment an object is placed in a category, we have opened up the whole vista of possibilities for "going beyond" the category by virtue of the superordinate and causal relationships linking this category to others.[10]

Thus, we can conceive of our beliefs as patterned in sets. We can speak of the listener as having a cognitive system composed of the beliefs and expectancies, that represent the world in which he lives. This system *is* reality for him.

Suppose that a speaker is interested in analyzing the attitude of a listener toward a political candidate. The listener's attitude will be determined in part by the nature of the concepts he associates with the candidate. For example:

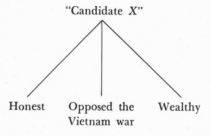

"Candidate X"

Honest   Opposed the   Wealthy
              Vietnam war

The figure gives us little insight, however, into the attitude of the listener toward our hypothetical candidate.

Martin Fishbein, in his Summative Theory of Attitude Change,[11] says that we must consider at least two factors in order to understand attitude. First is the belief-probability factor. The listener believes, at some level of probability, that certain elements both exist and are related to a concept. Returning to our example of the candidate, we would want to know whether the listener believes that opposition to the Vietnam war is conceivable human behavior (that it can exist), and how strongly opposition to the war is associated (related) with the candidate in the mind of the listener. For example, the listener may be uncertain about the candidate's degree of opposition to the war. He may have heard from a friend

[10]Bruner *et al.*, *A Study of Thinking*, p. 13.

[11]Martin Fishbein, "A Behavior Theory Approach to the Relations Between Beliefs about an Object and the Attitude Toward the Object," in *Readings in Attitude Theory and Measurement*, ed. Martin Fishbein (New York: John Wiley & Sons, Inc., 1967), p. 394.

that the candidate was anti-Vietnam, but have no real knowledge of the candidate's past voting record. Second, we must consider the evaluative factor. That is, we must know something of how the listener evaluates beliefs that he associates with the candidate. For example, if our listener favors the American commitment to Vietnam, knowing that the candidate opposes the war will reduce the listener's evaluation of him. Conversely, if the listener evaluates opposition to the war positively, association of this belief with the candidate will enhance the listener's evaluation of him.

Thus, Fishbein conceives of attitude toward a concept as equal to the sum of the probability dimension of each associated belief times the evaluative loading of the associated belief. The concept is expressed algebraically as follows:

$$A_o = \sum_{1 = i}^{n} a_i \, b_i$$

WHERE:

A_o = attitude toward some object "o."

B_i = belief i about o, that is, the probability that o is related to some other object X_i.

a_i = the evaluative aspect of b_i.

n = number of beliefs

Applying the formula to our example, let us suppose that each of the three traits associated with the candidate has been assessed by administration of Fishbein's AB Scales.[12] The results might be as follows:

CANDIDATE "X"

Honesty	(Belief level = 10)	× (Evaluative level = 15)	= 150
Opposition to Vietnam war	(Belief level = 4)	× (Evaluative level = 15)	= 60
Wealthy	(Belief level = 14)	× (Evaluative level = 2)	= 28
Etc.	. . .	. . .	. . .

12Martin Fishbein and Bertram Raven, "The AB Scales: An Operational Definition of Belief and Attitude," in *Readings in Attitude Theory and Measurement*, ed. Martin Fishbein (New York: John Wiley & Sons, Inc., 1967), pp. 183–89.

Attitude toward this candidate = 150 + 60 + 28 + other products.

This view of attitude is "unidimensional." That is, following Fishbein, we see attitude as simply the amount of affect for or against a concept.[13] This does not mean that beliefs and associative bonds are not important, but that they are seen as relevant to the formation and determination of attitude. Attitude itself, however, is the evaluative dimension of meaning.

The listener may thus be said to possess a structured cognitive map which represents reality for him. Fishbein's theory of the role of attitude within cognitive structures has important practical consequences for the speaker who wishes to influence the evaluative dimension of concept meaning—that is, change attitudes. Fishbein's view allows us to formulate the speaker's task in more specific terms. We will enumerate three of those tasks:

1. The speaker adds new beliefs to the listener's cognitive structure. Referring again to the example of our hypothetical candidate, assume for simplicity that your listeners hold only the three beliefs shown in the previous figure. Assume further that you as a speaker wish to persuade the listener to reject this candidate in the coming election. You may wish to tell the audience that this candidate consistently votes against educational funding and approves of the present military draft. If the listener perceives these two beliefs as negative characteristics, his evaluation of the candidate will be lowered. Thus, attitude change is in part dependent on the informing function of the speaker.

2. The speaker builds or attacks associations between concepts. It will not matter that the audience evaluates "voting against educational funding" negatively if they do not associate this concept strongly with the candidate. Thus, the speaker uses the forms and materials of discourse to establish the association. For example, you may cite a source trusted by the audience that shows the speaker's voting record on the issue. The source testifies to the existence of a relationship between the concepts "candidate" and "voting against educational funding." The strength of the association will depend on several factors, such as the listener's faith in the speaker as an honest reporter, belief in the trustworthiness of the source cited, and confidence that voting against the specific bill in question is a

13Martin Fishbein, "Attitude and the Prediction of Behavior," in Fishbein, *Readings in Attitude Theory,* p. 479.

good index of attitude toward educational funding in general. You may also wish to attack an association that you believe to be present in the mind of your listener. You might attack the association between "honesty" and "candidate" by arguing as follows: Those with something to hide vote against the public disclosure of all campaign contributions by law. This candidate votes against requiring such public disclosures. Therefore, this candidate probably has something to hide. Or you might refute an association drawn by the candidate in one of his speeches. If he argued that he is a strong antiwar candidate because he voted against a specific military appropriation bill, you might try to show that this one vote is not generally indicative of the candidate's general voting behavior on most bills related to the Vietnam war.

3. The speaker assesses the listener's cognitive system and plans in light of that assessment. The speaker must know something about the system of related beliefs held by the listener. Later in this chapter we will present suggestions for the systematic analysis of an audience, but now let us consider the ramifications of failing to analyze the cognitive system of the listener. Suppose that you plan to prove candidate X to be dishonest. You might choose to quote *The New York Times* to that effect. This is good strategy if your listeners hold positively evaluated beliefs about the values of *New York Times* reporting. Think what might occur if the audience holds very different beliefs about the *Times*. Suppose the listeners believe that the *Times* is biased, intent on destroying all "true American" candidates, and a tool of the Communist Party. If you tell this audience that *The New York Times* opposes candidate X, you may expect three results:

1. Candidate X will not be associated with dishonesty, since *The New York Times* will not be trusted to certify a relationship between the concepts candidate X and dishonesty.

2. The audience's attitudes toward the candidate will actually become more positive. They will probably see a categorical association between candidate X and the class of "true Americans" opposed by the *Times*.

3. The audience will probably hold your views in less esteem during the remainder of the speech. If they believe that those who trust "biased, Communist sources" are not very intelligent, they will associate you with those who trust such worthless sources. They will have a new negative belief associated with you.

This simplified example is meant to show that failure to assess your audience may result, not merely in failure to influence the listeners as you desire, but in moving them to an opposite point of view *and* significantly inhibiting your own future attempts to persuade. An excellent example of this kind of failure to analyze was provided by a student in a beginning public speaking class at the University of Massachusetts. The student, attempting to persuade the class that a particular candidate for governor should be supported, simply enumerated the legislative proposals that the candidate espoused. Many of these were highly sophisticated measures dealing with taxing powers, automobile insurance, and pollution control. The class was totally unmoved. Why should anyone prefer a candidate because he favors a certain proposal? Why should the proposal be positively evaluated by the audience? Some students took the speaker's word for the association between the concepts "candidate" and "auto insurance act," but, not knowing the nature of the insurance act, they simply associated the candidate with a belief that was essentially neutral in its evaluative dimension.

The speaker should have begun with the class's beliefs about auto insurance. They believed that it was extremely expensive and necessary. The speaker could have argued with reason and evidence that the new proposal was associated with reduction of insurance rates and availability of insurance. By first associating the bill itself with positively evaluated beliefs, he could have associated his candidate with a positively evaluated concept. This example of a classroom disaster should remind us to look at our listeners as active processors of information. They must make sense out of communication situations with the information they have on hand and the information that the speaker can convince them to accept. Speakers must make use of the experiences and attitudes possessed by the listener in planning persuasive messages.

FURTHER IMPLICATIONS OF STRUCTURE: CENTRALITY

We have observed that our beliefs are patterned in sets, and that certain beliefs underlie other beliefs in a hierarchical arrangement. A bit of reflection will indicate that some beliefs must, therefore, be more central than others. We may have three beliefs about one candidate, as in the previous examples. But this one candidate and others may all be related to the concept "Democrat," as shown below:

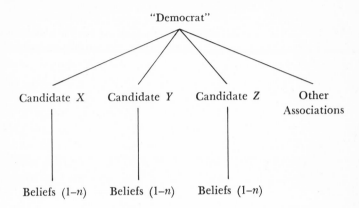

The concept "Democrat" may itself be more or less central to an individual's whole cognitive structure. Let us assume that a given individual's self-identification as a Democrat is highly central. Most of his beliefs and behaviors in business, social gatherings, politics, and so on, are in some way related to this central self-defining concept. If this is so, one of the hardest things to attempt would be to change this individual's attitude toward "Democrat" from positive to negative. If he should change his mind about "Democrat" he would have to alter the way he thinks and behaves in all of his social, business, and political dealings. More importantly, he would have to conclude that his whole image of himself is in error, that he has been a bad player in the game of life.

We have said that a listener's cognitive structure represents the world for him. It is a set of organizing categories that allows him to make sense out of the diversity of his environment. Hence, the more central a concept, the more beliefs and subsystems of belief are related to it, and the more likely it is that a change in the evaluation of the concept will have ramifications for the individual's whole world outlook. If a central notion about the world is admitted to be false, the individual is left with the problem of trying to make sense out of disorganized experience.

Conversely, we may examine the situation in which a given belief is peripheral to the individual. Political identification may be of central importance to one man's world view and self-image, but for another it may be a peripheral concern. For a businessman whose self-image is tied to economic success, and whose social and business associates rarely discuss politics, a change in party affiliation would have little effect.

The idea of cognitive structure thus provides the speaker with another dimension to be considered when planning a persuasive message. He must ask himself: Is the attitude I am trying to change central or peripheral for my listeners? Research evidence provided by Sherif, Sherif, and Nebergall support the hypothesis that central beliefs are the most difficult to change.[14] If the attitude you plan to alter is highly central, it is often best to reduce the scope of the goal that you set for any particular speech. It would be better to attempt alteration of one or more of the less central beliefs that underlie the major concept than to try altering the listener's whole world view at once. Such highly central beliefs will only be altered in the course of a long, gradual campaign. A single threat to an individual's whole perspective on self and life will probably result in the listener deciding to avoid the threat by not paying attention.

FURTHER IMPLICATIONS OF STRUCTURE: CONSISTENCY

We do not have to posit a totally rational model of the listener to accept the notion that there is some tendency toward consistency in the human cognitive system. A large number of researchers have employed the concept of consistency in their attempts to construct models of attitude change.[15] We are not arguing that consistency is the sole or even the paramount principle of cognitive dynamics, but only that the listener's need for consistency exists and has valuable explanatory power for helping us to understand how listeners may respond to communications.

Probably no individual has a totally consistent cognitive system. Abelson and Rosenberg point out that "there are innumerable

[14]Muzafer Sherif, Carolyn Sherif, and Roger Nebergall, *Attitude and Attitude Change* (Philadelphia: W.B. Saunders Co., 1965).

[15]The interested student will find an excellent review and critique of the major consistency theories in Chester A. Insko, *Theories of Attitude Change* (New York: Appleton-Century-Crofts, 1967).

inconsistencies in anyone's belief system that may lie dormant and unthought about."[16] Although the human cognitive system may be described as an organization of parts, there is no reason to assume that there is communication between any specific elements in a set, or between given sets. As Rokeach notes, however, the potential for communication is there.[17] Thus, we may conceive of the listener as having the capacity to isolate given beliefs. He may, for example, express hatred for "all dirty college kids," and total admiration for "my wonderful son the college student." By keeping these two concepts separate, this hypothetical listener can avoid confronting the inconsistency of his views, and thus maintain a kind of psychological consistency. He is not disturbed by the realization that his view of the world is incoherent from a logical view point. William McGuire's studies indicate that such individuals may be induced to reevaluate concepts if they are sensitized to the inconsistencies that they hold.[18] A speaker may take advantage of the fact that there is potential for communication among the parts of this individual's cognitive system by making the listener aware of his two isolated concepts at nearly the same time. He may ask the listener, "Do you have a son in college? Are you proud of him? Is he part of the class 'all college students' that you despise?" The listener may respond that his boy is one of the good college students, and in so doing he has agreed to reclassify so as to maintain consistency. He forms two classes of college students, "good" and "bad," placing his son in the former group. This seems a small change, but the listener has been led to reject blanket condemnation of all college students as a way of organizing his view of reality.

The foregoing illustration is meant to illuminate two points: (1) Our listeners have a tendency to prefer consistency, but may employ nonrational cognitive procedures (such as isolation) to achieve a sort of consistency; (2) Rational procedures can be effective in inducing consistency that more nearly approaches a rational model. This is not to say that such rational appeals will always be effective. An individual may face great pressures to find consistency

[16]Robert Abelson and Milton Rosenberg, "The Resolution of Belief Dilemmas," *Journal of Conflict Resolution*, Vol. 13, No. 4 (1959), 343–52.

[17]Rokeach, *The Open and Closed Mind*, pp. 33–34.

[18]William A. McGuire, "A Syllogistic Analysis of Cognitive Relationships," in *Attitude Organization and Change*, ed. Milton J. Rosenberg *et al.* (New Haven: Yale University Press, 1960), pp. 65–111.

through such nonlogical means as isolation rather than more rational means. Our hypothetical listener with a son in college may find that his social group wishes him to join them in blanket condemnations of college students when he is with them in the union hall; if he takes a more moderate view he is socially ostracized. If the social contacts are important to him, the new way of categorizing college students will have proven a less useful way of viewing the world. It is not unreasonable to assume that an individual will prefer to adopt a way of looking at the world that maximizes those rewards that are of importance to him.

Consistency needs should not be construed as simply a tendency for "proper" logical relationships. Research by McGuire indicates that there is both a tendency for "a person's beliefs (expectations) on related issues to be in accord with each other in the pattern required by the rules of formal logic," and a tendency "for a person's beliefs on a given issue to be in accord with his desires on that issue."[19] McGuire calls the latter form of consistency "wishful thinking." Thus, an individual's belief that pollution control is a Communist plot may depend, in part, on his belief that all movements supported by the university community are Communist plots, and upon the knowledge that the movement for pollution control is supported by the university community. The conclusion, however, will also depend on the extent to which the individual wants to believe that pollution control is a Communist plot. The combination of logical thinking and wishful thinking provides a significantly better prediction of attitude than does the logical thinking factor alone.[20]

The extent to which the kind and degree of one's cognitive consistency approaches a rational model is thus moderated by the tendency to bring reality into accord with desires and situational pressures. Two additional factors also affect the tendency toward cognitive consistency. First, individuals make logical errors in categorical relationships, hence, they accidentally create inconsistencies. In addition, individuals differ in their need for consistency. Arthur Cohen writes:

> . . . the need for cognitive clarity [is] the need to impose meaning, organization, integration, reasonableness on one's experiential world.

[19]*Ibid.*
[20]*Ibid.*

It may be that a person develops this need because he finds that achieving clarity is instrumental in satisfying other needs and because demands are made upon him . . . to comprehend, figure out, organize, see through, and relate information.[21]

In brief, an individual who drives a truck for a living and never discusses political science has little pressure to systematize these views, while a professor of political science has greater need for consistency in such matters.

If a speaker succeeds in getting a listener to accept data that is discrepant from a prevailing attitude, the listener may then behave in a variety of ways to reduce the degree of inconsistency that now pervades his world. Although research in the resolution of inconsistency is still in its infancy, speculation does indicate at least seven modes of cognitive behavior that may be employed.[22]

reevaluation. The listener may obtain greater cognitive consistency by reevaluating concepts, that is through attitude change. Suppose we are talking to a listener who is extremely negative toward the concept "Republicans." If we convince him that Lindsay, Goodell, and Javitz are all desirable candidates and all Republicans, he would then face an inconsistent situation as diagramed below:

The situation can be brought into balance by reevaluating the concept "Republican," as shown below:

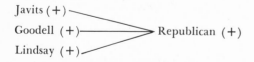

stop attending. If the information is disturbing because it creates inconsistency, a listener can simply "turn off," that is, stop attending to the whole problem.

[21]Arthur Cohen, *Attitude Change and Social Influence* (New York: Basic Books, Inc., Publishers, 1964), p. 49.
[22]The distinctions drawn here are based primarily upon the work of Abelson and Rosenberg, "The Resolution of Belief Dilemmas."

bolstering. Robert Abelson says that when an individual notes
an inconsistency between two of his beliefs, he can amass a great
number of other beliefs that are consistent with the conflicting
belief.[23] For example, a preacher might tell a listener that he is a
sinful man because he drinks, but the listener may consider himself a very good man, although he admits to imbibing on special
occasions (like the setting of the sun, high noon, and so on). The
listener faces this inconsistency in his cognitive structure:

Self (+) ————— Drinking (−)

To avoid any major readjustment of his self-image, our imbibing
listener may choose to see drinking as one extremely small aspect
of his many-faceted personality. The inconsistency is not removed,
but it is submerged so as to reduce its import and minimize the
amount of reevaluation that the self-concept must undergo. This
is accomplished by "bolstering" the positive concept with all of the
consistent beliefs that the individual can muster. The technique is
diagramed below:

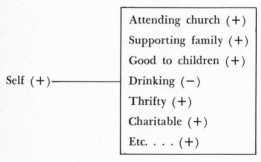

Self (+)————————

Attending church (+)
Supporting family (+)
Good to children (+)
Drinking (−)
Thrifty (+)
Charitable (+)
Etc. . . . (+)

This device can successfully reduce inconsistency so long as the individual consciously or habitually attends to many positive associations with "self" whenever he attends to the association "drinking."

compartmentalizing. Compartmentalization is the mode of
maintaining internal consistency by keeping conflicting beliefs in
logic-tight isolated compartments.[24] Earlier we considered the case
of an individual who compartmentalized his view of "all college

---

[23]*Ibid.*

[24]In addition to Abelson and Rosenberg, see McGuire, "A Syllogistic
Analysis of Cognitive Relationships."

students," and kept this concept dissociated from the concept "my son." The individual knows that one of these concepts is the genus (all college students) and the other the species (my son). He simply avoids attending to the association that is implicit in his own category system.

   differentiating.[25] We see differentiation as a mode of maintaining consistency distinct from compartmentalizing. Again refer to the example of the listener who hated all college students but professed to value his son very positively. We showed how that individual might be sensitized to the inconsistency implicit in his own method of categorizing. Once sensitized, he found the method of compartmentalizing inadequate, but instead of reevaluating the concept "all college students," he chose another mode of inconsistency reduction. He divided the single concept "all college students" into two coordinate categories, as shown below:

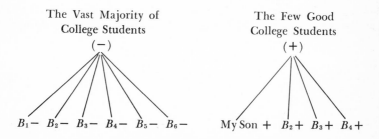

Where: B = Belief

Note that this mode of inconsistency reduction is another way of avoiding a genus-species relationship that would class "my son" with "all college students." By differentiating between two coordinate classes of students, the individual has so reordered his concepts that he does not have to avoid attending to the logical relationship that is inherent in his own classification system. If we asked this hypothetical listener, "How do you feel about students generally?" he might reply as follows: "I can't answer that question, because there are two distinct groups that cannot be meaningfully discussed as a composite."

   [25]See the work of Roger Brown, *Social Psychology* (New York: The Free Press, 1965), pp. 555-57.

transcending.[26] This technique may be viewed as the opposite of differentiating. The listener faced with two contradictory bits of data may create a new general concept that reconciles them. For example, we may like the personality of a given candidate, but find that he makes statements with which we agree when he speaks in the North, and statements with which we disagree when he speaks in the South. If we don't wish to declare him a charlatan, we might just create a new category that reconciles the discrepant beliefs he expresses. We might class these inconsistencies as part of the concept "necessary winning strategy." Since nothing can be better than to have our "good candidate" win, we can erect a wholly consistent cognitive structure as follows:

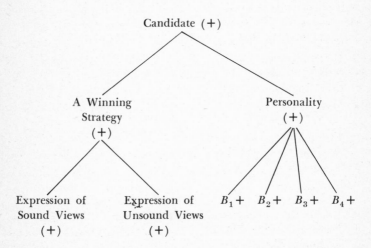

The "winning strategy" category transcends the contradictory expressions of the candidate. It allows us to see the expression of views with which we disagree as positively evaluated events within a strategy to win office, rather than as negatively weighted information about the ability or honesty of the candidate.

decentralizing.[27] This additional means of partial resolution involves shifting a set of beliefs to a less central place in one's view of reality. Faced with inconsistencies in his political outlook, an individual might shift his hierarchy of political beliefs to a more

[26]Abelson and Rosenberg, "The Resolution of Belief Dilemmas."
[27]*Ibid.*

peripheral position in his cognitive structure. Suppose that in the past this hypothetical individual made many decisions about social relationships, club memberships, and other activities on the basis of his self-concept as "a Democrat." Unable to make coherent sense out of the political spectrum, this individual may choose to base his concept of self and his day-to-day decisions on his economic or religious beliefs, which form a more coherent system. He thus decentralizes the place of the inconsistent set of beliefs. The inconsistency remains, but no longer has such great import for the problems of daily living.

The foregoing possibilities should serve to reemphasize the active role of the listener in rhetorical settings. We have implicitly portrayed the human respondent as a creature who creates categories, relates or disrelates them, and evaluates them. Since some of this behavior is beyond the direct influence of the speaker, its existence should serve to disabuse us of the view that public speaking is a kind of all-powerful weapon that controls the minds of men.

Our discussion of cognitive consistency also suggests some practical advice for the speaker:

1. If you believe that the view you are attacking contains inconsistencies, strive for the explicit illumination of inconsistencies in order to sensitize listeners to them.

2. When you are presenting information that is discrepant from the information they already have, emphasize the relative importance of the discrepant information. This might help combat behavior on the part of the listener that will bolster his previous information.

3. Do not begin by raising a direct threat to the listener's whole world view. Here is a sure way to get an audience of middle-aged conservative people to stop attending:

   (INTRODUCTORY MATERIAL): Good evening. Today I intend to show how your stupid, ill-conceived, middle class values led us into the Vietnam mess. But first I pause to relate an amusing anecdote . . .

4. Show your listeners how they can make consistent sense out of the world through the perspective you offer.

While the need for consistency is an important general principle in cognitive dynamics, we must avoid the temptation to see it as the single operating principle in attitude change. People often seek novelty, even at the risk of encountering discrepant information; individuals can and do cope with conscious inconsistencies in their world view.[28] The author of this chapter prefers to live with the often confusing mass of contradictory findings in persuasion theory in the hope that a coherent picture will someday take shape.

FURTHER IMPLICATIONS OF STRUCTURE: SALIENCE

We have discussed at some length the idea that beliefs are patterned in sets. We have also discussed the theory that attitude is equal to the sum of the affective values of associated beliefs times the probability dimension of those beliefs (see page 73). Now consider a concept that has a vast number of associations. Think about the concept "mother." Many associations are brought to mind. Notice that the longer you think about it, the greater the number of associations you recall. If you think about this concept again a few hours from now, it is possible that you will bring to mind still other associations. Some of your associations with the concept are more salient than others, that is, they are more dependably elicited whenever you think of the term. This is a function of the probability dimension of our associations and the position of beliefs in our response hierarchy.

Consider the problem of salience when we deal with terms that have many equally strong associations. Which associations will be salient at a given time to influence our evaluation of a concept? Research indicates that only six to eleven of our associations with a term are salient for us at one time, and therefore only six to eleven associations function to determine our attitude toward the main concept.[29]

Fishbein saw the implications of this line of research for his

---

[28]Cohen, *Attitude Change and Social Influence.*

[29]Milton J. Rosenberg, "Cognitive Structure and Attitudinal Affect," in *Readings in Attitude Theory and Measurement*, ed. Martin Fishbein (New York: John Wiley & Sons, Inc., 1967), pp. 325–331; R.S. Woodward and H. Schossberg, *Experimental Psychology* (New York: Holt, Rinehart and Winston, Inc., 1954); G.A. Miller, "The Magical Number Seven," *Psychological Review*, Vol. 26 (1956), 81–97.

own formulation and modified his model of attitude to make attitude equal to the sum of the affective values of salient beliefs. If a belief is not salient for us at a given time, it is not contributing to our evaluative behavior.

Think about the notion of belief salience as you read the following speech, delivered during a prohibition crusade early in the century:

I bear no malice toward those engaged in the liquor business, but I hate the traffic.

I hate its every phase.

I hate it for its intolerance.

I hate it for its arrogance.

I hate it for its hypocrisy; for its cant and craft and false pretense.

I hate it for its commercialism; for its greed and avarice; for its sordid love of gain at any price.

I hate it for its domination of politics; for its corrupting influence in civic affairs; for its incessant effort to debauch the suffrage of the country; for the cowards it makes of public men.

I hate it for its utter disregard of law; for its ruthless trampling of the solemn compacts of State constitutions.

I hate it for the load it straps to labor's back; for the palsied hands it gives to toil; for its wounds to genius; for the tragedies of its might-have-beens.

I hate it for the human wrecks it has caused.

I hate it for the almhouses it peoples; for the prisons it fills; for the insanity it begets; for its countless graves in potters' fields.

I hate it for the mental ruin it imposes upon its victims; for its spiritual blight; for its moral degradation.

I hate it for the crimes it commits; for the homes it destroys; for the hearts it breaks.

I hate it for the malice it plants in the hearts of men; for its poison, for its bitterness, for the dead sea fruit with which it starves their souls.

I hate it for the grief it causes womanhood—the scalding tears, the hopes deferred, the strangled aspirations, its burden of want and care.

I hate it for its heartless cruelty to the aged, the infirm and the helpless; for the shadow it throws upon the lives of children; for its monstrous injustice to blameless little ones.

I hate it as virtue hates vice, as truth hates error, as righteousness hates sin, as justice hates wrong, as liberty hates tyranny, as freedom hates oppression.

I hate it as Abraham Lincoln hated slavery, and as he sometimes
saw in prophetic vision the end of slavery, and the coming of the
time when the sun should shine and the rain should fall upon no
slave in all the Republic, so I sometimes seem to see the end of this
unholy traffic, the coming of the time when, if it does not wholly
cease to be, it shall find no safe habitation anywhere beneath Old
Glory's stainless stars. [30]

We could say that the function of this brief speech was to
"remind" (that is, to make salient) a great number of negative associations with liquor. The speaker makes no attempt to prove that
these evil events are associated with the sale of liquor; he assumes
that the audience already believes the associations hold. Modern
research makes us doubt that the speaker, in a single speech, can
really make all of these associations salient for very long. Any change
in the way in which the listener habitually thinks about liquor
would probably require a long systematic campaign aimed at rein-
forcing recall of certain negative associations. A listener may regularly go to church and hear short speeches like the one above, at
which times he will feel very negative toward liquor, since his strong
negative beliefs are salient. He may express his anger and feel the
social approval of others. If sufficiently reinforced, he may make the
same negative associations salient in a number of situations, even
carrying the habit over into the voting booth, where he will vote the
prohibitionist ticket. However, if our listener is getting a very different kind of reinforcement from his friends at the local bar on week-
days, the associations that will be salient at the voting booth are
harder to predict.

In general, when a large number of beliefs relatively equal in
probability are associated with a concept, we may expect that cues
from outside the listener, such as situation, message, and the rein-
forcing effects of repeated trials, will influence which associations
become salient.

The concept of salience also bears some practical implications
for the public speaker:

1. The speaker should not assume that the beliefs an individual
   associates with a concept are always salient. He may have to

---

[30]J. Frank Hanly, "I Hate It," in *Speeches of the Flying Squadron* (Indianapolis: Hanley and Stewart, n.d.), pp. 27–28.

remind listeners of certain associations before using them as a basis for reasoning to new conclusions.

2. The stability of one's attitude across situations is influenced by the level of probability with which one thinks a given belief to be associated with a concept. Thus, a speaker must attend carefully to the development of associations. He must show, for example, good reasons for associating liquor with economic loss. The stronger the new association, the more reliable the listener's evaluative responses will be.

3. The speaker must not assume that the listener will manifest the same initial attitude toward every concept in every situation. Some attitudes will be more stable than others. For example, if our associations with a concept are all strongly associated positive beliefs and weakly associated negative beliefs, we may expect that a positive response will be reliably elicited by the major concept. If, however, the major concept is associated with many beliefs of equally strong association, some of which are negative and some positive, attitude in a given situation will be less predictable. Simply put, what is salient about liquor in church may not be salient in the local bar. Your analysis of audience must therefore account for the setting in which your speech is to be delivered.

THE ROLE OF MOTIVES

Although theorists differ in their conception of motives, they generally agree that motives function to direct and drive behavior. "Drive" refers to "an internal process that goads a person into action."[31] The "directing" influence refers to the role of motives as goal states or rewards, which, if reached, reduce the drive. Of what relevance are motives to the study of public speaking?

The study of motives aids us in understanding how attitudes function for the individual. If the speaker assesses incorrectly the function that an attitude performs for the listener, he may develop a wholly inappropriate strategy for bringing about attitude change. Although there are many ways that motives may be classified, one motive common to many theorists is "social adjustment," or the

[31]Edward J. Murray, *Motivation and Emotion* (Englewood Cliffs, N.J.: Prentice-Hall, Inc., 1964), p. 7.

need to be accepted by a socially attractive group. People may adopt a set of beliefs in order to obtain social approval; a successful campaign of this sort would have to allow some device by which the individual can still obtain social approval. The so-called "bandwagon" technique in propaganda functions to assure the individual that adoption of a new set of beliefs will not lead to social ostracism. Cronkhite goes so far as to essentialize the process of persuasion as the establishment of a relationship between a motivational concept and an object concept.[32] "Social adjustment" would be a motivational concept; "voting for candidate Jones" might be an object concept. In Cronkhite's view, the speaker attempts to demonstrate that these concepts are related. Obviously, if the speaker cannot demonstrate that the view he espouses will lead the listener to anything he desires, there is no reason why the listener should adopt the view. If the speaker can demonstrate the existence of a relationship between an object concept and a motive, then the stronger the motive, the more attractive the new attitude should be.

Let us explore the importance of this analysis by referring to two quite different types of motives. First, consider the motivation for "ego-defense," which refers to the individual's need to protect himself from harsh truths about himself and reality. Second, we will focus on the "knowledge" motive, involving the individual's need to find structure, meaning, explanations, and organizations in his world. Assume that it is our task to deliver a series of speeches in the Deep South, our goal being to improve the attitude of southern Whites toward Blacks. In a question of this nature, analysis of motives is central. Perhaps in a given audience the dominant motive for negative attitudes toward Blacks is the need for ego-defense. Some of our listeners may be poor Whites who avoid the harsh reality of their personal position by dividing the world into two simple classes—the good intelligent Whites and the bad unintelligent Blacks. Thus, no matter how ignorant or impoverished the listener is, he sees himself as part of the good, intelligent, significant part of the world. It would probably be useless to spend much time arguing that Blacks are as intelligent as Whites, that Blacks have contributed significantly to the arts and sciences, or that Blacks have made significant contributions to government. Such arguments would be a good strategy if the listener's attitudes toward Blacks

[32]Gary L. Cronkhite, *Persuasion: Speech and Behavior Change* (Indianapolis: The Bobbs-Merrill Co., Inc., 1969), pp. 74–92.

served to make consistent sense of reality (the knowledge motive). But this data will not help the listener to achieve the ego-defense goal; he will probably stop attending. If the speaker is to obtain any real shift in listener's perspective, he must create a communication strategy that shows the poor White how he can defend his ego and hold new attitudes toward Black Americans at the same time. Our failure to evolve such a strategy probably accounts in part for the persistent failure to achieve political alliance between poor Whites and Blacks in the South.

We have discussed the relationship between a particular attitude and a single motive, but the speaker will be even more successful if he can associate a particular object concept with a number of strong motives. The diagram below indicates how an individual's attitude toward the concept "booze" might be related to several motives:[33]

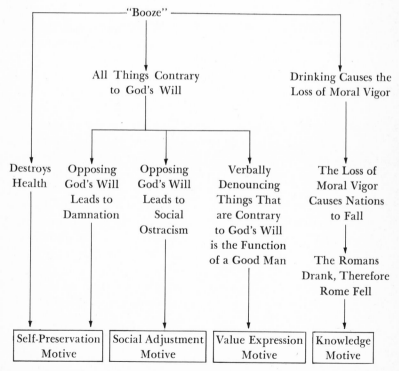

[33]The motives described in this diagram correspond to the attitudinal functions outlined by Daniel Katz, "The Functional Approach to Attitude Change," *Public Opinion Quarterly*, 24 (1960), 163–204.

Motives have been classified in many different ways. Later we will present a classification system developed by Abraham Maslow that seems particularly useful for the public speaker.[34] For now, let us summarize this brief introduction to the role of motives with some practical advice to the beginning public speaker: Audience analysis is not complete after assessing the prevailing beliefs and attitudes of listeners. To fashion an appropriate communication strategy, the speaker must attempt to account for how such beliefs function to fulfill the listener's motives.

THE EFFECTS OF ATTITUDES AND BELIEFS

Having defined attitude as the evaluative dimension of a concept's meaning, we must now ask how a changed attitude is likely to affect an individual's functioning. We will treat this question from two perspectives: How existing attitudes affect the way an individual perceives outside stimuli, and how they affect the way an individual overtly behaves toward his environment. Existing research literature allows us to be more informative about the former than the latter.

attitudes and receptive behavior

An individual's cognitive system functions to reduce the infinite diversity of his environment to manageable categories.[35] These categories not only constitute a systematization of past experience, but also a way of understanding new stimuli. A given way of systematizing the environment means that the individual will attend in specific ways. Bruner offers the following explanation and example:

> The use of cues in inferring the categorical identity of a perceived object . . . is as much a feature of perception as the sensory stuff from which percepts are made. What is interesting about the nature

[34]Abraham Maslow, *Motivation and Personality* (New York: Harper & Brothers, Publishers, 1954).

[35]Bruner *et al.*, *A Study of Thinking*, pp. 1–3.

of the inference from cue to identity in perception is that it is in no sense different from other kinds of categorical inferences based on defining attributes. "That thing is round and nubbly in texture and orange in color and of such-and-such size—therefore an orange. Let me now test its other properties to be sure."[36]

Notice how, in this example, stimuli attained meaning for the beholder through comparison with categories that were already in existence. The hypothetical "orange beholder" also used his category system to derive certain tests to ensure correct categorization of the new stimuli. The individual might look for a certain degree of hardness and find that his orange belongs in the class "artificial orange." Thus, he has selectively attended to certain stimuli in order to attain a given end, employing strategies of selective attention. We can say that the individual "tunes" his cognitive apparatus to attend in a way that is conducive to solving the problem at hand.[37] We can now apply our analysis of the fine art of perceiving oranges to the practical problem of public discourse.

Simon and Garfunkel sing a song called "The Boxer" which includes the line: "But a man hears what he wants to hear, and disregards the rest." A number of investigations show that our perceptions are highly influenced by our attitudes and beliefs. We attend to messages and events selectively in accord with our expectations. One interesting study indicates that attitudes so affected the way in which a football game was perceived by the fans of rival schools that the researchers concluded that it was almost senseless to say that the fans all "saw" the same game.[38] In another study, the same message was attributed either to a source believed to be moderate or a source believed to be more radical. As you might expect, the message was perceived as significantly more radical when attributed to the more radical source.[39]

Researchers also indicate that our prevailing attitude toward

[36]Jerome Bruner, "On Perceptual Readiness," *Psychological Review*, Vol. 64 (1957), 125.

[37]Robert Zajonc, "The Process of Cognitive Tuning in Communication," *The Journal of Abnormal and Social Psychology*, Vol. 61 (1960), 159.

[38]A. Hasdorf and H. Cantril, "They Saw A Game: A Case Study," *Journal of Abnormal and Social Psychology*, Vol. 49 (1954), 129–34.

[39]Michael Burgoon, "The Effects of Response Set and Race on Message Interpretation," *Speech Monographs* (1970), 264–68.

a subject functions as an "anchor" for the perception of other messages about that subject. This research, which goes under the name of "assimilation-contrast effects,"[40] indicates that individuals assess a speaker's position on an issue in light of their own positions. The assimilation-contrast view holds that when a speaker takes a position near the listener's own position, the speaker's position will be "assimilated," that is, perceived as more nearly identical with the listener's position than a disinterested party would perceive it to be. Conversely, discrepant views are "contrasted," that is, perceived to be more distant from the listener's position than a disinterested party would perceive them. In general, we may say that a listener's perception of what is said in a persuasive message is determined in part by his own attitudes and beliefs. This is important, because what the listener perceives is the message for him.

Verbal communication also displays strong evidence of cognitive tuning similar to that described in the orange perception example. An individual's beliefs and attitudes at a given time cause him to apply a strategy of receptive behaviors in order to handle the situation. One study indicates that when listeners believe that they must actively defend the conclusions reached on the basis of a communication, they attend to specific data and categorize it in more sophisticated ways than when their post-communication task is merely to make a decision.[41] The need to defend one's views requires specific well-organized data, so the listener tunes his cognitive apparatus to attend to the kind of information needed. Another study indicates that people tend to recall those statements in a message that provide plausible support for their own positions and implausible support for opposing positions.[42]

The importance of attitudes and beliefs for receptive behavior may be summarized as follows. One's habitual way of looking at reality, his cognitive structure of associated beliefs and attitudes, allows him to size up a situation and select a set of receptive strategies for filtering out the useful information in that situation. The

[40]Muzafer Sherif and Carl I. Hovland, *Social Judgment: Assimilation and Contrast Effects in Communication and Attitude Change* (New Haven: Yale University Press, 1961).

[41]Zajonc, "The Process of Cognitive Tuning in Communication."

[42]Edward E. Jones and Rita Kohler, "The Effects of Plausibility on the Learning of Controversial Statements," *Journal of Abnormal and Social Psychology*, Vol. 57, No. 3 (1958), 315–20.

category system that we bring to the situation, plus the tuned up filtration strategy, determine the way in which external stimuli are perceived. These perceptions, if assimilated into the cognitive structure, may then influence the nature of the cognitive system and cause the tuning up of new filtration strategies. The process may be modeled as shown in the figure.

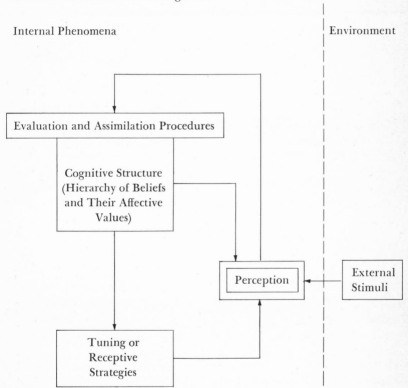

Note that this model places perception within the mental processes of the listener, not out in the external world. The cognitive functions of the listener interact with external stimuli to determine perception. Note also that the model describes a continuing functional process without terminal points. As Hartly put it, new information functions as new instructions for selecting out and assigning meaning to subsequent information.[43] To put the matter another

[43]R.V.L. Hartly, as cited in Colin Cherry, *On Human Communication* (Cambridge, Mass.: The M.I.T. Press, 1957), p. 172.

way, a change in attitudes and beliefs entails a change in the way in which the individual will perceive subsequent communications.

The problems of perceptual distortion suggest some strategies for the speaker.[44]

1. The speaker should use language that is familiar and consistent with the listener's linguistic labels for cognitive categories.
2. The speaker should strive to avoid highly loaded language when his audience is generally opposed to his position. Do this to minimize the "contrast" effects which increase the perceived gap between your position and that of your listeners.
3. Since opposing evidence is likely to be filtered out, restate crucial ideas and evidence in a number of ways when the audience holds views very different from your own.

attitudes, beliefs, and overt behavior

Several theorists have been concerned about the lack of correlation between measures of attitude and overt behavior. Some of the "slippage" between attitudes and overt behavior is the result of measuring attitude toward one concept and behavior toward a different concept. LaPiere measured attitudes toward the stimulus concept "Chinese" and behavior toward a specific well-dressed Chinese couple.[45] The failure of attitude toward one concept to predict behavior toward another should not surprise us, since it is likely that the subjects of the study had different salient beliefs about "Chinese in general" than they had about the specific Chinese couple that they saw.

Even if we are careful to measure attitudes and behaviors toward the same concept, we should not expect these measurements to be a sufficient predictor of overt behavior. Both Doob and Fishbein have noted that we do not just learn attitudes and beliefs about a concept, we also separately learn how and under what circum-

---

[44]The strategies cited here were suggested by Howard H. Martin and Kenneth E. Andersen, "Communication Strategies," in *Speech Communication: Analysis and Readings*, ed. Howard H. Martin and Kenneth E. Andersen (Boston: Allyn & Bacon, Inc., 1969), pp. 127–47.

[45]Richard T. LaPiere, "Attitudes Versus Actions," *Social Forces*, Vol. 13 (1934), 230–37.

stances to express our attitudes and beliefs.[46] If you are finding a textbook laborious reading, you will probably not stand up in class tomorrow and announce, "I think this book is a bore!" You may be concerned about the role you play in the classroom situation and about the impact of role playing on your grade. However, one of your friends may be more accustomed to full display of his attitudes and announce his displeasure loudly. He might not really care about his grade, or may have a different conception of his social role in the classroom. Thus, although you and your friend may have the same attitudes and beliefs toward the material, your classroom behavior toward it may be different. In the dorm, under different role conditions, you and your friend may both respond the same way.

To understand overt behavior, we must consider more than attitudes and beliefs. A real theory of persuasion and behavior change would probably have to account for at least the following factors:

1. The individual's motives in a given situation.
2. The individual's social role in a given situation.
3. The individual's repertory of behavioral intentions.

We have already discussed briefly the importance of motives, noting that they serve to drive and direct activity, and thus function as goal states, in that the individual's behavior is directed to fulfillment of the motive.

The idea of "role" has not yet been discussed. Roles may be studied as "norms" that apply to categories of people.[47] Of course, a person can and does assume different roles, and thus has reference to a number of sets of norms. You can take the roles of "student" and "campaigner" at different times. In the example in which two individuals applied different norms in a classroom, they were probably playing different roles. One may have conceived of his role as "All-American College Student," while his more vociferous friend may have conceived of his role as "campus radical."

It seems reasonable to speculate that assumption of a given role would influence the arousal of specific motives. For example,

[46]Fishbein, "Attitude and the Prediction of Behavior," pp. 477–92.
[47]Roger Brown, *Social Psychology* (New York: The Free Press, 1965), p. 154.

the role of "All-American College Student" would hardly seem compatible with the motive of obtaining social approval from radical students. More likely is the possibility that social roles are adopted in order to fulfill certain motives; desire for social acceptance may account for assuming the role of "campus radical" in some situations. Thus, we may posit an interaction between motives and roles.

The role that an individual assumes must also interact with his cognitive structure of beliefs and attitudes. Certain perceptions when compared to the individual's cognitive system lead the individual to conclude that he is in a situation calling for a certain role. Our mental category system allows us to interpret our perceptions to mean that we are in a classroom, hence we select the appropriate role of student.

Once a role has been derived and assumed, it interacts with our cognitive structure and our repertory of behavioral intention. We see behavioral intentions as a catalogue of "plans for action" that may be executed in response to a concept or situation.[48] In light of a given role, the individual selects a set of behavioral intentions that seem appropriate to the fulfillment of motives. This selecting operation must be with reference to the individual's beliefs about: (1) the situation, (2) concepts under discussion in the situation, and (3) people present in the situation. In large, the norms associated with a role function as a system of rules that tell the individual how to relate the following factors:

1. Beliefs and attitudes about situations, people, and other concepts.
2. Motivational goal states.
3. Selection of behavioral intentions.

Suppose that you have observed that you are in a classroom with your rhetoric teacher and several classmates, and the teacher has just asked, "What do you think of the material on attitude change?" Your primary motive might be to gain the approval of your teacher. In your cognitive system you hold the beliefs the material is dull, that your rhetoric teacher probably likes this material, and that your rhetoric teacher dislikes those who criticize the text. If asked, "How did *you* like the material on attitudes?" you

---

[48]Fishbein "Attitude and the Prediction of Behavior."

might think to yourself, "It was an awful bore," but you might also think that in light of your role as a student and what you know about your rhetoric teacher, it would be unwise to express your attitude openly. Given your motive, you might select the behavior intention of uttering some innocuous phrase about how "interesting" the section was. Then, seeing the need to respond, you might implement the plan by saying, "It was rather interesting." The relationship among attitudes, beliefs, roles, and behavioral intentions may be roughly modeled as shown below:

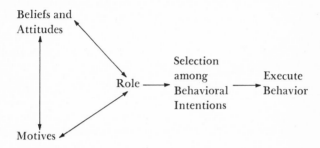

There is no reason to assume that a changed attitude will consistently cause specific change in behavior in every situation.

the speaker as respondent

Many studies confirm that the individual most likely to be significantly persuaded in a rhetorical situation is the speaker himself.[49] A common phenomenon is the case in which a speaker begins with a position that he thinks is only possibly true, develops a speech, presents it, and emerges convinced that the position he advocated is correct. There are several possible reasons for this self-persuasion effect. First, the audience may provide positive reinforcement for the speaker in the form of feedback. The speaker manipulates the message in order to get positive feedback; when he gets it, he learns that the position he advocated is positively related to his need for social approval and self-esteem.

There is another possible reason for self-persuasion. A message

[49]Carl I. Hovland, Irving Janis, and Harold Kelly, *Communication and Persuasion* (New Haven: Yale University Press, 1956), Chapter 7.

designed to change a listener's attitudes and beliefs may entail assumptions about the listener's prior beliefs, attitudes, and knowledge level that are entirely in error, with the result that the listener may perceive the message in a way different from that which the speaker intended. The speaker, on the other hand, can only use terms that he already knows, and concepts that he generally understands, and thus is more likely to use beliefs that are salient in his own cognitive system. In the process of writing a speech, he takes these beliefs and orders them to form a consistent system of support for the view he advocates. Hence, from the perspective of comprehension, belief saliency, and consistency needs, we should expect the speaker to be more readily persuasible. He proves to himself in the speech he has written that a consistent system can be developed to support a specific view. The speaker's expression of this view is then given reinforcement in the rhetorical situation via feedback. Arthur Schlesinger vividly described John F. Kennedy's realization of self-persuasion effects. He tells of the effect of the "Ich bin ein Berliner" speech on President Kennedy as the "crowd shook itself and rose and roared like an animal. . . . The hysteria spread almost visibly through the square. Kennedy was first exhilarated, then disturbed; he felt, as he remarked on his return, that if he had said, 'March to the wall—tear it down,' his listeners would have marched. . . ." So exhilarated by the excited, impassioned mass Kennedy allowed his words to become "unwontedly harsh. . . ."[50]

toward a theory of persuasion

In the foregoing discussion of attitude and belief we have not attempted to formulate a single theory of persuasion. None exists as yet. We have simply attempted to provide a set of concepts that are useful to the practicing public speaker and representative of current directions in attempts to formulate this theory. It is our hope that some beginning students of public address will become sufficiently intrigued with the problem of formulating a theory of communication to pursue it in further work.

It is essential that you recognize the rhetorical situation as a complex process that includes only active participants, not passive

[50]Arthur Schlesinger, Jr., *A Thousand Days* (Boston: Houghton Mifflin Company, 1965), pp. 737–38.

receivers. While for the sake of simplicity we have spoken of speakers and listeners, these are obviously not two distinct classes. Speaker and listener are roles that we constantly exchange every day in the course of every conversation.

approaches to audience analysis

Audiences may be classified in a variety of ways. For example, in our media age we often see speeches being given thousands of miles away, and some of us have participated in communicative events from spaceships orbiting the earth, and even from the surface of the moon. Speakers have always had not only face-to-face audiences, but audiences removed in time and space from the immediate rhetorical situation. The speeches of Demosthenes were not discussed only in Athens, and are still read in the 1970s.

Today, an auditor sitting in a sun-drenched, crowded football stadium to hear a commencement speaker will respond somewhat differently from the auditor listening to the same speaker in the air conditioned comfort of his own home. Still, speakers attempt to reach both audiences simultaneously; for example, Martin Luther King's "I Have a Dream" speech was not only addressed to the several hundred thousand gathered before the Lincoln Monument, but also to television viewers of the 1963 event. It was also, one may argue, addressed to future audiences as well.

Speakers often acknowledge their multiple audiences. Consider a televised speech during one of evangelist Billy Graham's Crusades in East Tennessee. The call to repentance in the end was not only to those actually physically present at the evangelistic meeting, but also to the television audience. Graham asked:

> Why not come today, now, and receive Him? . . . I'm going to ask you to do that. I'm going to ask hundreds of you to leave your seats in the stands right now and come and stand on this field. . . . You get up and come from all over the stadium. . . . There are many of you who have been watching by television and you see these hundreds of people who are coming here in this stadium in Knoxville, Tennessee, to receive Christ as their Lord and Saviour. You can

receive Him right now where you're watching. He'll come into your heart there.[51]

SOCIAL RELATIONSHIPS

In addition to classifying audiences as immediate face-to-face audiences and those distant in space or time, we can also categorize them in terms of who is addressed by the speaker. Sociologist Hugh Duncan categorizes five types of audiences: "these are, first, general public ('they'); second, community guardians ('we'); third, others significant to us as friends and confidants with whom we talk intimately ('thou'); fourth, the selves we address inwardly in soliloquy (the 'I' talking to the 'me'); and fifth, ideal audiences whom we address as ultimate sources of social order ('it')."[52]

Even the child recognizes that he must talk to different people in different ways, not only in what he says, but often in how he phrases it and the tone of voice he uses. The child speaks to his mother in the presence of his father, brothers and sisters, family friends, or strangers. Moreover, he soon realizes that he may speak to different audiences at the same time. By being especially agreeable with his parents he can irritate his brothers and sisters, or if he talks too much with his teacher he may be considered an "apple polisher." Even at an early age, what we say to one audience is in large measure conditioned by the presence of other audiences. We also realize that there are sometimes different sets of demands by inner and outer audiences. What we say to the boss or a dean in our inner dialogue may not be what we say in our actual public dialogue. These inner conflicts are often the result of our natural impulses in conflict with social or cultural needs.

This book is most concerned with the first two audiences ("they" and "we"), and of those two, most with the second ("we"). The "they" is the audience reached by mass appeal, whether they are being sold a box of soap or a political candidate. Hitler staged spectacular dramas in which the people could participate, but we participate in huge dramas, via television, far beyond Hitler's

[51]Transcribed from a tape made from the national telecast in June 1970.

[52]Hugh Duncan, *Symbols in Society* (New York: Oxford University Press, 1968), p. 81.

imagination. An agitator in California can reach hundreds of thousands of people instantly on the evening news. Thus, we not only have huge spectacles to which we may go (in football stadiums, the Astrodome, Madison Square Garden, Chicago's Cow Palace), but spectacles may come to us at home. Some confrontations may be staged primarily for a mass audience via television, and only secondarily for the people who are actually physically present.

Perhaps you as a speaker are most concerned with the second audience (the "we"), an audience largely of peers who consistently act as jurists, because we are subject daily to judgments by them. Not only do we talk most often with them, but also most of our talk is face-to-face; a large share of our day is spent in making and supporting general statements to our peers. It is they whom we most often advise and from whom we most often seek advice. With peers, as with friends, we talk with, not at. Even the child learns that a parent is a "superior," a younger brother an "inferior," but a peer is an equal. In a democracy, there is great pressure for even the President to justify his decisions to his constituency, on the assumption that, despite its bureaucratic character, it remains a government *of* the people, *by* the people, and *for* the people.

POSITION

Audiences may also be analyzed according to how they regard the speaker in general, and how they regard his position on a particular topic. Recall one of the first points mentioned about audiences: They do not assemble in a vacuum, nor have they come from one, so they may well have attitudes toward you and toward your point of view on any given topic.

Speakers may have their greatest impact on the neutral audience. Audiences may be neutral for one of several reasons. They may be informed on the speaker's topic but not yet ready to take sides, or they may be uninformed. If there is any group that may be persuaded by a single speech, it is the latter, which may be uninformed because they lack interest in the topic; that is, they do not relate the topic to an important motive. Thus, the speaker's first task is to motivate them. Only then can he provide the audience with the information that will help shape their opinion, and only then can he interpret the information in a way favorable to his position.

The informed neutral is rarer and more difficult to persuade. The speaker facing this audience needs to pose such questions as: How can I strengthen the audience's conviction on those points which support my position? How can I weaken any barriers that may stand in the audience's way of accepting my view? Then, because the informed neutral may be wary of attempts to persuade him, the speaker might next consider the following sorts of questions: How can I reassure the audience about the accuracy of my information? How can I alleviate suspicions they may have about the rigor of my arguments? How may I allay their fears of emotional involvement? How can I avoid the appearance of "rabid partisanship?" Should I admit opposing arguments to demonstrate my open-mindedness and fairness?

Partisan audiences are those who already favor the speaker's position, so he raises somewhat different kinds of questions: How can I work to maintain or strengthen the audience's commitment to this opinion? Is this audience also exposed to speakers and other forces in the environment which will generate counterarguments? How may I inoculate my audience against such counterarguments? To what types of appeals will this audience be most responsive?

Opponent audiences already disagree with the speaker's position. Thus, he will realize the futility of trying to persuade them with only one speech, and raise such questions as: How can I weaken my opponent's commitment to his position? How can I neutralize my opponent? If his opposition is deeply entrenched, how can I raise doubts about certain evidence or arguments that tend to support the opposing view? How may I avoid further alienating the audience from my position? Since this audience is likely to be very critical, how may I reassure them of my proof and documentation?

This grouping of audiences is broad, and usually the speaker will face various mixtures. Thus, the previous lists of questions can only suggest some general strategies. There are times, of course, when the audience's position on a partisan-neutral-opponent continuum is highly complex. For example, suppose the audience basically likes the speaker but does not agree with his position on a given topic. The speaker may well have to deal with an audience that, in schematized fashion, looks like this:

Audience's Attitude Toward Speaker in General	Audience Attitude Toward Speaker's Stand on Particular Issues	
Generally Favorable	WATER POLLUTION CONTROL	favorable
	AIR POLLUTION CONTROL	favorable
	LAND USE POLICY	favorable
	SST	unfavorable
	CONSERVATION CORPS	favorable

The audience is favorably impressed with the speaker's *general stance with regard to environmental control*; for example, he is well-regarded for his participation in the effort to secure clear air and waters, and for his initiation of certain land-use policies. But the audience disagrees with the speaker's *particular stance with regard to development of the supersonic transport plane, the SST*. The ways listeners may go about resolving this inconsistency between their general impression of the speaker (favorable) and their impression of his stance on a particular issue (unfavorable) have been discussed. They were, as you will recall: re-evaluation, stopping attention, bolstering, compartmentalizing, differentiating, transcending and decentralizing.

MOTIVATIONAL FUNCTION

Whatever kind of audience he faces, the *motivational states* of his listeners, his coparticipants in the communicative event, must necessarily concern the speaker. His knowledgeable guesses about how his audience will respond help to sharpen his decision about what he hopes to accomplish with any given message. A clear understanding that not all people respond to the same message in the same way will also remind him to proceed with careful deliberation.

Principles that help to explain differences in responses made by listeners in essentially the same situation have been synthesized by Bettinghaus.[53]

[53]Erwin P. Bettinghaus, *Persuasive Communication* (New York: Holt, Rinehart and Winston, Inc., 1968), p. 54.

1. Individuals differ in their *ability* to respond.
2. Individuals differ in their *readiness* to respond.
3. Individuals differ in their *motivation* to respond.

These principles suggest certain clusters of questions to the speaker: How much should I attempt to accomplish with my speech? How shall I limit my purpose? How much restatement should I include in order to be clear, but not boring? How much do my listeners know about the topic? How can I get and keep their attention? Do the physical surroundings and preliminaries to the speech facilitate attention? What are the dominant motives? What is likely to motivate my particular audience to listen and respond?

The term "motivation" becomes, as this set of questions indicates, a key concept for the speaker. How many different ways have you used the word "motivate"? Several common ways are:

1. I am really motivated to try for a place on the team.
2. Merit pay raises generally motivate better work.
3. A future salary of $15,000–$20,000 per year is what motivates me to stay in school.

When the person uses the word in these instances, he is saying: A certain salary level is an attractive goal; I really desire to reach an attractive goal (a place on the team); a merit pay system generates an environment that facilitates better work (and hence helps me reach a goal).

Although motives may be classified in a variety of ways, one scheme is to separate them into three categories:[54] (a) biological in import (emotion, force, drive, instinct, need); (b) mental in import (urge, feeling, wish, impulse, want, striving, desire, demand); and (c) those having reference to objects or states in the environment (purpose, interest, intention, attitude, aspiration, plan, incentive, goal, value). The list of readings at the end of the chapter will provide further useful materials for those of you particularly interested in motivation and related concepts. Here we will simply provide a definition of motivation and an example of how speakers appeal to motives in their speeches.

[54]C.N. Cofer and M.H. Appley, *Motivation: Theory and Research* (New York: John Wiley & Sons, Inc., 1964), p. 5.

Cofer and Appley stress the *dynamic* aspect of motivation. As they put it: "It is often said that *all* behavior is motivated and that behavior serves the organism's needs. Without motivation an organism would not behave; it would be an inert lump, doing virtually nothing. Galvanized into action by a need, it would engage in actions motivated by that need, and its actions would continue until the need was satisfied. The actions *serve* the need; the behavior is the instrument by which the need is satisfied. Behavior is a means, not an end."[55]

Notice the *goal motives* suggested by Richard Nixon's "Veto Message" (Appendix). In one of the initial statements, Mr. Nixon is apparently embracing a goal ("There are no goals which I consider more important"): "To improve education and to provide better health care for the American people."

GOAL A: To improve education and to provide better health care for the American people

GOAL B: To consider what is best for all the people in the United States

GOAL C: To avoid raising prices or taxes

Thus, Mr. Nixon suggests that his audience behave in a certain way (support his veto) in order to satisfy the combination of goals suggested above. Some analysts have suggested that he proposes that the audience relinquish or subordinate Goal A and B in favor of Goal C. If Mr. Nixon has correctly assessed the functions these goals (motives) perform for his listeners, then the speech will be persuasive. If, on the other hand, his assessment is incorrect, his audience may simply consider the message as unpersuasive. You may want to recall pages 62–102 at this point, concerning the role of motives.

DEMOGRAPHIC PROFILE

Knowledge of the general properties of his audience will also prove helpful to the speaker. This includes properties such as age, occupation, income, sex, religion, political affiliation, marital status,

[55]*Ibid.*, p. 10.

educational level, and place of residence. He may also want to raise such questions as: How homogeneous or heterogeneous is my audience in terms of these characteristics? Do they possess common interests? How alike are they in terms of environmental and cultural backgrounds? To what general social group do they belong? In what specific groups and organizations do they hold membership?

Knowledge of a group's demographic characteristics per se will not be especially beneficial to the speaker, but demographic analysis can be used as the *basis for inferences.* It is important to ask not how much information can I find out about my audience, but what information about my audience is most relevant to my particular needs. Not all characteristics are equally important in each act of analysis. If you are advocating the proposition: "Low-cost housing should be distributed throughout the city rather than centralized in one location," you might need to know:

> *where* your audience lives
> *what* their median income is

rather than:

> religion
> sex
> marital status

A demographic analysis is, consequently, only as good as the speaker's capacity to make inferences from the data that will be useful to his particular speech situation.

purpose and lines of argument

Since most of us speak to achieve certain responses from our hearers, the audience assumes that each speaker has a reason for giving his particular speech. The speaker's primary purpose is to elicit a response; included in this is his general purpose of establishing the commonness of which we spoke earlier, to share an idea, an attitude, some information. The first question the speaker asks here is: What do I want my audience to think? To understand? To say? To feel? To do? To value?

If the speaker's topic concerns the concept of economic community, the desired response may be an understanding of the term. The specific statement of purpose could be to describe the concept of economic community. If a speaker wants to persuade the audience to support U.S. membership in an economic community, his specific purpose would be to show the advantage of the United States' forming a close trade alliance with the European Economic Community. In any event, the purpose must be limited by what can be done in the time allotted for the speech, what can be done at the time of the speech (the stage in the life of the problem under discussion), and what approaches can be taken with the audience hearing the speech.

Every speaker wants to see his purpose fulfilled, but no premium can be placed on success in the narrowest sense of the word. The speaker's effectiveness is judged not only by how many boxes of Zap Soap Powder he can sell in one year, but also by the quality and long-term effects of his speech. Many times the odds are against immediate accomplishment of purpose. For example, although Franklin Roosevelt's "Happy Warrior Speech" nominating Al Smith for the presidency was much cheered and well-received, Smith was not nominated. Burns comments: " . . . no speech could affect that convention. Ballot after ballot dragged on in the smoky heat of Madison Square Garden until it became clear that neither the forces centered in the East supporting Smith nor the forces centered in the South and West behind McAdoo could muster the vital two thirds. . . . [T]he 103rd ballot gave John W. Davis the nomination."[56] In a political campaign, although an audience does not vote the way a particular candidate wants, it may be considering new problems and different solutions to old problems.

Very few rhetorical events are so simple that they do not confront the speaker with a critical question: How does one measure the effectiveness of a message? Audiences generally do not vote or prepare shift of opinion ballots immediately upon hearing a speech. Recall what we said earlier. A message may have different effects upon different listeners, and even a relatively short message may have more than a single effect upon any given member of the audience.

How, for example, would you go about measuring the effects

---

[56]James MacGregor Burns, *Roosevelt: The Lion and the Fox* (New York: Hartcourt, Brace, Jovanovich, 1956), p. 94.

of one of Billy Graham's crusades? Various people have suggested such measures as: (a) the size of the crowds attending; (b) the general interest manifested, as measured by the size of the Graham permanent organization; (c) the number of "decisions" at the end of each sermon; and (d) the increase in local church membership immediately after the crusade. But none of these is a truly acceptable way of going about measuring effectiveness. How do you measure, for example, the "spiritual lift" that the crusades bring to their audiences? Are there negative effects; that is, does the evangelism of Graham turn off some listeners? "Who can know," as Nichols asks, "how many sinners were 'almost' saved?"[57]

Moreover, the effects of a speech may not be readily or immediately apparent. How many conversations have you participated in, how many books read, that have had profound long-range effects, even though they were, on first hearing or reading, dismissed as insignificant?

The point of this brief discussion is merely to alert the speaker to some of the problems he will face when he asks himself the questions: Have I fulfilled my purpose? Has my speech been "successful" or "effective"? How can I measure my speech's effectiveness? What, in fact, constitutes fulfillment of purpose? Is fulfillment of specific purpose the only test of my speech? What other tests might I also use when judging the quality of my speech?

After the speaker has considered his audience and determined his specific purpose, he is ready to select the particular lines of argument suitable for his unique speech situation. The lines of argument can best be approached by raising a series of questions about the basic nature of the situation in which the speech is going to be given. Relevant questions would include: To what is my speech a response? Is there a problem which should be considered? Is one solution better than another for this problem? What kinds of difficulties will be met in trying to solve the problem? Does the problem involve an immediate and serious threat? Does some worthwhile cause or group need support? Can some group profitably use information on a process, a place, a concept?

[57]Marie Hochmuth Nichols, "The Criticism of Rhetoric," in *History and Criticism of American Public Address*, ed. Marie K. Hochmuth (New York: Longmans, Green & Co., Inc., 1955), Vol. III, p. 13.

We shall discuss six situations[58] which are likely to prompt speeches:

1. The information-giving situation
2. The difficulty situation
3. The goal-oriented situation
4. The barrier situation
5. The threat situation
6. The identification situation

I. In the information-giving situation the audience wants to learn something new for the sake of acquiring new knowledge if not for the sake of changing its opinions and attitudes. A speaker may choose:
A. To describe a process, place, person, or event
B. To tell about his personal experiences
C. To clarify concepts, material, ideas
D. To discuss the specific works of someone such as a writer, painter, or composer

II. In the difficulty situation an audience suspects that a problem may exist. A speaker may:
A. Recognize that a problem exists
1. By locating and more precisely defining the problem
2. By pointing out the importance of the problem
3. By pointing to the causes of the problem
or
B. Argue that a problem does not exist
1. By denying that there is a problem
2. By belittling the importance of the problem

III. In the goal-oriented situation the audience is concerned (or ought to be concerned) with a solution. A speaker may:
A. Urge the acceptance of a certain solution by pointing out
1. That the solution will meet the need
2. That the solution is practicable
3. That the solution holds certain advantages
or
B. Urge the rejection of a certain solution by pointing out

---

[58]This scheme represents, in part, a modification of a method suggested by Otis M. Walter in "Toward an Analysis of Motivation," *Quarterly Journal of Speech*, Vol. XLI, No. 3 (October 1955), 271–78.

1. That it will not meet the need
2. That it is impracticable
3. That there are more disadvantages than advantages
4. That another solution is better

IV. In the barrier situation the solution may become complicated by a barrier between the audience and its goal. Here, the speaker may urge:

A. That the barrier is not a deterrent to action, because
1. The goal is worth achieving regardless of the barrier
2. The barrier has been unnecessarily raised
3. The barrier can be overcome

or

B. That the barrier is a deterrent to action because
1. The barrier is insurmountable
2. Even if the barrier can be surmounted, the goal is not worth the time and energy
3. Even if the barrier can be surmounted, disadvantages would result that would make the situation worse, rather than better

V. In the threat situation action is needed because of some threat. Here, the speaker may point out:

A. That the threat is great, because
1. The threat is dangerous
2. The threat is immediate

or

B. That the threat is not really great, because
1. The threat is not dangerous
2. The threat is not immediate

VI. In the identification situation one group acts for the sake of another group. The speaker may urge:

A. That Group A help Group B, because
1. There is a relationship between the two groups
2. There should be a relationship between the two groups
3. The group deserves to be helped—it performs useful tasks

or

B. That Group B not be helped by Group A, because
1. There is no relationship between the two groups
2. The problem faced by the other group is not really serious —they can solve it themselves
3. Helping the other group would weaken this group

In each motivational situation there are other alternatives, other lines of argument. The information situation is, in a way, present in all the others. The difference is one of dominant purpose. In the first case the speaker gives information to acquaint the audience with new materials and new facts that can be assimilated and become useful. In the others he gives information to persuade people to accept a specific course of action or way of thinking.

An interesting example of how a variety of lines of argument operate to support the speaker's main line of argument may be found in John F. Kennedy's "Cuban Missile Address" (see Appendix). We will follow the precise chronology of President Kennedy's speech, using his own words whenever possible.

Thesis: In order to maintain "both peace and freedom, here in this Hemisphere," the course of action I suggest, a blockade of Cuba, must be taken immediately.

I. A problem exists. (Para. 1)
   A. The general nature of the problem is that there is a "Soviet military build-up on the island of Cuba."
   B. The precise nature of the problem is that there is, on the island of Cuba, "a series of offensive missile sites."
   C. The cause of the problem is the Soviet's desire "to provide a nuclear strike capability against the Western Hemisphere."

II. The problem is so major, it can properly be termed a "threat."
   A. The precise nature of the threat can be summarized as follows (Paras 2–4):
      1. There are two distinct types of installations.
         a. Medium range ballistic missiles capable of carrying a nuclear warhead for a distance of more than 1,000 nautical miles and thus are capable of striking:
            1) Washington, D.C.
            2) Panama Canal
            3) Cape Canaveral
            4) Mexico City
            5) Other cities in the southeastern part of the U.S., Central America, and the Caribbean Area
         b. Intermediate range ballistic missiles capable of traveling twice as far and thus capable of striking most of the major cities in the Western Hemisphere from

Hudson Bay, Canada, to Lima, Peru. There are also
jet bombers capable of carrying nuclear weapons being
uncrated and assembled in Cuba.

B. The threat constitutes a flagrant and deliberate defiance of
certain agreements and traditions. (Para. 5)
1. Rio Pact of 1947
2. Traditions of this nation and the Hemisphere
3. A Joint Resolution of the 87th Congress
4. Charter of the United Nations
5. My own public warnings on September 4 and 13

C. The threat contradicts the repeated assurance of Soviet
spokesmen, both publically and privately, that only defensive
weapons would be placed in Cuba. (Paras. 6–8)

D. The existence of these weapons alone constitutes a threat,
for: "We no longer live in a world where only the actual
firing of weapons represents a sufficient challenge to a nation's security to constitute maximum peril. Nuclear weapons
are so destructive and ballistic missiles are so swift that any
substantially increased possibility of their use or any sudden
change in their deployment may well be regarded as a
definite threat to peace." (Para. 9)

[Here you will note that the speaker was also faced with the necessity
of giving information in order to convince his audience fully that
a threat did exist and that it was, in fact, dangerous and immediate.]

III. The cause of the problem is clear: " . . . this sudden, clandestine
decision to station strategic weapons for the first time outside
of Soviet soil—is a deliberately provocative and unjustified
change in the status quo. . . ." (Para. 12)

IV. The threat calls for further action on our part.
A. The 1930s taught us a clear lesson: "Aggressive conduct, if
allowed to grow unchecked and unchallenged, ultimately
leads to war."
B. We are opposed to war.
C. We must keep our commitment to war.

V. The following action appears to be a viable solution. (Paras.
15–22)

VI. We identify with the interests of the Cuban people. (Paras.
26–28)

[The remainder of the speech consists of motivational appeals directed to the American people concerning need for courage and patience.]

A locus or line of argument may be found whenever there is potential disagreement. The point of disagreement may be called a *stasis*, a point beyond which discussion cannot proceed until one view is accepted as the one proved to be right. The reason for deciding upon a specific line of argument is that the speaker can at the beginning narrow the focus of what he intends to say to the point or points which specifically concern the matter he is discussing. Determining the *stasis* helps the speaker choose the line or lines of argument he will use in his speech. He should carefully select a few lines of argument, since maximum impact comes from developing the best arguments and making as vigorous a defense as possible.

establishing identification

In order to persuade a person, the speaker needs to identify his opinion (or the course of action he is suggesting) with one or more of the opinions or customary courses of action of his audience. Identification, which may be thought of as both end and means to that end, is, of course, the end of communication. The speaker and his audience establish identification with one another so they can act together to preserve the best of their world, or to bring about whatever changes they believe necessary to make it a better place in which to live.

Identification is also a means to the end cooperation. There are a variety of ways by which the speaker may seek identification with his audience:[59]

1. By "talking their language" through speech, gesture, attitude
2. By sharing some principle in common with them

[59]All of these are suggested in two of Kenneth Burke's books, *The Rhetoric of Motives* (Englewood Cliffs, N.J.: Prentice-Hall, Inc., 1950) and *Counter-Statement* (Chicago: University of Chicago Press, 1957).

3. By showing that his conduct or proposed act is like the conduct or actions they admire
4. By participating or appearing to participate in those specialized activities which make one a participant in some group
5. By use of certain stylistic devices
6. By aligning himself with whatever recurrent patterns of experience his audience has experienced.

Richard Murphy describes Theodore Roosevelt's sense of identification in this way:

> Everywhere he went he found things in common with his audience: some of his Rough Riders had come from the district, he had close friends in the area, he had read the history of the locality. He told an audience of Presbyterians that he often attended their services because they were so much like those of his own church, the Dutch Reformed. . . . He reminded the legislature in Texas that he had been a legislator. . . . At the Sorbonne, he interjected extemporaneous sentences in French to make meanings clear.[60]

This is not meant to suggest that the speaker compromise his own integrity, that he be subservient to his audience, but it does mean that people listen more easily when they see the common ground they share with the speaker. An audience needs to feel itself directly involved in the speaker's topic, so he should speak *with* them, not merely before them.

One of the most striking opening statements made by a student in a classroom speech urged the other members of the class to support a volunteer service program at one of the local mental hospitals:

> It has been estimated that one out of every ten people in the United States will, during the course of his lifetime, receive help of some kind for mental illness. If these figures are correct, and we have every reason to believe they are, that means three people in this room may some day suffer from one kind of emotional disturbance or another. So, the problem of caring for the mentally ill is a problem which you and I must face very seriously. It is *our* problem.
>
> Now, the first question which probably comes to your mind is this: How can I help care for the mentally ill? I am not a psychologist or

60Richard Murphy, "Theodore Roosevelt," in *History and Criticism of American Public Address*, Vol. III, pp. 338–339.

a psychiatrist. I am not a trained orderly. The answer to this question is one which dozens of students answer every Thursday night between the hours of seven-thirty and nine-thirty when they perform volunteer services at one of the local mental hospitals.

Today I'd like to tell you about our volunteer program, some of the things we have accomplished, and some of the things we can accomplish with your help.

This speaker found a very direct and attention-getting link between himself, his topic, and his audience. He established that the problem was not just his problem, or the problem of other people, but "our" problem. Thus, the audience became a direct participant in his speech. He kept the audience participating until the last portion, when he dealt with "some of the things which the volunteer services program can accomplish with *your* help." This speaker knew that the task of identification does not end with the opening remarks, that the common ground between the speaker and the listener must continually be established throughout the speech.

Observe a political speaker, campaigning across the country, establishing three different links with three different audiences:

1. In Minnesota: "I am grateful for the opportunity to talk with you about national farm policies. I won't waste your time this afternoon telling you . . . all about how I am myself a farmer. I own farm land in Illinois, and I come from a family that has lived in the heart of the Corn Belt for over a hundred years. . . . My first venture into public service was in Washington in the old Agricultural Adjustment Administration. . . ."

2. In Virginia: "Here in Richmond tonight, in Virginia, rich both in history and in the knowledge of its history, I am moved to talk for a few minutes of the past. . . . The South is a good place to take our bearings, because in no part of the country does the past—a past of great nobility and great tragedy—more sharply etch the present than in the South."

3. In Massachusetts: "I don't know why it is that an American, no matter where he was born or where he lives, has a feeling in New England of coming home. Perhaps it is because this country of yours looks so homelike; perhaps it is because the people and their welcome are always friendly; perhaps it is because so much of what we are as Americans came out of these valleys and these hills—our habit, for example, of making up our own minds in our

own way, and saying what we think—our habit of respect for each other, and for ourselves—our habit, if you please, of freedom."[61]

Identification can be affected either by the speaker's deliberate design or by unconscious factors of appeal. It is "a way of life," an "acting together," and, in acting together, men have common sensations, concepts, images, ideas, and attitudes. To catch a glimpse of the various levels on which identification operates, let's look briefly at related, but somewhat different, levels of identification used by Richard M. Nixon in his April 30, 1970, speech "On the Cambodian Decision."[62] We can see clearly how President Nixon tries to get his audience to "act together" with him, and that he tries to identify his life style with those he has included in his audience. But it is also clear that, by virtue of advocating one life style rather than another, he has excluded as well as included people from his audience. Thus, in identifying with only a portion of the mass audience, he is likely alienating another portion.

1. Identification with what the speaker presumes to be majority values.
    A. Most don't want to "clearly endanger the lives of Americans. . . ."
    B. Most want to be working for peace, to be "conciliatory at the conference table" but not "humiliated."
    C. Most do not want to "get peace at any price now" because a "peace of humiliation for the United States will lead to a bigger war or surrender later."

2. Identification with commonly held basic assumptions or premises, e.g.:
    A. " . . . only the power of the United States deters aggression."
    B. "If when the chips are down, the world's most powerful nation, the United States of America, acts like a pitiful, helpless giant, the forces of totalitarianism and anarchy will threaten free nations and free institutions throughout the world."
    C. "It is not our power but our will and character that is being tested tonight."

3. Identification with certain types of arguments. (You may want to return to this point after reading Chapter 4.)

[61]From *Major Campaign Speeches of Adlai E. Stevenson, 1952* (Copyright 1953 by Random House, Inc. Pp. 64, 149, 140. Reprinted by permission.
[62]All quotes are transcribed from a tape of the speech delivered over national television.

4. Identification of self with past Presidents and their policies; e.g., "In this room, Woodrow Wilson made the great decisions which led to victory in World War I. Franklin Roosevelt made the decisions which led to our victory in World War II. Dwight D. Eisenhower made decisions which ended the war in Korea and avoided war in the Middle East. John F. Kennedy, in his finest hour, made the great decision which removed Soviet nuclear missiles from Cuba and the Western Hemisphere."

5. Identification with certain character traits; e.g.:
   A. One does not "take the *easy* political path" [to "blame this war on previous Administrations and to bring all of our men home immediately regardless of the consequences"].
   B. One puts country above self: "I would rather be a one-term President than to be a two-term President at the cost of seeing America become a second rate power and to see this nation accept the first defeat in its proud 190-year history."
   C. One is strong but conciliatory.
   D. One is humble: "The decision I have announced tonight is not of the same magnitude [as those of Wilson, Franklin D. Roosevelt, and John F. Kennedy in their decisions announced in the same room]."

6. Identification with the men in the field with whom the President also identifies: "It is customary to conclude a speech from the White House by asking support for the President of the United States. Tonight I depart from that precedent. What I ask for is more important. I ask for your support of our brave men fighting tonight halfway around the world—not for territory—not for glory—but so that their younger brothers and their sons and your sons will be able to live together in peace and freedom and justice."

Whether the speaker has managed to identify his ways with those of his audience, is decided in the end by the audience.

a note on creative ideation

You have now read about some of the first steps a speaker takes as he prepares to give a speech. In many respects, the effectiveness with which you take these steps depends upon how well you develop a useful and productive view of speech preparation as a creative process and of the speaker as a creator. The truly creative speaker generally shares certain characteristics with other creative people: the capacity to use categories adapted from someone else; an openness to experience that usually rejects the view of the world in simple stereotypes; a tendency to enjoy complex and ambiguous situations with spontaneous exploration; and a tendency to possess an internal locus of evaluation. Besides these intellectual factors, the effective speaker may well possess another important character-istic, the capacity to care. At 87, shortly before his death, Pavlov wrote this advice on the requisites for "an effective pursuit" of science. "Third, passion. Remember that science demands from a man all his life. If you had two lives that would not be enough for you. Be passionate in your work and your searching." The speaker also must care, about the world in general and about his topic and his audience in particular.

Some years ago the cover of *Life* magazine showed a painter wearing a beret and a smock. His palette was full of paint and he stood with brush poised before a large blank canvas. "Now for an idea!" was the caption. That magazine cover not only presents the problem of all creative people, but it also tends to symbolize the attitude of many speakers toward ideas. When they are asked to come up with one, their minds may become as blank as the artist's canvas on the *Life* cover.

Ideas range in complexity from deciding how to open a closed lock to developing a theory of relativity. But whether creativity occurs in writing a poem or symphony, painting a picture, or in-venting a new jet propulsion system or a new marketing technique or a new wonder drug, the creative process appears to rest on the same fundamental ability—the ability to relate previously unrelated things. This seems to hold constant in fields as widely diverse as mechanical engineering and poetry writing. In fact, there is con-siderable support for the position that the creative process is facili-tated by the sheer number of things the potential creator has at his command. For example, some maintain that previous training which is general, broad, and nonspecific will facilitate a productive solution that does not reflect stereotyped thought. In fact, the proc-ess of creative ideation is most often associated with the capacity of people to free themselves from an immediate set of stimuli, for example, remembered facts of a specific subject. Creativity often requires that these stimuli be used as a point of departure, not as a stopping point, for while the acquisition of facts seems to be part of the creative process, it is probably not the beginning and certainly not the end of it. Very briefly, let us consider the levels of creativity and the stages in the creative process.

There have been many attempts to describe the creative process itself. We shall discuss a few of them, then make some observations about what these various descriptions have in common.

John Arnold defines the creative process as "primarily an intellectual process, a process whereby you combine and re-combine all your past experience or selected aspects of it—you may sort a bit, but you somehow end up with a new combination, a new pattern, a new configuration that somehow satisfies some basic expressed or implied need of a man."[63] He divides the creative process into three phases:

1. Preparation.
2. Production.
3. Decision-making.

In the first stage, a person questions and observes. In the second stage, he associates previously unrelated things with one another. In the last phase, he predicts; that is, he selects from alternative combinations the one that strikes him as most productive.

Osborn, on the other hand, describes the creative process as one of problem-solving:

1. Orientation: pointing up the problem.
2. Preparation: gathering pertinent data.
3. Analysis: breaking down the relevant material.
4. Hypothesis: piling up alternatives by way of ideas.
5. Incubation: letting up, to invite illumination.
6. Synthesis: putting the pieces together.
7. Verification: judging the resultant ideas.[64]

[63]John Arnold, "Creativity in Engineering," in *Creativity: An Examination of the Creative Process*, ed. Paul Smith (New York: Hastings House, Publishers, 1959), p. 35.

[64]A. Osborn, *Applied Imagination* (New York: Charles Scribner's Sons, 1953).

Wertheimer, in following the tenets of Gestalt psychology, also sees the creative process as a problem-solving process, but in a somewhat different light.[65] Generally speaking, a problem situation (S_1) begins the actual process. S_1 is "structurally incomplete"—that is, it contains some gaps, there is some flaw in its construction. The mind is frustrated by this sense of incompleteness, so a number of steps are taken to a second situation (S_2) where the gap is filled; in other words, the problem has disappeared.

Certain steps seem to be constant in all of these views of the creative process: (a) sensitivity or awareness of some lack of satisfaction with the status quo, analysis of the causes of this lack of satisfaction; (b) opening of the mind to ideational fluency; and (c) synthesis, not only a process of addition or reorganization, but a process whereby greater satisfaction is felt.[66] Old concepts are frequently brought together in some new combination, and the value achieved by the new combination is greater than the sum of its parts. So you can see that the essence of creativity may well be reorganization, the ability to relate previously unrelated things.

Now let us examine the stages in the creative process with a view toward seeing how the creative person reacts in each stage.[67]

1. EXPOSURE STAGE. In this first stage, the individual collects "raw material" from his environment. He observes, experiences, reads, and listens. It should be noted that quality and quantity of creative output may be determined by how much material is col-

[65]See particularly the discussion of Wertheimer in Jacob W. Getzels and Phillip W. Jackson, *Creativity and Intelligence: Exploitations with Gifted Students* (New York: John Wiley & Sons, Inc., 1962), p. 84.

[66]See, for example, Donald A. Schon, *Invention and Evolution of Ideas* (London: Tavistock Publications, 1967); J.P. Guilford, "Creativity," *American Psychologist*, Vol. 5 (1950), 444–454; W.J.J. Gordon, "Operational Approach to Creativity," *Harvard Business Review*, Vol. 34, No. 6 (1956), 41–51; C.R. Rogers, "Toward a Theory of Creativity," in *Creativity and Its Culmination*, ed. H.H. Anderson (New York: Harper & Row, Publishers, 1959); Morris I. Stein and Shirley J. Heinze, eds., *Creativity and the Individual: Summaries of Selected Literature in Psychology and Psychiatry* (New York: The Free Press, 1960); Bernard Berelson and Gary A. Steiner, *Human Behavior: An Inventory of Scientific Findings* (New York: Harcourt Brace Jovanovich, 1964).

[67]This follows the treatment of Irving A. Taylor, "The Nature of the Creative Process," in Smith, *Creativity: An Examination of the Creative Process*, pp. 64–66.

lected. The creative person is characteristically: (a) voracious in his consumption of his environment, and (b) independent in his interpretation of his environment; that is, he tends not to stereotype objects, events, people, and so on, into neat inventional pigeonholes. The creative person takes every opportunity to gather abundant data ("raw perceptual experience") and allows that data to be freely received. Thus, the exposure stage provides an abundance of unrestricted data with which he can work.

The noncreative person, on the other hand, pays little attention to the world about him (reads, listens, converses as little as possible) and categorizes what experience he does have into preconceived stereotypes. Thus, only a small portion of the environment is allowed to enter. Relatively few categories are accepted and only those perceptions which are easy to understand are admitted.

2. The Incubation Stage. During this stage the creative person allows experience to "mill and flow" freely. The milling parts interact dynamically with one another. Mentally undigested parts begin fitting together into new relations, new patterns. Of course, the larger the number of free parts the person has at his disposal, the greater the number of interactions which can occur during this stage. Whereas the creative person allows this freewheeling to occur, the noncreative person does not. He merely sorts his experiences into comfortable, tight mental compartments. What should be an uncomfortable phase is, for the noncreative person, comfortable. His old way of thinking is confirmed, not challenged and expanded.

3. The Illumination Stage. The creative person experiences insight during this period, when the incubated parts jell into a recognizable and meaningful new experience. Since this new organization represents a multiplying of values, not just an additive process, it may be termed *synergetic*. No new insight can occur for the noncreative person, since his hardening of categories or stereotyping permit him to remain relatively unchanged, even when he is exposed to new experience.

4. The Execution Stage. This stage involves the very difficult communicative task of transforming implicit experiences into objective symbolic form; e.g., a poem, a play, a painting, a speech. The noncreative person who has just copied material and then communicated it to some one may have recreated, but he has not created.

Where do ideas for a speech come from? They come from observing, experiencing, conversing, listening, and reading. The first prerequisite of good speaking is curiosity, questioning: What is going on? Why? How can it be changed or supported? Thomas Huxley once said, "No one who has lived in the world as long as . . . I have can entertain the pious delusion that it is engineered upon principles of benevolence. . . . But for all that, the cosmos remains always beautiful and profoundly interesting in every corner—and if I had as many lives as a cat I would leave no corner unexplored."[68] Exploring—through conversation, experience, reading— is the speaker's starting place. When a speaker says: I know something about the subject; I would like to learn something more about this subject; I think it should be talked about, he is in a sense saying: This subject is important to me.

It has been said of Lord Chatham, twice Prime Minister of England and defender of the rights of the American Colonists in Parliament, that his "mind [was] all aglow"[69] with a subject. We can not always be "all aglow" with a subject, but we can be genuinely interested in those subjects that have a natural urgency. What is being talked about? What needs to be talked about? If the speaker is not interested in his topic, how can he expect an audience to be or to become interested in it?

Since the speech occurs in a social situation, selection of subject is influenced by the audience for which it is intended. The speaker asks: What does my audience know? What are they talking about? What should they be concerned with? A potential speech subject can be found in the common ground of interest, feeling, and belief which exists between the speaker and his audience.[70]

The audience gains insight into the speaker's mind and his attitude toward his audience through the topic he selects. When a man speaks, he is occupying someone else's time and thoughts. Thus, the speaker assumes responsibility for using that time in a useful and productive manner. A trivial topic indicates that the speaker does not value the audience's time very highly. By selecting a topic

---

[68]As cited in "Is Liberal Education Still Needed?" a speech delivered by Gordon N. Ray. Printed in pamphlet form (Boston: Houghton Mifflin Company).

[69]Chauncey A. Goodrich, *Select British Eloquence* (Indianapolis: The Bobbs-Merrill Co., Inc., 1963), p. 73.

[70]James A. Winans, *Speech-Making* (New York: Appleton-Century-Crofts, 1938), pp. 335f.

of importance, the speaker brings to his audience a sense of dignity and respect.

Our ability to communicate through speech helps us do more than adjust to our environment; it enables us to change our environment, to reconstruct it so that we can bring it closer to the way we would like it to be. In our human context, the important subjects are those that allow us to discover what man can be. The speaker's task is to challenge his audience, in the tradition of civilized people everywhere, on the assumption that man can and will respond to an appeal of reason and imagination.

summary

Rhetorical invention begins with careful preliminary planning. From the moment the speaker decides on his topic he is faced with a series of questions. How well or how poorly he answers these may determine the success of his speech. A speech cannot succeed without careful consideration of the basis on which the speaker will build. We have discussed the steps in preliminary planning: Concern for and analysis of audience attitudes and beliefs, concern for purpose and lines of argument, and concern for establishing identification. Preliminary planning done, the speaker is ready to select the specific supporting materials of his speech.

rhetorical exercises

1. Give an eight to ten minute persuasive speech in which you: (a) make the audience aware of a problem area they may not have considered before, or (b) suggest a solution to a much discussed problem.

2. Recall the topics on which you have heard speeches lately. What were they? Could you gain insight into the speaker's mind by them? Did they reflect how he regarded his audience?

3. Stop to think over some of the topics you would like to speak about in class. How did you pick them? What areas of common ground can you find between you, your topics, and your audience?

4. Listen to the speeches in class with a view to answering this question: Did the speaker take into consideration the audience's attitudes and opinions on his subject? Then answer the question: Did the speaker understand those attitudes and opinions very well?

5. Select a problem area. Then discuss the nature of the problem, the causes of the problem, and the solution to it. How many different lines of argument can you find? Try doing this exercise in class and writing the lines of argument on the board. How would you determine which are the best? Is there general agreement in class on which lines of argument are the best? If there is disagreement, analyze why it has occurred. Finally, after each members of the class has delivered his speech, discuss the lines of argument used in each. Can you suggest others which might have been used?

6. Using a speech in the Appendix, analyze the motivational situation(s) the speaker seemed to feel he faced. Did he face it (them) effectively?

7. Keeping the topic constant, prepare speeches to be given to various kinds of audiences. What differences were there in the speeches? Why?

collateral readings

Berkowitz, Leonard, and Richard E. Goranson, "Motivational and Judgmental Determinants of Social Perception," *Journal of Abnormal and Social Psychology*, Vol. 66, No. 5 (1963), 405–12.

Brown, Roger, *Social Psychology*. New York: The Free Press, 1965. See especially Chapter 11, "The Principle of Consistency in Attitude Change."

Cohen, Arthur R., *Attitude Change and Social Influence*. New York: Basic Books, Inc., Publishers, 1964.

Cronkhite, Gary, *Persuasion: Speech and Behavioral Change*. Indianapolis: The Bobbs-Merrill Co., Inc., 1969. See especially Chapter 7, "Audience Characteristics."

Day, Dennis, "Persuasion and the Concept of Identification," *Quarterly Journal of Speech*, Vol. XLVI, No. 3 (1960), 270–73.

Fishbein, Martin, "A Consideration of Beliefs, Attitudes, and their Relationship," in *Current Studies in Social Psychology*, ed. Ivan D. Steiner and Martin Fishbein. New York: Holt, Rinehart and Winston, Inc., 1965, pp. 107–120.

Hovland, Carl I., Irving L. Janis, and Harold H. Kelley, *Communication and Persuasion*. New Haven: Yale University Press, 1953. See especially "Group Membership and Resistance to Change" and "Personality and Susceptibility to Persuasion."

———, and Muzafer Sherif, *Social Judgment*. New Haven: Yale University Press, 1961.

Katz, Daniel, "The Functional Approach to the Study of Attitudes," *Public Opinion Quarterly*, Vol. 24 (1960), 163–204.

Kelman, Herbert C., "Processes of Opinion Change," *Public Opinion Quarterly*, Vol. 25 (1961), 57–78.

Maccoby, Eleanor E., *et al.*, "Social Reinforcement in Attitude Change," *Journal of Abnormal and Social Psychology*, Vol. 63, No. 1 (1961), 109–15.

McGuire, William J., "Attitudes and Opinions," *Annual Review of Psychology* (1966), 457–514.

Nichols, Marie Hochmuth, *Rhetoric and Criticism*. Baton Rouge: Louisiana State University Press, 1963. See especially "Kenneth Burke: Rhetorical and Critical Theory."

Rosenberg, M.J., *et al.*, eds., *Attitude Organization and Change*. New Haven: Yale University Press, 1960.

Sherif, Muzafer, Carolyn W. Sherif, and Roger Nebergall, *Attitude and Attitude Change*. Philadelphia: W.B. Saunders Co., 1965.

Facts cannot be selected without some
personal conviction as to what is truth.

Allan Nevins

4

RHETORICAL INVENTION:
SELECTION
OF PROOFS

Invention is a process of coming-to-be. It refers not only to the
recovery of already existing facts, but also to the actual discovery
of facts and creative solutions. Thus, invention comes into play
long before the speaker has decided which proposition he will
advocate.

The speech at its best ought to be thought of as a productive
probe into the unknown because both the speaker and his audience
are in the process of generating the new. The rhetorical world is a
dynamic multi-directional flow of influence concerned with refor-
mation. As their perspectives interact to effect change, speaker and
audience are constantly concerned with making the world a "new"
place.

What we said earlier about communication may also be said
to be true of the process of invention: it is dynamic; it is a field of

interaction not a one directional S-R process, and it is creative; it is concerned with the replacement, evolution and nourishment of ideas.

The speaker's specific purpose is to speak with persuasive effect toward whatever end he has in mind. Thus, he is concerned both with the end and the means of securing that end. Martin Luther King aptly stated the relationship of ends and means when he viewed means as "the end in process." Further, the speaker is faced with the necessity for responsible commitment as he seeks to determine the available means of persuasion. What are the means of persuasion? Recall a basic fact about communication. When we speak, we assume the responsibility for usefully filling up the duration of our speech. Each time we say something, we are, in effect, asking people to listen to us, and we generally say one of these:

1. Listen to me because of who I am.
2. Listen to me because of what I know.
3. Listen to me because, as a human being, I share certain motives, emotions, and ambitions with you.

Most often we say all three of them together because they are inextricably associated with one another. Who can ultimately separate message source from what is said, or what is said from why it is said? *Who* is talking determines in large share what is said, and *what* is said is shaped by motives the speaker shares with his audience. So when we separate the ways of saying something, we do so only arbitrarily. These three kinds of materials may be called a speaker's credentials, his *proof* that he is using the time wisely, that what he is saying is of value.

the materials of proof

The word "proof" is closely bound to the Greek word *pistis*, which is associated with trust, faith. Proof is what we offer to secure belief. The term implies reciprocity: something must be offered and accepted to be rhetorical proof; somebody must show that he is reliable, and somebody else must trust.

SOURCE CREDIBILITY

Our discussion of ethical proof really began when we spoke of ethos or perceived credibility of source. We suggested that a speaker makes himself known in two ways: by what he brings to the speech (his character, his reputation), and by what he says in the speech (the judgments and commitments he makes through his choice of means and ends, and through his statements of fact and opinion as well as of value).

Many times, the audience may have formed their opinions about the speaker's integrity, sincerity, motive for speaking, and intelligence before he even begins to speak. As Isocrates admonished, ". . . the man who wishes to persuade people will not be negligent as to the matter of character . . . for who does not know that words carry greater conviction when spoken by men of good repute. . . ."[1]

However, as we have pointed out, a person's reputation may change as he speaks. Think of how we offer ethical proof almost constantly. Mary Jones has borrowed her roommate's sweater. If she returns it clean and intact, she may simply say, "May I borrow your blue sweater again this week?" because she has already established her reliability in borrowing sweaters. On the other hand, if she ripped the sweater, Mary may have to say, "If I can borrow your blue sweater this week, I promise to take better care of it." Thus, Mary has attempted to establish her reliability by or through the speech itself.

So, if a speaker is not known—or is known but wants to establish his reliability—he reminds the audience about his credentials and makes them stronger. He offers ethical proof by the choices he has made from the very onset of the rhetorical act, from the selection of subject to the actual delivery of the speech itself. He has:

1. Included certain details and facts and omitted others.
2. Drawn certain relationships between ideas.

[1]Isocrates, *Antidosis*, trans. George Norlin, The Loeb Classical Library (London: William Heinemann Ltd., 1929), p. 278.

3. Emphasized some ideas and not others.
4. Made a series of value judgments at each stage.

This last point cannot be emphasized too strongly, for surely when a speaker makes a public statement, he is making a public commitment.

It is difficult to find distinguished speakers who have told audiences what they themselves have not believed. To do so is, in effect, to be what Senator Albert Beveridge in 1924 called "a public liar."[2] No speaker ever has the right to try to influence the behavior of others until, as a result of careful thought and study, he decides his point of view is worthwhile.

In the following speeches, each speaker has manifested integrity, presented ethical proof (ethos): (1) through attempting to convey directly to the audience a favorable impression of his good will and character; and (2) through allowing the audience to form an impression through the total of the value judgments implied by his statements.

An example of the first type is this speech by Daniel Webster, speaking for the prosecution to the jury in the White murder case:

I am little accustomed, Gentlemen, to the part which I am now attempting to perform. Hardly more than once or twice has it happened to me to be concerned on the side of government in any criminal prosecution whatever; and never, until the present occasion, in any case affecting life.

But I very much regret that it should have been thought necessary to suggest to you that I am brought here to "hurry you against the law and beyond the evidence." I hope I have too much regard for justice, and too much respect for my own character, to attempt either; and were I to make such attempt, I am sure that in this court nothing can be carried against the law, and that gentlemen, intelligent and just as you are, are not, by any power, to be hurried beyond the evidence. Though I could well have wished to shun this occasion, I have not felt at liberty to withhold my professional assistance, when it is supposed that I may be in some degree useful in investigating and discovering the truth respecting this most extraordinary murder. It has seemed to be a duty incumbent on me, as on every other citizen, to do my best and my utmost to bring to light the

[2]Albert J. Beveridge, *The Art of Public Speaking* (Boston: Houghton Mifflin Company, 1924), p. 20.

perpetrators of this crime. Against the prisoner at the bar, as an individual, I cannot have the slightest prejudice. I would not do him the smallest injury or injustice. But I do not affect to be indifferent to the discovery and the punishment of this deep guilt. I cheerfully share in the opprobrium, how great soever it may be, which is cast on those who feel and manifest an anxious concern that all who had a part in planning, or a hand in executing, this deed of midnight assassination, may be brought to answer for their enormous crime at the bar of public justice.[3]

An example of the second may be found in the First Inaugural Address of Thomas Jefferson. After saying that ". . . it is proper that you should understand what I deem the essential principles of our government . . . ,"[4] Jefferson lists eleven clearly stated principles to which he commits himself. Why? The presidential campaign of 1800 was an unusually bitter fight between the Federalists and the Republicans. In addition, the two Republican candidates both polled the same number of votes, and the election was thrown into the House of Representatives. The whole speech is an attempt to manifest an ethos, to say, "Here is the manner of man I am," so he is very explicit: ". . . though the will of the majority is in all cases to prevail, that will, to be rightful, must be reasonable; that the minority possess their equal rights, which equal laws must protect, and to violate which would be oppression."[5]

The most interesting attempts of speakers to manifest an ethos occur when their reputations are in question. Two such cases were Richard Nixon's defense of his campaign expenditures in 1952 and Edward Kennedy's defense of his behavior in the Mary Jo Kopechne case.[6] In both incidents, the speakers were called to account via national television for their behavior. They both utilized several strategies: (1) to suggest that they were victims of events and forces surrounding their actions; (2) to present brief sketches of what they did; and (3) to place their futures in the hands of their audiences. Let's observe these strategies in action:

[3]Wayland Maxfield Parrish and Marie Hochmuth, eds., *American Speeches* (New York: Longmans, Green & Co., 1954), pp. 122–23.

[4]*Ibid.*, p. 98.

[5]*Ibid.*, p. 96.

[6]Excerpts from Senator Edward A. Kennedy's speech on July 25, 1969, transcribed from a tape; excerpts from Richard Nixon's speech as it appeared in *U.S. News and World Report* (October 3, 1952), pp. 66–70.

I. STRATEGY ONE: I AM A VICTIM OF THE SCENE

KENNEDY   NIXON

A. Denial of Illicit Actions

There is no truth, no truth, whatever, to the widely circulated suspicions of immoral conduct that have been leveled at my behavior and hers regarding that evening. There has never been a private relationship between us of any kind.

. . .

Nor was I driving under the influence of liquor.

Not one cent of the $18,000 or any other money of that type ever went to me for my personal use. Every penny of it was used to pay for political expenses that I did not think should be charged to the taxpayers of the United States.

. . .

It was not a secret fund. As a matter of fact, when I was on "Meet the Press"—some of you may have seen it, last Sunday—Peter Edson came up to me, after the program, and he said, "Dick, what about this fund we hear about?" And I said, "Well, there is no secret about it. Go out and see Dana Smith, who was the administrator of the fund. . . ."

. . .

. . . no contributor to this fund, no contributor to any of my campaigns, has ever received any consideration that he would not have received as an ordinary constituent. I just don't believe in that. . . .

B. Suggestion of Extraordinary Forces Operating

Little over one mile away, the car that I was driving on an *unlit* road went off a *narrow* bridge which had *no guard* rails and was built on a *left angle* to the road. The car overturned in a *deep pond* and immediately filled with water. [Italics added.] All kinds of scrambled thoughts—all of them confused, some of them *irrational*, many of them which I cannot recall and some of which I would not have seriously entertained *under normal circumstances*—went through my mind during this period.

.   .   .

They were reflected in the various inexplicable, inconsistent and inconclusive things I said and did, including such questions as . . . whether some *awful curse* did actually hang over all the Kennedys. . . .

. . . I know that this is not the last of the *smears*. In spite of my explanation tonight, other smears will be made. Others have been made in the past. And the purpose of the smears, I know, is to silence me, to make me let up. Well, they just don't know who they are dealing with. I'm going to tell you this: I remember, in the dark days of the Hiss trial. . . . [To understand fully the inference here, you might want to read up on the trial of Alger Hiss and the era of the Communist scare in the 1950's.]

II. STRATEGY TWO: BRIEF SKETCHES OF THE ACTIONS

SUBSEQUENT ACTIONS

The car overturned in a deep pond and immediately filled with water. I remember thinking as the cold water rushed in around my head that I was for certain drowning. Then water entered my lungs and I actually felt the sensation of drowning. But somehow I struggled to the surface alive. I made immediate and repeated efforts to save Mary Jo by diving into the strong and murky current but succeeded only in increasing my state of utter exhaustion and alarm. My conduct and conversations during the next several hours to the extent that I can remember them make no sense to me at all.

.   .   .

Instead of looking directly for a telephone after lying exhausted in

PRECEDING ACTIONS

. . . and there are some that will say, "Well, maybe you were able, Senator, to fake this thing. How can we believe what you say—after all, is there a possibility that maybe you got some sums in cash? Is there a possibility that you might have feathered your own nest?" And so now what I am going to do—and, incidentally, this is unprecedented in the history of the American politics—I am going at this time to give to this television and radio audience a complete financial history, everything I have earned, everything I have spent, everything I own, and I want you to know the facts.

I will have to start early. I was born in 1913. Our family was one of modest circumstances, and the grass for an underdetermined time, I walked back to the cottage where the party was being held and requested the help of two friends, my cousin, Joseph Gargan, and Phil Markham, and directed them to return immediately to the scene with me—this was some time after midnight—in order to undertake a new effort to dive down and locate Miss Kopechne.

. . .

Instructing Gargan and Markham not to alarm Mary Jo's friends that night, I had them take me to the ferry crossing. The ferry having shut down for the night, I suddenly jumped into the water and impulsively swam across, nearly drowning once again in the effort, and returned to my hotel about 2 A.M. and collapsed in my room.

I remember going out at one point and saying something to the room clerk.

In the morning, with my mind somewhat more lucid, I made an effort to call a family legal adviser, Burk Marshall, from a public telephone on the Chappaquidick side of the ferry and belatedly reported the accident to the Martha's Vineyard police.

most of my early life was spent in a store, out in East Whittier. It was a grocery store, one of those family enterprises. The only reason we were able to make it go was because my Mother and Dad had five boys, and we all worked in the store. I worked my way through college and, to a great extent, through law school. And then, in 1940, probably the best thing that ever happened to me happened. I married Pat, who is sitting over here.

We had a rather difficult time, after we were married, like so many of the young couples who might be listening to us. I practiced law. She continued to teach school.

Then, in 1942, I went into the service. Let me say that my service record was not a particularly unusual one. I went to the South Pacific. I guess I'm entitled to a couple of battle stars. I got a couple of letters of commendation. But I was just there when the bombs were falling. And then I returned. I returned to the United States, and 1946, I ran for Congress. When we came out of the war, Pat and I—Pat during the war had worked as a stenographer, and in a bank, and as an economist for a government agency—and when we came out, the total of our savings, from both my law practice, her teaching, and all the time that I was in the war, the total for that entire period was just a little less than $10,000. Every cent of that, incidentally, was in government bonds. Well, that's where we start, when I go into politics.

Now, whatever I earned since

I went into politics—well, here it is.
I jotted it down. Let me read the
notes. First of all, I have had my
salary as a congressman and as a
senator. Second, I have received a
total in this past six years of $1600
from estates which were in my law
firm at the time that I severed my
connection with it. And, incidentally, as I said before, I have not
engaged in any legal practice, and
have not accepted any fees from
business that came into the firm
after I went into politics. I have
made an average of approximately
$1500 a year, from nonpolitical
speaking engagements and lectures.
And then, fortunately, we have in-
herited a little money. Pat sold her
interest in her father's estate for
$3000, and I inherited $1500 from
my grandfather. We lived rather
modestly.

For four years we lived in an
apartment in Parkfairfax, Alexan-
dria, Virginia. The rent was $80 a
month. And we saved for the time
that we could buy a house. Now,
that was what we took in.

What did we do with this
money? What do we have today to
show for it? This will surprise you,
because it is so little, I suppose, as
standards generally go of people in
public life. First of all, we've got a
house in Washington, which cost
$41,000 and on which we owe
$20,000. We have a house in Whit-
tier, California, which cost $13,000,
and on which we owe $3000. My
folks are living there at the present
time. I have just $4000 in life in-
surance, plus my GI policy, which
I have never been able to convert,

and which will run out in two years. I have no life insurance whatever on Pat. I have no life insurance on our two youngsters, Patricia and Julie. I own a 1950 Oldsmobile car. We have our furniture. We have no stocks and bonds of any type. We have no interest of any kind, direct or indirect, in any business. Now, that is what we have. What do we owe?

Well, in addition to the mortgage, the $20,000 mortgage on the house in Washington, a $10,000 one on the house in Whittier, I owe $4500 to the Riggs Bank, in Washington, D.C., with interest at 4 per cent. I owe $3500 to my parents, and the interest on that loan, which I pay regularly because it is a part of the savings they made through the years they were working so hard—I pay regularly 4 per cent interest. And then I have a $500 loan, which I have on my life insurance.

Well, that's about it. That's what we have. And that's what we owe. It isn't very much. But Pat and I have the satisfaction that every dime that we have got is honestly ours.

I should say this, that Pat doesn't have a mink coat. But she does have a respectable Republican cloth coat, and I always tell her that she would look good in anything.

One other thing I probably should tell you, because if I don't they will probably be saying this about me, too. We did get something, a gift, after the election. A man down in Teaxs heard Pat on the radio mention the fact that our two youngsters would like to have a dog, and, believe it or not, the day before we left on this campaign trip we got a message from Union Station in Baltimore, saying they had a package for us. We went down to get it. You know what it was?

It was a little cocker spaniel dog, in a crate that he had sent all the way from Texas, black and white, spotted, and our little girl, Tricia, the six-year-old, named it Checkers. And, you know, the kids, like all kids, loved the dog, and I just want to say this, right now, that regardless of what they say about it, we are going to keep it.

III. STRATEGY THREE: AUDIENCE RESPONSIBLE FOR FUTURE

These events, the publicity, innuendo and whispers which have surrounded them and my admission of guilt this morning—raises the question in my mind of whether my standing among the people of my state has been so impaired that I should resign my seat in the United States Senate.

If at any time the citizens of Massachusetts should lack confidence in their Senator's character or his ability, with or without justification, he could not in my opinion adequately perform his duty and should not continue in office.

The people of this state, the state which sent John Quincy Adams and Daniel Webster and

And, now, finally, I know that you wonder whether or not I am going to stay on the Republican ticket or resign. Let me say this: I don't believe that I ought to quit, because I am not a quitter. And, incidentally, Pat is not a quitter. After all, her name was Patricia Ryan and she was born on St. Patrick's Day, and you know the Irish never quit.

. . . the decision, my friends, is not mine. I would do nothing that would harm the possibilities of Dwight Eisenhower to become President of the United States. And for that reason I am submitting to the Republican National Committee tonight through this television broadcast the decision which it is

Charles Sumner and Henry Cabot Lodge and John Kennedy to the United States Senate, are entitled to representation in that body by men who inspire their utmost confidence.

For this reason, I would understand full well why some might think it right for me to resign. For me this will be a difficult decision to make.

It has been seven years since my first election to the Senate. You and I share many memories—some of them have been glorious, some have been very sad. The opportunity to work with you and serve Massachusetts has made my life worthwhile.

And so I ask you tonight, people of Massachusetts, to think this through with me. In facing this decision, I seek your advice and opinion. In making it, I seek your prayers.

theirs to make. Let them decide whether my position on the ticket will help or hurt. And I am going to ask you to help them decide. Wire and write the Republican National Committee whether you think I should stay on or whether I should get off. And whatever their decision is, I will abide by it.

There is also a fourth major strategy, only briefly developed in each speech—the suggestion that despite the immediate judgment of their acts they hope to continue to make contributions to society:

KENNEDY

I pray that I can have the courage to make the right decision. Whatever is decided and whatever the future holds for me, I hope that I shall be able to put this most recent tragedy behind me and make some further contribution to our state and mankind, whether it be in public or private life.

NIXON

But just let me say this last word. Regardless of what happens, I am going to continue this fight. I am going to campaign up and down America until we drive the crooks and the Communists and those that defend them out of Washington, and remember, folks, Eisenhower is a great man, and a vote for Eisenhower is a vote for what is good for America.

We can glimpse the way in which these speakers attempted to reestablish an ethos largely by examining the scene in which their actions took place, by narrating events surrounding the action, and by manifesting a good will toward their audiences; that is, the audience will help them make their decisions, and even if their audiences should disapprove of them, they will continue to think of and work toward the public good.

As we continue to discuss ethical proof or source credibility, it becomes clear that it is not enough for the speaker to be sincere. He also has an obligation to be informed. Good intentions are meaningless unless the speaker is sure that his materials are accurate and his sources reliable. A mistake in statistics, a misquoted authority, whether motivated by ill will or an honest mistake, are in either case false and misleading. The use of an unrepresentative example, because the speaker is intent on trickery or has not read widely enough, is unethical. The character of the speaker cannot, in the end, be separated from the integrity of his materials.

What are the dimensions of ethos? Why are some speakers highly credible, and others not? You can begin to answer that question by relating it to speakers whom you admire or trust. Various experimenters[7] have suggested that ethos consists of at least four main dimensions:

1. A competency dimension.
2. A trustworthiness dimension.
3. A good will dimension.
4. A dynamism dimension.

The competency dimension appears to consist of such characteristics as knowledgeableness, expertness, and authoritativeness;[8] the truthworthiness dimension of truth telling, sincerity, and general reputation; the good-will dimension of motivation toward audience, and ability to find the common ground between oneself and audience;

[7]D.K. Berlo, J. Lemert, and R. Mertz, "Dimensions for Evaluating the Acceptability of Message Sources," mimeographed report (East Lansing, Mich.: Michigan State University, 1966); C.I. Hovland, I.L. Janis, H.H. Kelley, *Communication and Persuasion* (New Haven: Yale University Press, 1953), pp. 19–53. See also sources cited in following footnotes.

[8]See also section on "Authority" in this book, pp. 152–54.

and the dynamism dimension of dynamic delivery, liveliness of style, animation, and creativity of ideas.

Although it is difficult to know exactly how ethical proof operates, a large number of experimental studies support the position that the speaker's prestige significantly influences the persuasive outcome of a speech.[9] One study used a single tape-recorded speech and prepared two introductions to it. One introduction employed techniques to build the speaker's prestige, and the other did not. The audience hearing the speech with the favorable introduction changed their opinions more than did those who heard either no introduction or a poor one.[10]

In another experiment, a single tape-recorded speech was presented to three different groups. The speech was variously attributed to a Northwestern University sophomore, the Secretary of the Communist Party in America, and the Surgeon General of the United States. Not only was the Surgeon General rated as significantly more competent than the other two supposed speakers, but his speech was also the most effective in changing attitude.[11]

Still another experiment attributed a taped speech to either a political science professor or a college student. Women listeners demonstrated no large difference in the effects of the "two" speeches, but the proportion of males shifting opinion was larger in the group which thought it had been addressed by the professor.[12]

As pointed out earlier, not only may ethos be related to the position or reputation of the sources, but the internal message may vary in ethical elements. In an experiment which included or ex-

[9]Kenneth Andersen and Theodore Clevenger, Jr., "A Summary of Experimental Research in Ethos," *Speech Monographs*, Vol. XXX, No. 2 (June 1963), 59–78.

[10]Barbara Kersten, "An Experimental Study to Determine the Effect of a Speech of Introduction upon the Persuasive Speech that Followed," as cited in Andersen and Clevenger, "A Summary of Experimental Research in Ethos," pp. 69–70.

[11]Franklin Haiman, "An Experimental Study of the Effects of Ethos in Public Speaking," *Speech Monographs*, Vol. XVI, No. 2 (September 1949), 190–202.

[12]Stanley F. Paulson, "The Effects of the Prestige of the Speaker and Acknowledgement of Opposing Arguments on Audience Retention and Shift of Opinion," *Speech Monographs*, Vol. XXI, No. 4 (November 1954), 267–71.

cluded quotations by authorities in two versions of the same speech, both versions caused a significant shift in attitude, with a slight trend to favor the inclusion of authorities.[13]

High correlations have also been found between evaluations of authors and later judgments of passages to which authors' names were randomly attached; the author's name seemed to influence the ratings of passages.[14] Judgments of art are somewhat similar. One study cites results which indicated that recognition of the artist's name had some favorable effect on the evaluation of pictures.[15]

There continue to be a large number of experimental studies attempting to relate ethos to the impact of the message.[16] However, as Andersen and Clevenger point out: ". . . the scope of this concept is such that the findings are not yet sufficiently numerous and sophisticated to permit definitive conclusions about the operation of ethical proof."[17] Still, in their summary of research in ethos they conclude: "The finding is almost universal that the ethos of the source *is related in some way* to the impact of the message. This generalization applies not only in some way to political, social, religious, and economic issues but also to matters of aesthetic judgment and personal taste."[18]

[13]Howard Gilkinson, Stanley F. Paulson, and Donald Sikkink, "Effects of Order and Authority in an Argumentative Speech," *Quarterly Journal of Speech*, Vol. XL, No. 2 (April 1954), 183–92.

[14]Muzafer Sherif, "An Experimental Study of Stereotypes," *Journal of Abnormal and Social Psychology*, Vol. XXIX, No. 4 (1935), 371–75.

[15]Paul Farnsworth and Issei Misumi, "Further Data on Suggestion in Pictures," *American Journal of Psychology*, Vol. XLIII, No. 2 (1931), 632.

[16]Bradley Greenberg and Gerald R. Miller, "The Effect of Low-Credible Sources on Message Acceptance," *Speech Monographs*, Vol. XXXIII, No. 2 (1966), 127–36; James C. McCroskey, "Scales for the Measurement of Ethos," *Speech Monographs*, Vol. XXXIII, No. 1 (1966), 65–72; Murray A. Hewgill and Gerald Miller, "Source Credibility and Response to Fear-Arousing Communications, *Speech Monographs*, Vol. XXXII, No. 2 (1965), 95–101.

[17]Kenneth E. Andersen and Theodore Clevenger, Jr., "A Summary of Experimental Research in Ethos," in *Speech Communication: Analysis and Readings*, ed., Howard H. Martin and Kenneth E. Andersen (Boston: Allyn & Bacon, Inc., 1968), p. 199.

[18]*Ibid.*

SUBSTANTIVE PROOF

Supporting materials may be presented in two ways: verbally or visually. Both types of supports may be cast into different forms. The most common types of verbal support are: (1) events: historical and present, (2) statistics, (3) examples, (4) comparisons and contrasts, (5) definitions, and (6) authority. The most common types of visual supports are: (1) actual objects or models, (2) diagrams and graphs, and (3) maps and charts. We shall discuss each type and then suggest some tests to determine whether your supporting materials do, in fact, operate as evidence to help prove the points you want to make.

events: historical and present

A fact is material which may be verified independently of the speaker. There is no question about its existence and its nature, and it is not open to interpretation and evaluation. Of course, such statements have to be made with the clear understanding that, as Boulding suggests: "We do not perceive our sense data raw; they are mediated through a highly learned process of interpretation and acceptance."[19] That is why facts are dependent on no one person's "filtering system." We now know that we can label something a fact only with considerable caution:[20]

> We know that what used to be regarded as primary sense data are in fact highly learned interpretations. We see the world the way we see it because it pays us and has paid us to see it that way.

One of the most useful facts for the speaker is a statement about an event or groups of events, either from the past or from contemporary life, such as:

[19]Kenneth Boulding, *The Image* (Ann Arbor: University of Michigan Press, 1961), p. 14.
[20]*Ibid.*, p. 50.

1. On December 20, 1606, the *Susan Constant, Godspeed,* and the *Discovery* set sail from London for Virginia under the command of Captain Christopher Newport.
2. Talleyrand was born in Paris on February 2, 1754.
3. Dylan Thomas was twenty years old when his first book of poems was published in 1934.
4. There are 751 in this year's freshman class.

All these statements can be easily checked and verified. Since the speaker says them, we assume he is accurate; that is, that Talleyrand *was* born in 1754, and not in 1753. If any of these statements is being disputed, the speaker should say so.

statistics

The word "statistics" in common usage is synonymous with data: for example, the statistics of a football game or of automobile accidents. They denote description recorded in numerical form, such as this description of the funds appropriated to the Bureau of Indian Affairs for 1970:

Education and Welfare Services	$192,502,000
Resource Management	$ 59,620,000
Construction	$ 26,264,000
Road Construction	$ 20,000,000
General Administration Expenses	$ 5,526,000
Indian Health Activities	$104,017,000
Construction Indian Health Facilities	$ 20,952,000

Since statistics are often badly abused, the audience may well ask: "How do we know these figures are accurate?" "What makes them acceptable?" The question can be answered in advance by naming the source. The statistical material concerning funds appropriated to the Bureau of Indian Affairs was taken from *Statement of Appropriated Funds for Fiscal Years 1969 and 1970* (U.S. Department of the Interior). It can also, of course, be verified in a variety of reference works.

Several sources for statistics are especially helpful; they include *The Statistical Abstract of the United States, World Almanac, Information Please Almanac, Statistical Yearbook of the United*

Nations, and *Demographic Yearbook of the United Nations.* Publications of various bodies concerned chiefly with statistics are also helpful: for example, The United Nations Statistical Office, The United States Bureau of the Census, and The United States Bureau of Labor Statistics.

When necessary, the method used for arriving at the statistics should be indicated. For example, in comparing the per capita Gross National Product of the United States with the per capita Gross National Products of the European Common Market countries, it would be necessary to note two things: (1) that the dollar aggregates have (or have not) been divided by converting national aggregates into dollars at official exchange rate (that is, that you are actually comparing the same things); and (2) that European currencies have a larger domestic purchasing power than is indicated by exchange rate conversion. Consequently, the total, when compared with the United States, will be understated. In short, the speaker should tell the audience what it needs to know to guarantee accuracy of information and to make the material more meaningful. It is generally better to round off the numbers, unless small differences are crucially important, since round numbers are usually easier for an audience to assimilate.

examples

An example is the use of one particular instance to clarify or vivify a more general statement. Examples may well be the best remembered expression of the ideas in a speech. A speaker may be explaining the concept that languages have "signals" which give clues as to whether or not an object is animate or inanimate, large or small. He may choose to cite either: (1) an instance (a short, undetailed example). or (2) an illustration (a longer, more detailed example:

1. *Instance*: In the Algonquin language, small animals are often assigned to the class of inanimate objects, while particularly important plants are assigned to the animate class.
2. *Illustration*: In Liberia's Gola language, a noun which normally takes another prefix, takes the o-prefix of humans and animals if it is particularly large, valuable, or outstanding in some way. These qualities put it in the class of living creatures. Instead of

kesie, oil palm, one would say *osie*, which characterizes this palm as one of the most important trees; not *kekul*, tree, but *okul*, a particularly large and beautiful tree; not *ebu*, field, but *obuo*, a very beautiful and luxuriant field.

One determines the length of an example by asking "Is my example complete enough to be clear? Is it long enough to be meaningful to my audience?" The speaker may also use hypothetical examples, which are attempts to explain ideas which cannot be exemplified by referring to an actual experience. Although they may occasionally dramatize the speaker's point more effectively than a real example, they nevertheless remain grounded in imagination rather than in empirical (observed) evidence.

A speech should not be overburdened with examples, but should have a sufficient number of them to illustrate the point. Cicero, in one of his orations against the tyrant Verres, could have revealed the latter's despicable character by giving two, three, or even five or six examples of the crimes he had committed; but after Cicero had listed six or seven dozen, the listener probably was too tired to be impressed by anything.

comparison and contrast

These two types of supporting material are based on the same process—putting two or more things together and studying them to see how they are alike (comparison) and how they are unlike (contrast). The speaker is calling attention to certain aspects of one object, event, or person, through the copresence of another object, event, or person.

analogy. One important type of comparison is the analogy, which is especially useful in showing a similarity or resemblance of relations in two or more objects. It is this notion of relationship which is the mark of an analogy. For example, whenever we draw a diagram, such as the map of a given area, we are drawing a logical picture of something. This relationship of map to actual location is one of analogy. The black dots on the map are not really like actual cities, nor are the lines on the map tall like actual mountains or wet like actual rivers. However, the structure of a good map corresponds to the structure of the country it represents. The shapes of the actual states are like the shapes on the map, and the relative distances between the dots on the map are like the relative distances between the actual cities. In each analogy the speaker must indicate in what respects and to what extent the objects are analogous. In the comparison cited, the structures of the map and the landscape are similar. Suppose a speaker wants to compare the cost of the Louisiana Purchase with something today. He might say: "Though $15,000,000 would not even buy one aircraft carrier today, the sum was more than double the $7,000,000 it cost to run the entire government (including the Army and Navy) in 1800." Obviously the comparison here involves only cost. But take a more complicated comparison. The speaker wants to compare two poems: Dylan Thomas' "The Force that through the Green Fuse" and Gerard Manley Hopkin's "Spring and Fall: to a Young Child." From the outset he should make clear that the one similarity they share is central theme, while they are unlike in tone and method. He has thus acknowledged the *area* of similarity (and the scope of difference).

Suppose that a speaker suggests a solution to a problem and states that because it has solved a similar problem in City A, it will solve one in City B. Here the speaker infers that the two cities are more *alike* than they are different. We suppose that they are alike in size, government, functioning, location, social groupings, and so forth, *and* that the two problems were initiated by similar causes and exhibit similar symptoms. If there are differences in any of these characteristics serious enough to interfere with the solution, then the speaker should acknowledge and clarify the conditions under which his analogy (in this case, his proposed solution) could not hold true. Every analogy must break down at some point, since the objects, events, and other elements are only similar, and not identical.

Of great importance then is *fairness of sampling*. Are there more similarities than dissimilarities? Have I acknowledged the conditions under which the analogy would not hold true? The soundness of an analogy depends both upon the number of positive characteristics as compared to the number of negative characteristics, and upon the relative essentialness of the resemblances. Obviously, the number of dissimilarities between the particulars must not be more numerous or more significant than the similarities. This is not to suggest that *only* numbers of similarities and dissimilarities are relevant. One really crucial difference may be far more significant than many less important similarities.

One of the results of faulty analogy is *stereotyping*, which occurs when we group people, objects, or events together and treat them as a unit simply because they share one or a few properties in common. Lippmann defines a stereotype as "an ordered, more or less consistent picture of the world, to which our habits, our tastes, our capacities, our comforts and our hopes have adjusted themselves. They may not be a complete picture of the world, but they are a picture of a possible world to which we are adapted. In that world, people and things have their well-known places, and do certain things. . . . There we find the charm of the familiar, the normal, the dependable; its grooves and shapes are where we are accustomed to find them."[21] Our stereotypes of hillbillies, Southerners, mid-Westerners, jazz musicians, and psychiatrists are to a large extent based on faulty analogies.

metaphors and similes. Short compressed comparisons are called *metaphors* and *similes*. These have often been thought to be the semiexclusive property of creative literature, but they are an important and effective tool of the speaker. Let us note several examples:

1. Jonathan Edwards: "The sovereign pleasure of God, for the present, stays his rough wind; otherwise it would come with fury, and your destruction would come like a whirlwind, and you would be like the chaff of the summer threshing floor."[22]

2. Patrick Henry: "Has Great Britain any enemy, in this quarter of the world, to call for all this accumulation of navies and armies? No, sir, she has none. They are meant for us: they can be meant for no other. They are sent over to bind and rivet upon us those chains which the British ministry have been so long forging."[23]

3. Martin Luther King, Jr.: "In a sense we have come to our nation's capital to cash a check. When the architects of our republic wrote the magnificent words of the Constitution and the Declaration of Independence, they were signing a promissory note to which every American was to fall heir. This note was a promise that all men, yes, black men as well as white men, would be guaranteed the unalienable rights of life, liberty, and the pursuit of happiness. It is obvious today that America has defaulted on this promissory

[21]Walter Lippmann, *Public Opinion* (New York: The Macmillan Company, 1922), p. 95.

[22]Parrish and Hochmuth, *American Speeches*, p. 81.

[23]*Ibid.*

note insofar as her citizens of color are concerned. Instead of honoring this sacred obligation, America has given the Negro people a bad check; a check which has come back marked **insufficient** funds."[24]

Here, as in the literal analogy, credulity should not be stretched. A good test of the figurative analogy is to break it down into a ratio with four terms. Here the relationship can be checked more easily, more directly for an equality of ratios. For example, "My experience [as an Apprentice Seaman] thus provided me with a very special view—what could be called a worm's-eye view—of the service."[25] The ratio would then be—worm's-eye view: world:: apprentice seaman's view: service. We shall discuss metaphor and simile at length in Chapter 7.

definition

Since the speaker assumes responsibility for the audience's understanding, definition is especially important. The speaker asks himself: Am I using words which are new or unfamiliar to my audience? Am I using words with vague and/or ambiguous meanings? Am I using a familiar word in a unique way?

Good definitions include all that is necessary for clarity and interest. A definition is an inquiry into the nature of a thing. In effect, it answers the question, "What does it mean to say that something is government, that something is Socialism, that something is matter?" The answer should describe the basic characteristics and not the accidental or irrelevant properties. When we give a word meaning, when we have circumscribed its uniqueness, we have defined it.

There are numerous methods of defining, but perhaps the soundest scheme is suggested by Ehninger and Brockriede: (1) definition by classification; (2) definition by necessary conditions; and (3) definition by operational description.[26]

[24]Martin Luther King, Jr., "I Have a Dream," address delivered on August 28, 1963, in Washington, D.C.

[25]From *Major Campaign Speeches of Adlai E. Stevenson, 1952* Copyright 1953 by Random House. Reprinted by permission, p. 17.

[26]Douglas Ehninger and Wayne Brockriede, *Decision by Debate* (New York: Dodd, Mead & Co., 1963).

Definition by classification consists of placing a term within a class of similar phenomena and showing how it differs from others in the same class. This may be done by: (1) straightforward classification and differentiation; (2) placing a term in a continuum; (3) comparison and contrasts; (4) negation; and (5) etymology.

When Aristotle defined "Rhetoric" as "the faculty for observing, in any given case, all the available means of persuasion,"[27] he placed rhetoric in a class (faculty) which is differentiated from other faculties in that it has a different function: It observes (not necessarily uses) all available means of persuasion. He further differentiated it from all the processes which observe means of persuasion by adding, "in any given (particular) case"; that is, with reference to time, place, and audience. When we suggest that chartreuse is "yellow-green" we have placed it in a continuum—in this case the color spectrum.

Bertrand Russell's definition of "matter" illustrates defining by comparison and contrast: "We commonly mean by 'matter' something that is opposed to 'mind,' something which we think of as occupying space and as radically incapable of any sort of thought or consciousness."[28]

Definition by negation uses contrast to indicate what a term does not mean. *De facto* recognition of a government is not the same as *de jure* recognition. *De jure* recognition carries with it the implication of approval, whereas *de facto* recognition does not. It implies only the awareness that a given government is *in fact* controlling the affairs of the state.

We have already used the method of definition by etymology when we defined the terms "communication" and "proof." The critic Sainte-Beuve uses this method in his essay "What is a Classic?" He points out:

A classic, according to the usual definition, is an old author canonised by admiration, and an authority in his particular style. The word *classic* was first used in this sense by the Romans. With them not all the citizens of the different classes were properly called *classici*, but only those of the chief class, those who possessed an income of a certain fixed sum. Those who possessed a smaller income were de-

[27]Aristotle, *Rhetoric*, trans. W. Rhys Roberts (New York: Random House, Inc., 1954), 1355b 26–27.

[28]Bertrand Russell, *The Problems of Philosophy* (New York: Oxford University Press, 1959), p. 13.

scribed by the term *infra classem,* below the pre-eminent class. The word *classicus* was used in a figurative sense . . . and applied to writers: a writer of worth and distinction, *classicus assiduusque scriptor,* a writer who is of account. . . ."[29]

Definition by necessary conditions, as the name implies, is an enumeration of the conditions that must be met before the term can be used properly. For example, a monopoly exists only if there is exclusive control (however obtained) of the supply of any given commodity in any given market.

Lincoln's "First Inaugural Address" used the definition by necessary condition to meet the contention of the secessionists that the Constitution nowhere authorized the federal government to take forcible measures against the withdrawing states. "Perpetuity is implied, if not expressed, in the fundamental law of all national governments";[30] that is, it is a fundamental feature of, condition to, "national governments." Lincoln thus suggests that whatever is recognized as a "government" has the obligation to defend itself from without and from within.

Winston Churchill, distinguishing between "Liberalism" and "Socialism," demonstrated operational definition by pointing out how they function. In this example, operational description is set in the context of comparison and contrast:

Socialism seeks to pull down wealth; Liberalism seeks to raise up poverty. Socialism would destroy private interests; Liberalism would preserve private interests in the only way in which they can be safely and justly preserved, namely, by reconciling them with public right. Socialism would kill enterprise; Liberalism would rescue enterprise from the trammels of privilege and preference. Socialism assails the pre-eminence of the individual; Liberalism seeks, and shall seek more in the future, to build up a minimum standard for the mass. Socialism exalts the rule; Liberalism exalts the man. Socialism attacks capital; Liberalism attacks monopoly.

In addition to these kinds of definitions, there are definition by example and authoritative definition. Both could probably be used in defining a term by any of the methods discussed above.

[29]C.A. Sainte-Beuve, "What is a Classic"? in *Great Essays,* ed. Houston Peterson (New York: Pocket Books, Inc., 1954), p. 228.

[30]Parrish and Hochmuth, *American Speeches,* p. 36.

[31]F.B. Czarnomski, ed., *The Eloquence of Winston Churchill* (New York: The New American Library of World Literature, Inc., 1957), p. 16.

authority

Authority is support drawn from the experience and judgment of someone other than the speaker. The speaker may have to rely on the experience of others to supply him with the substantive data (e.g., statistics) that he needs, or he may use the opinion of someone more expert at interpreting relationships among data. C. Wright Mills has aptly pointed out how much our lives are governed by opinion and authority:

> The first rule of understanding the human condition is that men live in second-hand worlds. They are aware of much more than they have personally experienced; and their own experience is always indirect. [That is, they view reality through a perceptual screen]. The quality of their lives is determined by meanings they have received from others. . . . Their images of the world and of themselves, are given to them by crowds of witnesses that have never met and shall never meet. Yet for every man these images—provided by strangers and dead men—are the very basis of his life as a human being.[32]

In form, the use of authority may mean solely an interpretation or value judgment, or it may involve factual material of all kinds with interpretation or judgment by an expert whose relationship with the facts makes him particularly qualified to observe and interpret them. For an example of testimony which includes statistics and contrast, consider the statement of Senator Mark Hatfield, member of the Senate Committee on Interior and Insular Affairs:

> At the federal level there is little doubt that there is need for unification of the environmental effort. With some 13 congressional committees, 90 separate Federal environmental programs, plus 25 quasigovernmental bodies and 14 interagency committees already involved in the environmental action, it is high time that formal recognition take place in order to insure some coherent form for environmental protection.[33]

[32]C. Wright Mills, *Power, Politics and People* (New York: Ballantine Books, 1963), p. 405.

[33]Statement by Senator Mark O. Hatfield on "Environmental Quality," April 1970, Mimeo, p. 2. Text supplied by the Senator's office.

Observe how a speaker can use an authority within an authority; for example, Catherine Bowen's reflections about an event which gives insight into another historian, Bernard DeVoto:

> Bernard DeVoto lived with history, read history at night and in the morning, talked history, and was restless when other people did not want to talk history. When I began to write about John Adams, I asked DeVoto if I should buy the *Dictionary of American Biography*. There are twenty-one volumes and it is not cheap. DeVoto was surprised at my question and surprised that I did not already own the volumes. "Of course, buy it," he said. "It's good to read in bed at night before you go to sleep."[34]

What makes an authority credible? We shall indicate the kinds of questions the speaker will want to ask about the authorities he cites. They are the questions the more alert members of his audience may be asking themselves as he speaks.

expertise. Is he an expert on the subject being discussed? Is he in a position to get at the facts? Has he directly observed that which he testifies to, or is he using materials observed and reported by others than himself? If the authority is a firsthand observer, how contemporaneous is his reporting? Has a considerable time-lapse occurred between his observing and reporting? When he relies upon secondary sources, does he choose wisely? Does he reveal his dependencies on the testimony of others?

lack of bias. How objective is the authority? Does the material of the authority appear free of bias? Is he a member of a group whose purpose is to persuade the general public to their point of view? Does the group with which the authority is associated have a disqualifying bias or indeterminate bias? To what extent does the authority acknowledge his bias? Does he pretend bias does not exist in the case at hand?

past reliability. Has the authority made statements in the past that have proved reliable and accurate?

relationship to other experts. Do other reliable authorities agree with him? Do other reliable authorities make claims counter to his?

relevancy. Is the authority an expert on the subject under

[34]Catherine D. Bowen, "The Historian," in *Four Portraits and One Subject: Bernard DeVoto* (Boston: Houghton Mifflin Company, 1963), p. 23.

discussion? Or is he a generally knowledgeable person who may have no special expertise in the particular topic?

type of task. What is the expert doing? Is he making descriptive generalizations? Causal explanations? Drawing historical analyses? Predicting? Is this the type of task which the expert is best able to do?

situational variables. Was the situation in which the authority made his observations conducive to accurate observations? To what extent was the situation free of tension? If the situation was not relatively tension-free, to what extent may the observer have perceived what was expected either by himself or some agency to which he was reporting? In times of considerable tension, to what extent may the observer have been affected by affective feelings? Habitual stereotypes? Suspicions? Fears?

Now that we have suggested questions that the speaker and audience may ask about the testimony cited in a speech, let us make a few observations about how testimony is used. First, use of authority does not take the place of substantive or motivational proof; it is supplementary to them, and may often reflect them. Second, the use of authority ought not be separated from the type of task the speaker has undertaken. The expert in one field often holds no claim to universal wisdom, and "expert" testimony may not provide the best guide in the task the speaker is undertaking. Sorensen, for example, has observed: "The trained navigator . . . is essential to the conduct of a voyage, but his judgment is not superior in such matters as where it should go or whether it should be taken at all."[35] The answer to such a question as, "Should we have sent troops to Vietnam?" is not likely to be answered by the authority who cites the SEATO Treaty and the Eisenhower letter to President Diem on October 23, 1964. Such questions are to be answered by recourse to values, costs of the policy in human and material terms, relationships to U.S. goals other than treaty obligations, and so on. The makers of nuclear weapons, who may know most about them in technical terms, may not be the ones to determine whether and in what ways those weapons may be used. Thus, expert testimony needs to be considered in light of the overall task of the individual speaker or of society as a whole.

[35]Theodore C. Sorensen, *Decision-Making in the White House* (New York: Columbia University Press, 1963), p. 66.

visual aids

One of the criteria for selecting all the materials for a speech should be potential interest and attention value. Change, both in terms of variety among types of verbal supporting materials and from presenting supporting material verbally to presenting such material through visual aids, generally helps maintain attention. Visual aids in a speech add interest chiefly because they *do* involve a change from one activity (hearing) to another (seeing).

The other basic difference between visual and verbal support is this: words are discursive, they are temporal in nature and are heard one at a time, with the complete meaning withheld until the entire sentence, paragraph, or even the whole speech has been delivered. Visual symbols, on the other hand, are presentational; their complete meaning is presented all at once.

Many people are more "eye-minded" than "ear-minded." One study reports that 85 percent of learning is gained through the eyes. Subjects learned one-third faster through visual instruction than through aural instruction only, and material that was seen was remembered 55 percent better than material that was only heard. So visual aids not only have attention value, but they strengthen understanding as well, since they serve to promote clearness. It is hard to compare more than two numbers when hearing them, but when they are presented in a graph or chart it is easy to understand the interrelationships among them.[36]

Some students discovered these two effective uses of visual aids in a classroom speech. When discussing the campaigns of General Washington, one student made the speech more meaningful and vivid by pointing out the campaigns on a large, multicolored map. Another student, discussing the plight of slum children, evoked much more feeling and compassion and a clearer belief in the need for action by showing photographs taken from a weekly news-magazine.

Whether you are using models, diagrams, charts, maps, graphs, or objects, there are two major criteria for selecting them: (1) Are they easy to use? To handle? To explain? and (2) Are they large

[36]Reported in Robert T. Oliver, Harold P. Zelko, and Paul D. Holtzman, *Communicative Speech* (3rd ed.; New York: Holt, Rinehart and Winston, Inc., 1962), p. 250.

enough to be seen by everyone in the audience? Unless your aids meet both criteria, they are more hindrance than help and will distract attention from your speech. Visual aids are, as the name implies, aids which supplement, not supplant, the spoken word.

If the visual aid hinders the speaker's direct relationship with his audience, if the speaker talks to the diagram instead of to his audience, his actions detract from the speech rather than help it. Practice with the aid will help the speaker use it efficiently without giving it his complete attention at the audience's expense.

tests of effective supporting material

We have been suggesting some criteria for selecting different kinds of supporting material. Now, let us list the questions the speaker needs to ask about all of his supporting material:

1. Is my material relevant to my speech?
2. Is my material accurate? Does it come from a reliable source?
3. Is my material recent enough?
4. Is my material fairly stated? Are my examples typical? Is my information sufficient in scope to present an accurate picture?
5. Is my material appropriate to this particular audience? Will it be meaningful to them?
6. Is my material interesting and vivid?

If the supporting materials meet the first five requirements, it will be acceptable as rhetorical proof. If it also meets the sixth, it will have still a better chance of actually being accepted by the audience.

MOTIVATIONAL APPEALS

In substantive proof, materials are drawn from a body of data in the external world (statistics, examples, and so on). When source credibility is used as proof, materials are drawn from what the audience knows about the speaker (his intelligence, good will, credibility). But when motivational appeals are used as rhetorical proof, the materials are drawn from the audience's motives, emotions, and values. At this point it might be helpful to review our discussion of motive and values appearing on pp. 66–102.

In the section that follows we will attempt to do two things: (1) to point to the wide range of motivational appeals; and (2) to point to the variety of ways motive appeals are often associated with source credibility and substantive proof. As before, we will use the schematization of human motives suggested by Abraham Maslow.[37]

physiological needs

Gratification of physiological needs frees the human being from being dominated by them, thereby permitting other more social goals to emerge and predominate. The dominating goal (here the fulfillment of some basic physiological need) operates as "a strong determinant not only of his current world outlook but also his philosophy of the future."[38] Thus, an audience whose attention is dominated by any one or a combination of physiological needs is probably unable or unwilling to turn their attention to other subjects.

The relationship of speeches to these needs is quite interesting. For example, one can talk about blood sugar level or some other homeostatic control, but words don't directly affect it. The speaker would, in this instance, give his audience information on how it operates, urge people to have it checked regularly, and talk to diabetics about the importance of diet, schedule, and so on. One can urge those who live in arid lands to insist on the canalization of water resources to their areas, but words will not directly affect their thirst. Speeches will just provide them with knowledge and hope that their basic needs for water can be fulfilled.

Although most of you reading this book are not forced to go hungry or thirsty, we are all increasingly aware of the vast pockets of poverty in our abundant society, of the "outs" who want "in," not just in on the "good life" but in on the basic requirements to meet their physical needs. However, much of the rhetoric that reaches us is about hunger; it is not addressed to the hungry. Ap-

---

[37]Abraham Maslow, *Motivation and Personality* (New York: Harper & Row, Publishers, 1954).

[38]*Ibid.*, p. 84.

peals of this kind are to these needs by virtue of empathetic responses, by virtue of our common humanity.

The "out" groups are also increasingly being addressed by organizers from their own groups, or by politicians who are just beginning to recognize the clout of "poor power" at the voting booths. Thus, you will likely be able to find a growing body of rhetoric directed to those who have yet to fulfill their basic human needs.

safety

The variety of safety appeals ranges from direct physical threat to more subtle and less easily observed threats; for example, from the dangers of environmental pollution and guerrilla warfare in our cities to presumed political infiltration of governmental structures. Let us consider several examples by well-known speakers. We can make certain assumptions about the type of audience the speaker is addressing by the threat he chooses to discuss and by the way he describes and discusses that threat.

Consider two recent instances from speeches concerning environmental pollution. In the first, the speaker talks of air pollution:

> Two years ago, Los Angeles had five micrograms of lead per cubic meter of air—highest in the nation at that time. But last year, New York City earned this dubious distinction—seven and one-half micrograms. And scientists estimate San Diego may exceed even that this year—eight micrograms. The level of ten micrograms, but a short span away, is the maximum tolerable limit set by the United States Public Health Service.[39]

Note the straightforward reporting of the information. The speaker gently points the way to interpretation ("a short span away"), but leaves it largely up to the audience to draw their own inferences about the direct application of this information. In the next example, information is also given, but the speaker openly suggests that the materials also have emotive-connotative attachments:

[39]Senator Frank Church, "Give Earth a Chance," address delivered on April 22, 1970, at Ricks College and Idaho State University.

> Every major river system in America is seriously polluted, from the Androscoggin in Maine to the Columbia in the far Northwest. The rivers once celebrated in poetry and song—the Monongahela, the Cumberland, the Ohio, the Hudson, the Delaware, the Rio Grande— have been blackened with sewage, chemicals, oils, and trash. They are sewers of filth and disease.[40]

Here the speaker draws the interpretation: The rivers "are sewers of filth and disease." Whereas the first speaker talks in terms of "micrograms of lead per cubic meter," the second speaker deals with rivers that "have been blackened with sewage . . ." Further, he is not just speaking of rivers, but "rivers once celebrated in poetry and song. . . ."

In the next example, the speaker either assumes that his audience already knows the facts, or that they will accept his interpretation of them:

> Let's consider the matter of guerilla warfare. The central fact in this situation cannot be denied or avoided. It is that the United States has been included among the nations of the world against which guerilla warfare tactics are to be employed for revolutionary purposes. Another fact is that responsible agencies of federal government were aware that such a decision has been made. For example, they knew of the conference of world guerilla warfare chieftans in Havana, Cuba, where the decision was made—and the identity of individuals and organizations from the United States at that meeting. It was known (in and out of federal government) that these plans called for employment of guerilla warfare tactics in heavily populated urban areas of the United States.[41]

This audience is either largely dependent on their own special knowledge of the facts, or the speaker assumes that his credibility as a person who has access to the facts ranks high with them. The motivational appeal to safety seems more tied to the source credi-

[40]Senator Gaylord Nelson, in an article reprinted in the *Congressional Record* (November 18, 1969).

[41]George C. Wallace, "Address on Law Enforcement," delivered August 29, 1967, to the Fraternal Order of Police, Miami, Florida. As quoted in James C. McCroskey, *An Introduction to Rhetorical Communication* (Englewood Cliffs, N.J.: Prentice-Hall, Inc., 1968), p. 272.

bility of the speaker than in either of the two previous examples.

In the following appeal to safety against a Communist threat, the speaker reminds the audience of his credibility in fighting the Communist threat and invites them to join with him:

> The Communists, Communists you know don't wear, they don't wear their party membership on their coatsleeves. They work, the only time they can work, effectively, is secretly in the dark recesses. . . . So I have been fighting night and day, for months and years, to expose and get Communists, and Communist-line thinkers out of positions of power in Washington. Tomorrow, you the American people will either get rid of the Communists and fellow-travelers, or you will vote more of them into power. . . . If you want to get rid of the Communists and the corrupt mess in Washington, your task is to work . . . to make sure that we elect Eisenhower. . . . If . . . you are sick way down deep inside at the deliberate sell-out of America, a sell-out according to the plans, to the careful plans of the red-printed-tinted crowd who have been so bad for America and so good for Communist Russia . . . [you] can do it tomorrow by voting for Eisenhower. . . .[42]

The appeal is not only to safety, but also obliquely to the sense of belonging to part of a national crusade.

love and belonging

These appeals range from "Do this because you love your children" (as in certain advertisements sponsored by the American Cancer Society in their antismoking campaign) to appeals concerning groups far larger than the immediate family. First consider an example in which the speaker appeals to his audience to join their country's interests to those of his country as they fight a common enemy, the Axis Powers:

> We in Britain had the *same* feeling in our darkest days. We, too, were sure that in the end all would be well. You do not, I am certain,

[42]Joseph McCarthy, "The Red-Tinted Washington Crowd," address delivered in November, 1952, in Appleton, Wisconsin. As quoted in Charles Lomas, ed., *The Agitator in American Society* (Englewood Cliffs, N.J.: Prentice-Hall, Inc., 1968), pp. 160–62.

underrate the severity of the ordeal to which *you and we* have still to be subjected. The forces ranged against *us* are enormous.

.   .   .

Here we are *together* facing a group of mighty foes who seek *our* ruin. Here we are *together* defending all that to free men is dear. [Italics added][43]

The italicized words indicate the speaker's sense of togetherness between England and America: the two countries have common feeling in their "darkest days." They are both optimistic "that . . . all would be well." Neither of the countries underestimate their peril; the "enormous" forces of their common enemy seek to ruin both countries, and the countries find themselves together upholding "all that to free men is dear."

Consider another circumstance and the way in which the speaker (Abraham Lincoln in this instance) tries to appeal to a sense of "national belonging." In this example, he appeals to both the North and the South:

Physically speaking, we cannot separate. We cannot remove our respective sections from each other nor build an impassable wall between them. A husband and wife may be divorced and go out of the presence and beyond the reach of each other, but the different parts of our country cannot do this. They cannot but remain face to face, and intercourse, either amicable or hostile, must continue between them. Is it possible, then, to make that intercourse more advantageous or more satisfactory *after* separation than *before*? Can aliens make treaties easier than friends can make laws? Can treaties be more faithfully enforced between aliens than laws can among friends?[44]

The speaker is arguing that geographical proximity makes complete separateness impossible, and that friends can deal better with one another than enemies or aliens. The common ground shared by the speaker and both his audiences is quite literally the ground on which they stand.

[43]Winston Churchill, "Address to Congress," delivered on December 16, 1941. As quoted in Goodwin Berquist, Jr., ed., *Speeches for Illustration and Example* (Glenwood, Ill.: Scott, Foresman & Company, 1965), pp. 93, 97.

[44]Abraham Lincoln, "First Inaugural Address." As quoted in Berquist, *Speeches for Illustration and Example*, p. 138.

The next speaker urges two races to recognize the common ground they share of freedom and the rights that accrue from that freedom:

> The marvelous new militancy which has engulfed the Negro community must not lead us to a distrust of all white people, for many of our white brothers, as evidenced by their presence here today, have come to realize that their destiny is tied up with our destiny and they have come to realize that their freedom is inextricably bound to our freedom. We cannot walk alone.[45]

"Inextricably bound" leaves no room for doubt as to the philosophical ground that the speaker is asking both his White and his Black audience to share with him.

We are used to hearing, especially during election campaigns, politicians and admen ask us to support and work for a political party because we accept a given party's platform (the ground on which the party stands). Or we are asked to share one political ideology or set of policies rather than another. Politicians usually try to include as many people in their camps as possible, but occasionally they establish very strong common ground with their coworkers when they suggest that only a certain type of person should be committed to the campaign team:

> The ordeal of the twentieth century—the bloodiest most turbulent era of the Christian age—is far from over. Sacrifice, patience, understanding and implacable purpose may be our lot for years to come. Let's face it. Let's talk sense to the American people. Let's tell them the truth, that there are no gains without pains, that we are on the eve of great decisions, not easy decisions, like resistance when you're attacked, but a long, patient, costly struggle which alone can assure triumph over the great enemies of man—war, poverty and tyranny—and the assaults upon human dignity which are the most grievous consequences of each.
>
> .   .   .
>
> That, I think, is our ancient mission. Where we have deserted it we have failed. With your help there will be no desertion now. Better, we lose the election than mislead the people; and better we lose than misgovern the people.

[45]King, "I Have a Dream."

Help me do the job in this autumn of conflict and of campaign. . . .[46]

Here the speaker asks his listeners to belong to that group of people who would join him in a "mission," in a campaign that would be waged in a certain way.

esteem

Just as with the other motives, the range of appeals to esteem needs is large. Appeals range from advertisements for hair rinses and automobiles through pleas for ethnic and national esteem. The more obvious ones are readily available in the major weekly magazines or on television. Below are several examples to indicate appeals to group esteem needs. First, consider an example from a speech by Louis Lomax to a Black audience:

This white man is crazy. He may not know it, but I'm somebody. He doesn't know with whom he is about to tangle. Because, if the truth were told, I was somebody before I even got here. If you go back deeply enough into my African past—I don't know about you, but I can tell from the way I walk and the way I feel some mornings that my old folks way back in Africa were kings and princes. And when I dig back into my past, I find out that I was teaching mathematics and geometry and plotting the course of the stars in the skies when the white man of Europe was still living in the caves of England and running from the Romans. . . . When this country was ready to die, to break the chains of colonialism, I, Louis Lomax, black man, in Crispus Attucks, was the first man to die on Boston Commons to set these white folks free from England. I'm somebody. In Phyllis Wheatley I taught them how to write poetry. In Paul Lawrence Dunbar I taught them the rhythm of anguish. In Frederick Douglass I taught them the meaning of oratory. In Sojourner Truth I taught them the meaning of militancy. In Booker Washington I gave them one of the first philosophies of American education . . . in Jesse Owens I beat him running. In Marian Anderson I beat him singing. In Joe Louis I beat him fighting. In Jackie Robinson I

[46]Adlai E. Stevenson, "Acceptance Address," delivered on July 26, 1952, at the Democratic National Convention in Chicago, Illinois. Transcribed from a tape of the speech.

beat him playing baseball. And in Charles Drew I took the blood
bank. And in Ralph Bunche I'll run the world if you'll move over
and get out of the way. I'm somebody.[47]

Note how the speaker works through example and comparison to
support his esteem appeal. Especially effective is "I, Louis Lomax,
black man, in Crispus Attucks, was . . ." because it combines the
belongingness and esteem motive appeals.

The esteem appeal has also been attempted with some regularity in speeches concerning the Southeast Asian conflict. Consider
how it was used in this speech on Vietnam. These appeals are aimed
at the President's included audience; they will often be offensive to
the audience he excludes, particularly in his use of the Good
Samaritan parable:

> Two hundred years ago this nation was weak and poor. But even
> then, America was the hope of millions in the world. Today we
> have become the strongest and richest nation in the world. The
> wheel of destiny has turned so that any hope the world has for the
> survival of peace and freedom in the last third of this century will
> be determined by whether the American people have the moral
> stamina and the courage to meet the challenge of free world leader-
> ship.
>
> Let historians not record that when America was the most power-
> ful nation in the world we passed on the other side of the road and
> allowed the last hopes for peace and freedom of millions of people
> on this earth to be suffocated by the forces of totalitarianism.[48]

Here again the motive appeal to esteem is helped by a variety of
supporting strategies: (1) contrast and comparison (once poor, now
rich—but always the "hope of millions in the world"); (2) "destiny"
is on our side—a kind of mystical force has made the United States
the "hope the world has for the survival of peace and freedom";
(3) we are now facing a test of "moral" stamina that must be faced
by the free world "leader"; (4) allusion to the Good Samaritan, a

[47]Louis E. Lomax, "I am Somebody," address delivered in 1963 in Pacoima,
California. As quoted in Lomas, *The Agitator in American Society*, pp.
128–29.

[48]Richard M. Nixon, "Let Us Be United for Peace . . . Against Defeat,"
address delivered on November 3, 1969, over national television. Transcribed from a tape of the speech.

Christian example of one who would not leave his fellowman by the "side of the road" to perish; (5) metaphor—the United States must allow the world to "breathe" (they must fend off "suffocating" forces).

A similar motive appeal supported by a variety of strategies appears in another presidential speech, this one on Cambodia:

> If when the chips are down the world's most powerful nation, the United States of America, acts like a pitiful helpless giant, the forces of totalitarianism and anarchy will threaten free nations and free institutions throughout the world.[49]

Such appeals are aimed at a specific audience; the excluded audience will likely also find this metaphor repugnant. The point here is to show how speakers attempt to use these appeals; no doubt the intellectually rigorous person has examined or will want to examine them thoroughly for accuracy.

self-actualization

Maslow has defined self-actualization as that motive that impels man "to become everything [he] is capable of becoming."[50] This is not a newly discovered motive. You have undoubtedly heard it called by a variety of names: The unified personality, the autonomous person, the existential being, or creative becoming.[51] Clearly the nature and level of aspiration will be determined in large part by the individual's environment. For example, the level of a person's aspiration may be permanently lowered or even completely deadened; the self-actualizing goal may disappear and be lost forever if a person has continuously experienced life at a very low

[49]Richard M. Nixon, "Speech on Cambodia," delivered on April 30, 1970, over national television. Transcribed from a tape of the speech.

[50]Maslow, *Motivation and Personality*, p. 92.

[51]Prescott, Lecky, *Consistency: A Theory of Personality* (New York: Island Press, 1945); Rollo May, *Man's Search for Himself* (New York: W.W. Norton & Company, Inc., 1953); David Riesman et al., *The Lonely Crowd* (New Haven: Yale University Press, 1950); Gordon Allport, *Becoming: Basic Considerations for a Psychology of Personality* (New Haven: Yale University Press, 1955).

level. His self-image may so shrink that even his potential for becoming the best diminishes.

To a great extent, the rhetoric of the "War on Poverty" was filled with the recognition that basic needs must be at least minimally fulfilled (to provide an economic environment where people do not have to spend the whole of their lives intent upon survival) before higher needs can arise. Much of the rhetoric concerning the issue of disarmament also rings of this appeal: That the shadow of nuclear war be removed so man no longer is dominated by the quest for physical and psychological security, but can live in an atmosphere conducive to creativity and growth. In many respects the self-actualizing motive is the essential motive-appeal in the rhetoric of Blacks, Indians, the poor of all races, and women's liberation.

Consider, for example, the words of Vine Deloria, Jr., of the Standing Rock Sioux:

> The red man is neither white nor black; he is a fascinating and complex member of a culture that still lives, despite overwhelming odds. He does not want the American dream of homogeneous bliss; he does not want the rite of the Easter bunny to replace his own meaningful religions; he does not want a low-calorie non-culture to replace his own vital heritage. He *does* want what he was promised. Now.[52]

The same kinds of themes have echoed in Black rhetoric. Consider Stokely Carmichael and Louis Lomax:

> . . . number one, it is clear to me that we have to wage a psychological battle on the right for black people to define their own terms, define themselves as they see fit, and organize themselves as they see fit.

> And this is why . . . the ballgame is over. This is why the word "nigger"—you can forget it. If anybodys a nigger, he is. He created the word nigger. I didn't. He made the word nigger because he needed to have somebody he felt better than. He can forget it now, because God didn't make my sons and daughters to clean up his kitchen. And God didn't make my son so he could have chauffeurs and shoe-shine boys. But God made little black boys for the same

---

[52]*Custer Died for Your Sins: An Indian Manifesto* (New York: The Macmillan Company, 1969, back flap copy.

reason he made little white boys: so they can grow up like men, and some of them can work in kitchens, and some of them can be President of the United States.[53]

Appeals to the self-actualizing motive often occur in rhetoric about those institutions commonly thought of as trustees of our common culture, and by men whose reputation makes them keepers of that trusteeship. Consider first a passage from a speech (see Appendix) delivered by poet Archibald MacLeish at the opening of Hampshire College, and secondly a passage from the Nobel Prize Acceptance Speech of novelist William Faulkner:[54]

> . . . it is as trustee of the culture that the University has failed in these years in which the culture has lost its human values and deteriorated into a mere technocracy which exploits everything else, using even science itself not as a means for the advancement of civilization and the enrichment of life but as a ground for gadgetry and invention regardless of the human value of the thing invented, so that the triumphs of the epoch make no distinction between the glories of modern medicine and the horrors of modern war.
>
> .   .   .
>
> Without a center that can hold, the falcon cannot hear the falconer—things fall apart . . . Human liberty becomes an inhuman liberty to mutilate and murder. The liberated slave is liberated to another bondage.
>
> Only when freedom is human, as well as humanity free, can a nation of free men exist. Only when the balance between society and self is reestablished can the self be realized. . . .

> Our tragedy today is a general and universal physical fear so long sustained by now that we can even bear it. There are no longer problems of the spirit. There is only the question: when will I be blown up? Because of this, the young man or woman writing today has forgotten the problems of the human heart in conflict with itself which alone can make good writing because only that is worth writing about, worth the agony and the sweat.
> He must learn them again. He must teach himself that the basest

[53]Stokely Carmichael, "Black Power," and Louis Lomax, "I am Somebody," in Lomas, *The Agitator in American Society,*" pp. 129, 150.
[54]Transcribed from a tape of the speech delivered by Archibald MacLeish on October 3, 1970; William Faulkner, "Nobel Prize Acceptance Speech." The full text of both speeches are in the Appendix of this book.

of all things is to be afraid; and, teaching himself that, forget it forever, leaving no room in his workshop for anything but the old verities and truths of the heart, the old universal truths lacking which any story is ephemeral and doomed—love and honor and pity and pride and compassion and sacrifice. Until he does so, he labors under a curse. He writes not of love but of lust, of defeats in which nobody loses anything of value, of victories without hope, and worst of all, without pity or compassion. His griefs grieve on no universal bones, leaving no scars. He writes not of the heart but of the glands.

Perhaps self-actualization ought to be thought of as a transitive process rather than an end product. Jung and Allport, for instance, defined the personality in terms of some "ideal state of integration toward which the individual is tending."[55] They observe that while "it has some stable features, it is at the same time continually undergoing change."[56] This may well be in our collective, societal interests as well as our personal interests, because the finished structure tends to be static; it is the unfinished structure that has dynamic power.

An illuminating example of the thin line between motivational appeal and substantive proof occurs in this passage from a speech by Vice-President Agnew criticizing television on its coverage of the news.[57] Let's compare two versions of one passage, the first as actually delivered by Mr. Agnew. The passage concerns the fact that one network offered a commentary by Averell Harriman on one of President Nixon's Vietnam speeches:

> To guarantee in advance that the President's plea for national unity would be challenged, one network trotted out Averell Harriman for the occasion. Through the President's message, he waited in the wings. When the President concluded, Mr. Harriman recited perfectly.

Now suppose that Mr. Agnew has wanted to use this example as substantive proof only. He could have said:

> To ensure discussion of the President's speech, Averell Harriman appeared on one network. His analysis and commentary occurred immediately after the President's speech.

[55]Allport, *Becoming*, p. 90.

[56]*Ibid.*, 19.

[57]Vice-President Spiro Agnew, as quoted in *The New York Times* (November 14, 1969), 24.

But notice how the choice of the words by the speaker evoke emotive-connotative meanings. They are not purely referential.

the President's speech	the President's plea for national unity
would be discussed	would be challenged
one network presented	one network trotted out
he listened	he waited in the wings
he offered his analysis and commentary	he recited perfectly

the anatomy of proof

Now that we have looked briefly at the materials of proof, let us turn to a discussion of its anatomy.

INFERENCE

An inference is that which is derived by *implication*. Inferences are often drawn when the speaker wants to go beyond empirical evidence. The types of supporting material which we have just discussed become the basis of an inductive generalization; the speaker wants the audience to make an "inductive leap" beyond the known. Let us illustrate by showing how statistics can be used as the basis of inference. A newspaper reporter questions twenty-five people in a town about their opinions of proposed legislation. Twenty are in favor of it, and five are opposed. If the reporter records that twenty out of twenty-five people were in favor of the legislation, he is only describing what he has observed. But if his story reports that 80 per cent of the town's people favor the legislation, he is *inferring* that the percentage of the population favoring the legislation is basically the same as in his small sample. The question becomes: Is the sample large enough in scope to allow the inference? In this case, probably not.

The reporter could have said: "Since twenty of the twenty-five people I sampled were in favor of the legislation, I can be 95 per cent confident that the proportion of citizens in favor of it is somewhere between 54 per cent and 91 per cent." This may not be as dramatic, but it is more accurate. As soon as the speaker makes an inductive generalization, saying in effect that because this (that which can be empirically proven) is true, then this (that which cannot be empirically proven) is probably also true, the speaker is no longer describing—he is drawing an inference.

The most important thing for the beginning speaker to remember when drawing an inference is to limit his claim to the scope of the supporting material or evidence. Inferences, by definition, are limited in such ways as "much of the time," "most of the time," "80 percent of the time," "possibly," "there is a high degree of probability that what I say is in fact likely to hold true." The speaker must be sure that when he is moving from observed or known facts to a "prediction" (that which is unable at the moment to be observed or known), his claim is appropriate to the amount of support.

ARGUMENT

An argument may be defined as a movement from data (evidence) to claim. We will begin our discussion of argument by exploring a claim statement; for example, "It's going to rain tomorrow." Certain questions have already occurred to you, the first of which would probably be: "How do you know?" which is our general way of asking: "Based on what evidence?" Thus we have raised a question about the claim statement's starting point, its evidence.

"The weatherman on Channel 22 said so on the 11:15 weather forecast," might be a reply. So we know that the speaker's claim was based upon a piece of testimony. But suppose the listener is not satisfied by the speaker's reply. "What did the weather forecaster have to go on?" is the casual way of asking: "Do you have additional evidence?" At this point the maker of the claim statement might recall a weather satellite's photograph and/or related materials concerning wind currents, cold fronts, and so on.

"How accurate has the forecaster been in the past?" a curious listener who is aware of the fallible ways of weather forecasters might ask. This seemingly casual question has cut to the core of the speaker's "argument." Note that we have so far been told by the speaker that the weather forecaster (backed by evidence) tells us that it will rain. This supposes that the speaker is warranted in his unspoken assumption that the weather forecaster has generally been correct in the past, and is therefore likely to be specifically correct in tomorrow's forecast. The speaker's warrant is from whole (the general tendency of the weather forecaster to be correct) to the part (tomorrow's forecast will be correct). "Channel 22's weather forecaster is correct about 80 percent of the time," the speaker recalls. "Well," replies the unusually argumentative listener, "shouldn't your claim have a qualifier; that is, shouldn't your claim recognize that weather conditions change quickly and often unexpectedly, so the only claim you can really make is: 'It will *probably* rain tomorrow.'" The listener has forced the speaker to recognize the conditions under which his claim would not hold true (we shall later term this part of the argument the *rebuttal*) and, at the same time, forced him to qualify his claim to make it more in line with the evidence he has used.

Philosopher Stephen Toulmin has schematized the anatomy of an argument, taking into consideration the kinds of questions a listener might ask about a speaker's claim. In the discussion of argument that follows, we will classify arguments according to the type of warrant (the type of reasoning, the nature of the basic assumption that relates evidence and claim).[58] First, let us consider the types of warrants employed in substantive proof. They may be schematized as follows:

A. Warrants based on time relationships
   1. Cause to effect
   2. Effect to cause
   3. Sign

B. Warrants based on part-whole relationships
   1. Generalization
   2. Classification

C. Warrants based on similarity relationships
   1. Analogy
   2. Parallel case

[58]This treatment follows that suggested by Stephen Toulmin, *The Uses of Argument* (Cambridge: Cambridge University Press, 1959). See also Ehninger and Brockriede, *Decision by Debate*.

Now let us examine in skeletal form how these warrants appear to operate.

1. cause to effect

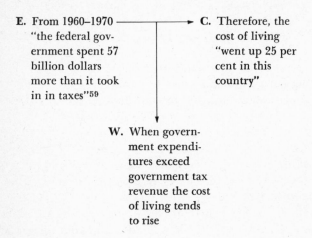

E. From 1960–1970 "the federal government spent 57 billion dollars more than it took in in taxes"[59]

C. Therefore, the cost of living "went up 25 per cent in this country"

W. When government expenditures exceed government tax revenue the cost of living tends to rise

2. effect to cause

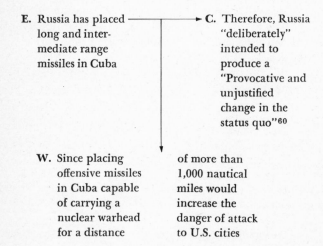

E. Russia has placed long and intermediate range missiles in Cuba

C. Therefore, Russia "deliberately" intended to produce a "Provocative and unjustified change in the status quo"[60]

W. Since placing offensive missiles in Cuba capable of carrying a nuclear warhead for a distance of more than 1,000 nautical miles would increase the danger of attack to U.S. cities

[59]From a transcription of a tape of Richard Nixon's "Veto Message." The entire speech is reprinted in the Appendix.

[60]From a transcription of a tape of John F. Kennedy's "Cuban Missile Address." The entire speech is reprinted in the Appendix.

3. sign

E. There exist in ――――――――→ **C.** Therefore, the
Cuba "large, "presence" of
long-range, and these missiles
clearly offensive constitutes an
weapons of "explicit threat
sudden mass to the peace and
destruction"[61] security of all
the Americas"

W. Since the build- tutes a threat to
up of offensive the security of
weapons by one other nations
nation consti-

4. generalization

E. "The people of
the U.S. individ-
ually could not
have developed
the Tennessee
Valley. Collec- ――――――――→ **C.** Therefore, in
tively, they could cases where
have"[62] individual action
"Seventeen mil- is ineffective,
lion Americans then national
who live over 65 governmental
on an average action will be
social security effective
check of about
$78 a month—
they're not able
to sustain them-
selves individ-
ually, but they
can sustain them-
selves through
the social security
system"

[61]*Ibid.*

[62]John F. Kennedy in nationally televised debate with Richard M. Nixon
on September 26, 1960. From a transcription of a tape of the broadcast.

↓

W. Since what is
true of a selected
sample is prob-
ably true of the
majority of
members in its
class

5. classification

E. The world com-   → **C.** Therefore, the
munity of nations   U.S. cannot
cannot "tolerate   "tolerate delib-
deliberate de-   erate deception
ception and   and offensive
offensive threats   threats" on the
on the part of   part of Cuba/
any nation,   Russia
large or small"[63]

W. Since what is   nations is prob-
true of the   ably true of
world com-   the U.S.
munity of

6. analogy

E. Appropriate pre-   → **C.** Therefore, ap-
cautions (quar-   propriate pre-
antine, vaccina-   cautions (under-
tions, etc.)   ground testing)
reduce the   would probably
hazards of infec-   reduce hazards
tious diseases   of nuclear weap-
                                        ons testing

[63]Kennedy, "Cuban Missile Address."

W. Since appropriate precautions against the hazards of infectious diseases are related to infectious diseases in the same way

that precautions against the hazards of nuclear weapons testing are related to nuclear weapons tests

7. parallel case

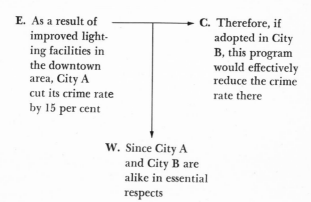

E. As a result of improved lighting facilities in the downtown area, City A cut its crime rate by 15 per cent

C. Therefore, if adopted in City B, this program would effectively reduce the crime rate there

W. Since City A and City B are alike in essential respects

Parallel case and analogy are closely related, but note that while argument from analogy involves a similarity of relationships (vaccination: infectious diseases:: underground testing: hazards of nuclear weapons testing), argument from parallel case is based on a similarity between two cases (City A to City B).

In each of the types of argument studied so far, the warrants can aptly be labeled *substantive* warrants. They assert relationships among various phenomena in the external world; that is, the phenomena reside outside the speaker and his listeners (e.g., amount of tax revenue, number of intermediate range missiles, the social security system, the lighting facilities in City A).

8. credibility warrant

Ethical proof often operates through the same kind of argumentative structure, but the warrant is of a different kind; it may be called a *credibility* warrant. Note first the evidence ⟶ warrant ⟶ claim structure operating:

E. Senator Henry Jackson says: ". . . I am not optimistic that the choice we are making today is going to lead to a quality environment and a better life for Americans. I am not sure that the commitments to expend effort and resources on environmental programs will be sustained, and I fear that the expenditure will be directed toward treating symptoms rather than the underlying causes"[64]

C. Therefore, the government may not have the necessary commitment to environmental programs that treat of causes rather than symptoms

W. Since Senator Jackson, who is Chairman of the Senate Committee on Interior and Insular Affairs, is a credible source of information about the national government's commitment to basic environmental programs, he is worthy of our belief

[64]"A View from Capitol Hill," address delivered at Princeton University on March 9, 1970. Mimeo, p. 4. Provided by Sen. Jackson's office.

One can see why the warrant here is called an authoritative or credibility warrant, because it makes an assumption about the credibility of the *source* of testimony which the speaker uses as evidence for his argument.

9. motivational warrant

In motivational proof, the warrant makes an assertion concerning the values, emotions, or motives which operate to shape the behavior of the audience. For example:

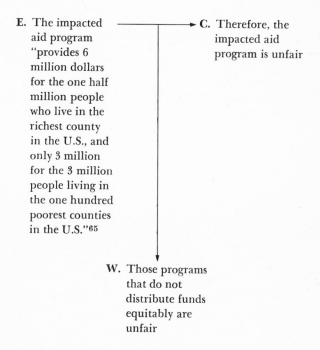

E. The impacted aid program "provides 6 million dollars for the one half million people who live in the richest county in the U.S., and only 3 million for the 3 million people living in the one hundred poorest counties in the U.S."[65]

C. Therefore, the impacted aid program is unfair

W. Those programs that do not distribute funds equitably are unfair

You have probably raised certain questions about some, if not all, of the preceding nine arguments, and may already be aware that, as they now stand, they seem incomplete. Thus, we need to add two additional parts to our anatomical sketch of an argument: reservation and qualifier. The finished outline looks like this:

[65]Nixon, "Veto Message."

EVIDENCE ⟶ (CLAIM QUALIFIER)

WARRANT ⟶ RESERVATION

Reservation, as the name suggests, sets forth whatever special circumstances or conditions under which the full force of the warrant on the claim may be reduced. Described as the speaker's "safety valve" or "escape hatch" clause, it allows the speaker to limit the scope of his claim.[66]

In planning his argument, a wise speaker might also consider this kind of silent rebuttal by some listener who raises the question: "But aren't there times when the warrant doesn't hold true?" The speaker may decide to attempt to eliminate possible refutations; for example:

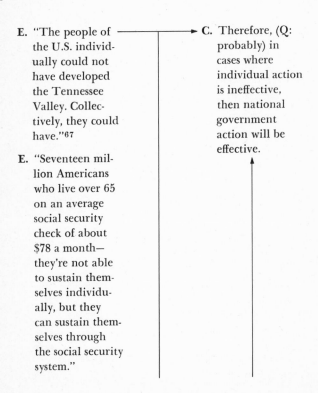

E. "The people of the U.S. individually could not have developed the Tennessee Valley. Collectively, they could have."[67]

E. "Seventeen million Americans who live over 65 on an average social security check of about $78 a month—they're not able to sustain themselves individually, but they can sustain themselves through the social security system."

C. Therefore, (Q: probably) in cases where individual action is ineffective, then national government action will be effective.

[66]Douglas Ehninger and Wayne Brockriede, *Decision by Debate* (New York: Dodd, Mead & Co., 1963), p. 106.
[67]Nixon-Kennedy Debate, September 26, 1960.

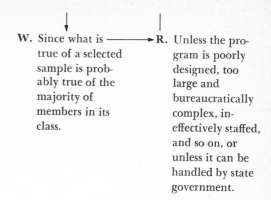

W. Since what is ⟶ **R.** Unless the program is poorly designed, too large and bureaucratically complex, ineffectively staffed, and so on, or unless it can be handled by state government.

W. Since what is true of a selected sample is probably true of the majority of members in its class.

Of course some claims may be proved without a reservation, or the speaker may not wish to state it explicitly. The point is that stopping at this point to think about possible refutation allows the speaker to check on the strength of his own claim.

Qualifiers are intimately related to reservations because they register the degree of force the speaker believes his claim holds. They are easy to recognize, for they usually consist of words such as *generally, probably,* or *almost certainly.* Note how the qualifier operates to limit the scope of the claim:

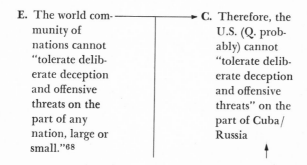

E. The world community of nations cannot "tolerate deliberate deception and offensive threats on the part of any nation, large or small."[68]

C. Therefore, the U.S. (Q. probably) cannot "tolerate deliberate deception and offensive threats" on the part of Cuba/ Russia

[68]Kennedy, "Cuban Missile Address."

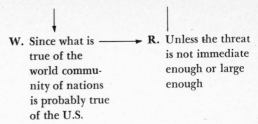

W. Since what is ——————→ **R.** Unless the threat
true of the   is not immediate
world commu-   enough or large
nity of nations   enough
is probably true
of the U.S.

It would be helpful at this point if you went back to reexamine the previous arguments with an eye to developing them fully.

CONFLICTING ARGUMENTS

The speaker will also need to consider whether to include, either by mentioning or by refuting, arguments that run counter to his position. The experimental literature has yielded somewhat conflicting results.[69]

To some extent, the decision appears to be related to the educational level of the audience. A one-sided approach seems to be more persuasive to audiences with lower educational levels; a two-sided approach appears to be somewhat more persuasive to audiences with higher educational levels. Such a two-sided approach apparently calls for *refutation* of opposing arguments rather then mere acknowledgement or mention of them.

However, the matter is not that simple, since the decision is also apparently related to whether the audience initially agrees or disagrees with the speaker. A two-sided message appears to be pref-

[69]D.L. Thistlethwaite and J. Kamenetzky, "Attitude Change Through Refutation and Elaboration of Audience Counterarguments," *Journal of Abnormal and Social Psychology*, Vol. 51, No. 1 (1955), 3–12; D.L. Thistlethwaite, J. Kamenetzky, and H. Schmidt, "Factors Influencing Attitude Change Through Refutative Communication," *Speech Monographs*, Vol. XXIII, No. 1 (1956), 14–25; A.A. Lumsdaine and I. Janis, "Resistance to 'Counterpropaganda' Produced by One-Sided and Two-Sided 'Propaganda' Presentations," *Public Opinion Quarterly*, Vol. XVII, No. 3 (1953), 311–18; C.J. Hovland *et al., The Order of Presentation in Persuasion* (New Haven: Yale University Press, 1961).

erable for audiences initially in disagreement with the speaker's arguments.

The decision on whether or not to deal with conflicting arguments also appears to be related to the degree of likelihood that an audience will be exposed to arguments counter to the speaker's position. Audiences that already know these arguments would either be hostile to the speaker's position or informed neutrals who know both sides of the topic; a two-sided approach would be best with them.

Even in the instance where the one-sided message appears preferable, that is, before an audience already in agreement with the speaker, there is a very important reservation. The speaker may want to "inoculate" his audience against possible later exposure to opposing positions by refuting them in advance. If the listener is not well informed about an issue, he might be caught off-guard by a new argument and, hence, especially vulnerable to it. As usual, the decision on whether or how to treat conflicting arguments is mainly influenced by what the speaker knows of his audience, and his understanding that his speech may be only one of many messages to which they will be exposed.

summary

Rhetorical invention concerns the content of a speech. It includes selection of subject, selection of purpose, and all the materials which the speaker uses to fulfill his purpose. He may say, "Listen to me because of who I am," "Listen to me because of what I know," "Listen to me because I share certain motives, certain values, and emotions with you." *Most often he will say all three because they are, in the final analysis, inseparable.* When a speaker says, "Listen to me because of who I am," he is saying, "Listen to me because of what I know." Any time one person speaks to another, he is in the act of trying to establish a common ground, saying, "Listen to me because I share basic motives and emotions with you."

All the speaker's materials, his proofs, are his way of establishing the fact that he has a right to speak on his topic; that is, that

he knows something about it and that what he says is worthy of
being accepted by those who hear him speak.

There are tests of evidence which both the speaker and the
audience can use to see whether or not his credentials are in fact
acceptable. If they are acceptable, then he can use them as the basis
for inference and argument, for moving beyond them to interpretation and speculation. The worth of the inference is limited by the
kind and the scope of evidence on which it is based. The worth of
both evidence and inferences determines the *acceptability* of the
speaker's proof.

rhetorical exercises

1. Give an eight to ten minute speech in which you support your
   thesis with a wide variety of kinds of substantive proof. Then
   give a speech on the same topic, including reference to source
   credibility and motivational appeals. What differences occurred
   during the planning of the two speeches? To which of the two
   speeches did the audience seem more receptive?

   In a discussion after the speech try to determine whether the
   audience could spot the motivational appeals. Did they label the
   kinds of proofs as you did in your planning?

2. Attend a speech or a debate on your campus. What kinds of supporting materials were offered? Were they acceptable as proof?
   Why or why not?

3. What effect is source credibility (ethical proof) likely to have on
   evidence? Can you point to specific examples to support your
   answers?

   List the speakers in class you consider as highly credible. What
   appear to be the main characteristics of the speakers listed?

4. Check through the weekly magazines and select advertisements
   that effectively utilize motivational appeal. To what motives do
   they appear to be appealing? Why do they appear to succeed in
   their appeal?

5. Check the *Quarterly Journal of Speech, Speech Monographs,* and
   other journals which your teacher can recommend for some other
   interesting experimental work with the materials of proof used
   in a speech.

6. Read one of the articles in the collateral reading list. Report on it to the class. Most of them will provoke discussion. Perhaps you would like to see if one of the experiments yields the same results in your class.

collateral readings

Bormann, E.G., "An Empirical Approach to Certain Concepts of Logical Proof," *Central States Speech Journal*, Vol. XII, No. 2 (1961), 85–91.

Cronkhite, Gary, "Logic, Emotion, and the Paradigm of Persuasion," *Quarterly Journal of Speech*, Vol. L, No. 1 (1964), 13–18.

Deiter, Otto, "Stasis," *Speech Monographs*, Vol. XVII, No. 4 (1950), 345–69.

Eagly, Alice, and Melvin Manis, "Evaluation of Message and Communicator as a Function of Involvement," *Journal of Personality and Social Psychology*, Vol. 3, No. 4 (1966), 483–85.

Ehninger, Douglas, and Wayne Brockriede, "The Unit of Proof and its Structure," in *Decision by Debate*. New York: Dodd, Mead & Co., 1963.

Haiman, Franklyn, "Democratic Ethics, and the Hidden Persuaders," *Quarterly Journal of Speech*, Vol. XLIV, No. 4 (1958), 385–92.

Lefford, A., "The Influence of Emotional Subject Matter on Logical Reasoning," *Journal of General Psychology*, Vol. 34, No. 2 (1946), 127–51.

McKeon, Richard, "Communication, Truth and Society," *Ethics*, Vol. LXVII, No. 2 (1957), 89–99.

Newman, Robert P., and Dale R. Newman, *Evidence*. Boston: Houghton Mifflin Company, 1969.

Pence, Orville L., "Emotionally Loaded Argument: Its Effectiveness in Stimulating Recall," *Quarterly Journal of Speech*, Vol. XL, No. 3 (October 1954), 272–76.

Rogge, Edward, "Evaluating the Ethics of a Speaker in a Democracy," *Quarterly Journal of Speech*, Vol. XLV, No. 4 (December 1959), 419–25.

Ruechelle, Randall, "An Experimental Study of Audience Recognition of Emotional and Intellectual Appeals in Persuasion, *Speech Monographs*, Vol. XXXV, No. 1 (March 1958), 49–58.

Toulmin, Stephen, *The Uses of Argument*. Cambridge: Cambridge University Press, 1959.

Utterback, William E., and Harold F. Harding, "Some Factors Conditioning Response to Argument," *Speech Monographs*, Vol. XXII, No. 5 November 1955), 303–8.

Wallace, Karl R., "An Ethical Basis of Communication, *Speech Teacher*, Vol. IV, No. 1 (January 1955), 1–9.

Wieman, Henry Nelson, and Otis M. Walter, "Toward an Analysis of Ethics for Rhetoric," *Quarterly Journal of Speech*, Vol. XLIII, No. 3 (October 1957), 266–70.

It is the capacity for organizing information into large and complex images which is the chief glory of our species.

Kenneth Boulding

5

ARRANGEMENT OF MATERIALS

Before beginning our discussion of how the speaker decides to arrange and proportion his materials, recall something basic about the nature of cognition. Man is naturally an organizing animal. He does not attempt to collect all the facts before he organizes them. As soon as he collects two or more facts, he begins to perceive them as organized into some kind of meaningful whole. So, in a sense, when the speaker began the selection of his topic and his proofs, he began the process of disposition. He may have eliminated some ideas, added others. The very attempt to arrange materials on any subject may suggest other materials, new lines of thinking. It is the process of arrangement that gives the speaker a complete view of the subject.

The closeness between the invention process and the arrangement process cannot be overemphasized. The process of invention has proceeded from a result of thinking according to some kind of method, either good or bad. Often, just in seeking the best method, pertinent and useful materials are suggested to the speaker. Skill in disposition lies in the capacity to see facts and ideas not as isolated and random, but in combination with other facts and ideas.

speech organization

A speech, whether informative or persuasive, is generally divided into three parts: Introduction, Discussion, and Conclusion. Each of these has a distinct function. The advice sometimes given to young men going into the clergy is useful to recall: "Tell the audience what you're going to say. Say it. Then, remind them of what you've said." Time and considerable skill are needed to construct a clear but interesting speech which has maximum chance of fulfilling its intended purpose. All parts of the speech are governed by what the speaker knows about the specific occasion and audience.

Arrangement of materials for a speech is more complex than simple determination of what materials will go in the introduction, discussion, and conclusion. It also consists of arrangement of main points, sequencing supporting materials under each main point, and proportioning the material for proper emphasis. We shall discuss each of these aspects of arrangement.

INTRODUCTION

The introduction serves to: (1) gain attention; (2) give materials which the audience may need to start thinking about and become oriented to the subject; (3) present a clear statement of purpose which permits the audience to see what the speaker hopes to accomplish; (4) provide a thesis which suggests the main point of the speech; (5) indicate the approach to the subject through a partition or division of the materials.

Although each speaker must learn to adapt this method for opening a speech to his own particular situation, the reasons for, and basic order of, all introductions remain very much the same. We shall discuss the reasons for this by explaining in some detail how each portion of an introduction functions.

attention-getter. Persuasion begins by gaining attention. The speaker cannot influence any audience unless he has first captured their attention. He can attempt to get attention by means of a striking fact of which most people are not aware, by means of a question, and by a variety of other strategies. The nature of the topic, the speaker's ingenuity, plus recognition of the importance of an attention-getter should provide such a device for a speaker.

A good attention-getter must be stimulating enough to make an audience focus its attention on the speech and not on some other aspect of its environment. It must somehow provide a contrast with what members of an audience have been thinking about before the speech. A good attention-getter attempts to involve the audience, letting them participate directly in the speech. The audience ought to be able to say about the attention-getter: "I never thought of that before!" or "That's happened to me, too," or "How interesting that is (to me)!" How much time the speaker spends in considering the problem of getting attention and how much freshness and vitality he brings to his subject determines how much attention he will get. Although an initial attention-getting device is necessary, the speaker should work throughout the speech to get and maintain attention.

orientation. Next, the speaker should recall the implication of the temporal nature of the speaking act. Time must be given for the intellect to deal vigorously with what is being said. At the beginning of his speech, the speaker must provide his audience with:

1. A clear statement of purpose.
2. A direct assertion, a thesis, a subject sentence which in effect summarizes the whole speech in one sentence.
3. A clear suggestion of the structural progression to be followed in the speech development.

Let us take an example. Suppose the speaker has chosen as his topic, "An Introduction to Alaska." His thinking might proceed along these lines:

Attention-getter and orientation to topic: If you had lived at the beginning of the eighteenth century, one of the questions which might have kept you guessing was: "Are America and Asia one continent or two?" To answer the question, Tsar Peter the Great sent Danish-born Vitus Bering east to Kamchatka in Siberia with orders to explore the waters off its coast. At that time, the North Pacific lay shrouded in mystery. In 1728 Bering sailed through the fog-bound strait that was to bear his name and proved that Asia and America were separate. Russia's claim to Alaska rested in Bering's discoveries. In the 1860s, Tsarist Russia, considering Alaska a financial and strategic liability, offered it to the United States. Secretary of State William H. Seward snapped at the $7,200,000 bargain, but the Senate ratified the purchase with reluctance, and wits called the deal "Seward's Folly" and the new possession his "ice box."

Statement of purpose: Today, I'd like to tell you why Seward's "ice box" is one of the best buys the United States has ever made. Subject Sentence: Alaska, with her tremendous natural resources and her strategic location, has a very great value as a state for the U.S.

specific statement of purpose. We have already considered the formulation of purpose under the heading of invention. After the speaker has selected one of the three general reasons for speaking (informing, entertaining, persuading), he needs to think more about a specific statement of purpose in relationship to the specific aim of his speech. Suppose you had chosen the general topic "Alaska" for a speech. Do you want to describe the discovery and exploration of Alaska? Do you want to discuss its economic potential? Do you want to describe its geography and climate? Do you want to recount tales of a trip to Alaska? Your answer to this kind of question will become an explicit statement of purpose—your audience will know exactly what aspect of Alaska you are going to talk about and will have its first specific clue about the direction of your speech. Then they will know what sort of information, ideas, and judgments to expect. It is not always necessary that a speaker state his purpose explicitly, especially when speaking to an unfriendly audience. He must, of course, state his purpose in his own analysis.

the thesis sentence. The audience's expectation should be fulfilled as soon as possible, or evidence offered that its expectations will be fulfilled. That is the function of the thesis, or subject, sentence. The purpose sentence tells the audience what you're going to do; the subject sentence does it. It is in effect a one sentence summary, the one statement in your speech which all others support, either directly or indirectly.

The subject sentence is the assertion of an idea or an opinion.

Consider the basic nature of an assertion. When someone coughs, you may suppose that he has a cold. You may feel sorry for him and may even say, "It's too bad you're catching a cold." But you would not say, "That's true." His cough shows that he has a cold; it does not say it. If he had said, "I am catching a cold," you could agree or disagree with him—but not with his cough. This cough is, in a way, similar to three types of sentences: interrogative, imperative, and exclamatory. You cannot judge any of them true or false.

A declarative sentence, on the other hand, is either true or false: "The temperature today is 45 degrees." "If I study harder, I may be able to improve my grades." "Deficit spending is a wise policy." These sentences make assertions. If the assertions are debatable, as "The Federal Government should guarantee an opportunity for higher education to all qualified high school graduates," then they are termed opinions. If the statements can be tested by direct observation, they are said to be facts; for example, "There are more students in this year's freshman class than in last year's class." Beardsley defines assertion in this way:

> When someone . . . utters or writes a statement in such a way (that is, with such a tone of voice, or in such circumstances) that he appears to believe what he is saying, and appears to invite others to believe it as well, we shall say that he is *asserting* the statement, or making an assertion.[1]

The subject or thesis sentence is the statement of your case—the point you intend to prove, the opinion you hope will be accepted, the particular policy you are asking your audience to adopt. All other statements in the speech are directed essentially at proving the thesis. They will show why your opinion is right or valuable or wise, and why the policy you are proposing is practicable or advantageous.

partition. After the thesis sentence, the audience may want to know exactly how the speaker is going to handle his subject. Often this is a preview of the main heads. One student, in a speech about contemporary French philosopher Gabriel Marcel, used this partition:

[1]Monroe C. Beardsley, *Thinking Straight: Principles for Readers and Writers* (2nd ed.; Englewood Cliffs, N.J.: Prentice-Hall, Inc., 1956), p. 10. This discussion follows Professor Beardsley's, pp. 8–12.

First, I want to tell you *who* Gabriel Marcel is. Then, I want to tell you *what* he has to say. And lastly, I want to tell you *why* I think everyone in this class should become familiar with his writings.

Often the partition is implicit in the statement of the thesis sentence itself. Consider this example: "In learning to play tennis, the beginner should concentrate on developing three basic strokes: the forehand, the backhand, and the serve." Whether the partition (or division) of the subject is included in the thesis sentence or stated separately, it provides the audience with insight into what to expect.

THE DISCUSSION: OUTLINING FOR A MOTIVATIONAL SITUATION

In Chapter 3 we discussed the notion of lines of argument as they are derived from six motivational situations: the information situation, the difficulty situation, the goal-oriented situation, the barrier situation, the threat situation, and the identification situation. The outline forms for speeches are determined primarily by the motivational situation. Each of the motivational situations suggests a series of questions you must ask in an attempt to discover what sorts of materials to offer to have your thesis accepted. Those questions necessary for the acceptance of your speech are called issues.

Let us suggest an approach to each of the situations in which you might be giving a speech. In each case we shall present a general outline and then a specific example.

the information situation. The need for information exists:

A. The first major portion of information is . . .

B. The second major portion of information is . . .

C. The third major portion of information is . . .

Thesis sentence: To become a good debater you must possess five basic skills.

    I. You must be able to analyze the topic for debate, searching out the essential areas of controversy.

   II. You must be able to support your position with adequate, well-documented materials.

  III. You must be able to organize materials clearly and efficiently.

  IV. You must be able to demonstrate skill in refuting what your opponents say.

   V. You must be able to present your materials fluently and with ease.

the difficulty situation. A problem exists:

A. The nature of the problem is . . .
B. The scope and magnitude of the problem is . . .
C. The cause(s) of the problem is (are) . . .

Thesis sentence: A very serious problem exists in higher education today.

   I. About half of the top 24 percent of high school graduates do not enter college.

  II. The problem is serious both to the students themselves and to the nation as a whole.

 III. The reasons for failing to enter college vary, but the primary one seems to be that prospective students cannot obtain the necessary finances.

the goal-oriented situation. This solution should be accepted:

A. Other solutions have been tried and have failed.
B. This solution does meet the problem.
C. It is practicable.
D. There are other advantages.

Thesis sentence: The Federal Government should guarantee an opportunity for higher education to all qualified high school graduates by means of a federally underwritten loan system.

   I. The solutions which have been tried in the past have not succeeded in diminishing the percentage of above average students who cannot attend college because of lack of finances.

  II. Under the proposed plan students could borrow at low rates of interest and thereby finance their college education.

III. A federally underwritten loan program could be carried out by already existing governmental departments at no extra cost to the Federal Government.

IV. There are two major advantages to such a program.

the barrier situation. Although such a solution may be difficult to achieve, it is necessary:

A. Its outcomes are worth achieving.
B. The objections to such a plan are not serious.
C. The objections can be met.

Thesis sentence: Although there may be objections to a federal loan system, it is vitally necessary.

I. The outcome would be beneficial to the well-being of both the individual and the nation.
II. The objections to such a plan are based on misconceptions.
III. The objections can be met and fear of federal control allayed.

the threat situation. A threat exists:

A. It is serious.
B. It is inherent in the present structure.
C. It is immediate.

Thesis sentence: The potential loss of this talent represents a serious threat of loss in terms of new ideas and economic gain.

I. The talent loss represents a potential of $177,000 in earnings to the persons who cannot attend college; it represents untold loss in human creativity.
II. This talent loss is due in large part to our current conception of the proper methods of providing means for needy students to go to college.
III. The nation cannot afford such a loss at a time when it is competing very directly with communist countries.

the identification situation. Group A should help Group B:

    A. They are related.

    B. Group B should be helped.

    C. Only Group A can do it.

Thesis sentence: The Federal Government should provide financial aid to students who cannot otherwise afford to go to college.

    I. The quality and quantity of national output depends on education.

    II. Higher education is a worthwhile cause to support as it allows the individual to fulfill his potential for growth.

    III. Since other resources have failed, the Federal Government must try.

By this time you have probably devised other lines of argument and ways to develop them. What are they? How did you arrive at them?

THE DISCUSSION:
OTHER TYPES OF OUTLINES

In addition to ordering material according to the motivational situation, it is also possible to outline according to the kinds of relationships that the speaker is trying to draw between ideas. Is it essentially a time relationship? A spatial relationship? A topical relationship? A cause-effect relationship? A problem-solution relationship? Let us explore a few examples.

time pattern. *Thesis sentence*: The history of trade unions in the United States is long and interesting.

    I. The National Labor Union was formed in 1836.

    II. The Knights of Labor was formed in 1869.

    III. The American Federation of Labor was formed in 1886.

    IV. The Congress of Industrial Organizations was formed in 1935.

    V. The A.F. of L. and C.I.O. memberships merged in 1955.

space pattern. *Thesis sentence*: The plan of our campus is like a wheel.

I. The administrative offices are at the center of the campus.

II. The classroom buildings are circled around the administrative offices.

III. The dormitories are circled around the classroom buildings.

topic pattern. *Thesis sentence*: Berdyaev, in his attempt to explore Dostoevsky's "world-vision," points to the main themes of his novels.

I. Dostoevsky's first concern is the nature of spirit.

II. Dostoevsky's second concern is the nature of man.

III. Dostoevsky's third concern is the nature of freedom.

IV. Dostoevsky's fourth concern is the nature of evil.

V. Dostoevsky's fifth concern is the nature of love.

causal pattern. *Thesis sentence*: A problem exists in the financing of higher education.

I. The problem originated from lack of interest in coordinated effort.

II. The lack of interest resulted in lack of funds.

III. The lack of funds is also partially due to past ways of deciding who should pay for higher education.

problem-solution pattern. *Thesis sentence*: A problem exists in the financing of higher education.

I. We must first realize the seriousness of the problem.

II. Then we must consider possible solutions.

III. From the possible solutions we must select the best one.

Whatever type of pattern the speaker selects, there is one point which should be remembered about each main heading within the pattern: It should directly support the subject sentence. A good test of directness of support is to see if the main heads can be joined to the subject sentence by such connectives as *for, because, in that.* Example subject sentence: John Smith is a better instructor than Bill Brown (for)

I. He has greater enthusiasm and interest in his subject.

II. He reflects greater understanding of student needs.

There is little evidence to support the position that any one of these patterns of organization is more effective than any other.[2] The main considerations seem to be: (1) that the materials be presented in an orderly manner for the audience, and (2) that they be suitable for the motivational situation that has prompted the speech.

Sample Outline One

Here is an example of an outline by a student facing a difficulty situation.[3] He proceeds primarily by the use of examples to point out some problems he sees in the policies of labor unions which would call for firm federal legislation.

THESIS STATEMENT: I think that *there is a need for the federal government to increase substantially its regulation of labor unions.*

I. A study of the activities and policies of labor unions reveals serious problems in both their internal and external activities. (because)

A. There are serious internal problems.   (because)
1. There are problems in admission policies.   (because)
a.
b.
c.
2. There are problems arising from compulsory membership. (because)
a.
b.

[2] Erwin P. Bettinghaus, *Persuasive Communication* (New York: Holt, Rinehart and Winston, Inc., 1968), p. 151.

[3] The material in these two sample outlines has been adapted from a brief prepared by student and faculty participants in the eighth annual Illinois Summer Debate Workshop held at the University of Illinois, Urbana. A fuller treatment of this same brief appears in Douglas Ehninger and Wayne Brockriede, *Decision by Debate* (New York: Dodd, Mead & Co., 1963).

3. Problems exist concerning the voting rights of union members. (because)
   a.
   b.
4. Problems are created by denial or evasion of union members' rights to protest. (because)
   a.
   b.
   c.
5. There is evidence of criminal activity in the administration of union funds. (because)
   a.
   b.
6. There are problems in the trusteeship system. (because)
   a.
   b.

B. There are serious problems arising from the external activities of unions. (because)
   1. Collective bargaining procedures and policies constitute a serious threat to effective unions. (because)
      a.
      b.
      c.
   2. Procedures for handling grievances of employees create serious problems. (because)
      a.
      b.
   3. The mishandling of welfare and pension funds is a serious problem. (because)
      a.
      b.
   4. Serious problems are present in union political activities. (because)
      a.
      b.

II. Problems in the internal and external affairs of labor unions are national in scope. (because)

   A. Union activities are widespread in geographical scope.

   B. Union activities affect a major portion of the economy. (because)
      1.
      2.

III. Problems of unions' internal and external affairs are inherent in the present extent of federal regulation.   (because)

   A. The problems will remain even if unions undertake self-regulation.   (because)
      1.
      2.

   B. State regulation cannot solve the problem.   (because)
      1.
      2.

   C. The problem will remain even if the federal government "slightly" increases its regulation of labor unions.   (because)
      1.
      2.

SAMPLE OUTLINE TWO

Here is an outline by a student facing a goal-oriented situation. Rather than refute directly the previous speaker, he has decided to talk about the disadvantages of increased federal legislation over labor unions.

THESIS STATEMENT: I believe that *a substantial increase in federal regulation of labor unions cannot be instituted without incurring four serious disadvantages.*

I. Such a policy would have the disadvantageous effect of weakening the powers of states to regulate unions.   (because)

   A. The states' power to regulate unions *would* be weakened. (because)
      1. Federal legislation may tend to discourage some states from acting because of an overreliance upon the federal government.
      2. The Supreme Court has made it clear that it will not permit state deviation from federal policy.   (because)
         a. An example occurred in the case of Bethlehem Steel Co. vs. New York Labor Board.
         b. An example occurred in the case of La Crosse Telephone Corporation vs. Wisconsin Labor Board.

B. If the states' power to regulate labor unions is weakened, this would constitute a serious disadvantage. (because)
  1. Multiform state legislation tests various proposals and provides experiments to guide in evolving solutions.
  2. A mistaken remedy at the federal level could have drastic repercussions on the entire labor movement.

II. Such a policy would have the disadvantageous effect of weakening the power of labor unions. (because)

  A. Such a policy would have the disadvantageous effect of threatening the stability and strength of union membership. (because)
    1. Such legislation may well hamper the organizing and operating of unions.
    2. If the strength and stability of union membership is threatened, this would constitute a serious disadvantage. (because)
      a.
      b.
      c.

  B. Such a policy would have the disadvantageous effect of weakening the power of labor unions in effective collective bargaining. (because)
    1. If such a policy is adopted, the power of labor unions to bargain collectively effectively *would* be weakened. (because)
      a. Authoritative testimony says it will.
        (1)
        (2)
      b. Centralized collective bargaining calls for authority by the national officers to enforce their commitments in labor-management negotiations without hindrance by governmental interference.
    2. If the power of labor unions to bargain collectively effectively is weakened, this would constitute a serious disadvantage. (because)
      a. Unless a union is strong it has little bargaining power and without strong bargaining power unions could not have made all of the favorable advances they have in the past.
      b. Labor unions must have substantial economic, political, and social power if they are to assume the social responsibilities that modern society has placed upon them.

C. Such a policy would have the disadvantageous effect of preventing the maintenance of stable industrial relations. (because)

   1. If such a policy is adopted, the maintenance of stable industrial relations *is* prevented. (because)

      a. Authoritative testimony says it is.

         (1)

         (2)

      b. Without a strong union shop agreement, many businesses would not enjoy the stable labor relations which have been conducive to their prosperity in the past.

   2. If the maintenance of stable industrial relations is prevented, this would constitute a serious disadvantage. (because)

      a.

      b.

      c.

III. Such a policy would have the disadvantageous effect of creating economic dislocation and competition among the various states. (because)

  A. If such a policy is adopted, economic dislocation and competition among the various states *is* created. (because)

    1. An example occurred in Kansas.

    2. An example occurred in Indiana.

  B. If economic dislocation and competition is created among the various states, this would constitute a serious disadvantage. (because)

    1.

    2.

    3.

IV. Such a policy would have the disadvantageous effect of giving the federal government excessive power in labor-management relations. (because)

  A. Authoritative testimony says so.

    1.

    2.

  B. There is no compelling national need at this time which overrides the basic value of federalism and justifies preferring national legislation over state legislation. (because)

    1.

    2.

    3.

TRANSITIONS

The audience must see how the speaker moves from one idea to another, that is, what relationships exist between the ideas. Transitions fulfill this function, serving to make evident the pattern of ideas. How they are phrased depends on what kind of outline pattern the speaker is using. You may want to use one of the following methods: (1) the flashback-preview device: for example, "not only" (what you have said previously), "but also" (what you are going to say); (2) conjunctive adverbs: "also," "in addition," "however"; (3) signposts: "first," "second," "third," "finally."

CONCLUSIONS

An effective conclusion generally consists of two parts: (a) a summary, and (b) a direct indication of how the speech may be used; that is, how it is the basis for further discussion. Because of the temporal nature of a speech, a summary is necessary to recount its main points and to remind the audience about the basic relationship which the speaker has drawn between his main ideas. The key here is repetition with variation. If the repetition of the main ideas is so unvaried as to be boring, the summary may do more harm than good.

The speaker should state his conclusions specifically and positively. It is most often ineffective to "let the facts speak for themselves." They may or may not. Or they may say one thing to the speaker and another to his audience. Thus, the speaker should interpret his facts for the audience and explain why his is a reasonable and valuable interpretation. A good speech should have more "life" to it than the three or fifteen minutes it takes the speaker to deliver it. Specific implications for its use after the audience has left the room should be indicated. One especially useful fact concerning the statement of the final appeal is that the positive statement is more likely to be heeded than the negatively worded conclusion; "Please be on time" is more likely to meet with success than "Don't be late."

The degree of emotional appeal in the conclusion must also be carefully considered. This is determined primarily by the nature of your topic, and of course by the particular audience. The most interesting research in the area of emotional appeal has concerned threat appeal. Generally speaking, if a strong appeal is made, the threat itself is remembered; if the appeal is weak, the source and explanation of the threat are remembered.[4] Thus, the strength of the appeal is determined by the specific response the speaker hopes to elicit from his audience.

sequencing materials

Yet another kind of order has to do with the sequencing of materials according to strength. There are three basic methods of sequencing materials:

1. Climax order—from the weakest to the strongest.
2. Anticlimax order—from the strongest to the weakest.
3. Pyramidal order—weak-strong-weak-strong.

Experimental studies of attitude change have resulted in apparently contradictory conclusions about which method is best. Some indicate that climax order was found to be superior, some favor anticlimax, and some, pyramidal order.[5] Most can find no great difference, but

[4]See, for example, "Fear-Arousing Appeals," in Howard Martin and Kenneth E. Andersen, *Speech Communication Analysis and Readings* (Boston: Allyn & Bacon, Inc., 1968), pp. 214–23; Gerald R. Miller and Murray A. Hewgill, "Some Recent Research on Fear-Arousing Message Appeals," *Speech Monographs* (November 1966), 377–91; Alan S. DeWolfe and Catherine N. Governale, "Fear and Attitude Change," *Journal of Abnormal and Social Psychology*, Vol. 69, No. 1 (1964), 119–23; Fredric A. Powell, "The Effects of Anxiety-Arousing Messages when Related to Personal, Familiar, and Impersonal Referents," *Speech Monographs*, Vol. XXXII, No. 2 (1965), 102–6.

[5]F.H. Lund, "The Psychology of Belief: IV. The Law of Primacy in Persuasion," *Journal of Abnormal and Social Psychology* (1925), 183–91; F.H. Knower, "Experimental Studies of Changes in Attitude: A Study of the Effect of Printed Argument on Change in Attitude," *Journal of Abnormal and Social Psychology*, Vol. XXX, No. 4 (1936), 522–32; C.I. Hovland *et al.*, *The Order of Presentation in Persuasion* (New Haven: Yale University Press, 1961); H. Gulley and D.K. Berlo, "Effects of Intercellular and Intracellular Speech Structure on Attitude Change and Learning," *Speech Monographs*, Vol. XXIII, No. 4 (1956), 288–97. See also Sponberg and Gilkinson articles in "Collateral Readings."

there is a slight tendency to favor the climax order. Bettinghaus, after surveying the experimental literature on this point, concludes: "Clearly, placing an argument or an important piece of material in the middle of a message does not seem to be as effective as placing it in either the first or last position. In choosing between first and last, however, the evidence seems to show some slight preference for a placement in final position."[6]

In most cases, few differences in learning were observed. If the audience is interested in the subject and favorable to it, climax order is probably best. If the audience is not interested or is unfavorable, anticlimax order is probably best. The pattern that best fits the topic and audience should be used. However, a speaker should try different patterns to see which one seems most effective. He must mold the organization of his materials to achieve the desired response and make sure that the pattern is clear enough (without being obtrusive) for the audience to grasp easily and follow the direction of the speech.

proportion

After the speaker has determined the direction and arrangement of his materials, he must proportion his material. Here the speaker chooses the amount of time he will devote to each point. There are several questions he might raise: (1) What ideas are most important and therefore need to be emphasized? (2) What ideas are most complicated and therefore need to be explained in more detail? (3) Which ideas are most readily accepted by the audience and therefore will need less time?

direct suggestion

If the speech is predominantly an attitude-modifying communication, the speaker must decide where his suggestion for change

---

[6]Bettinghaus, *Persuasive Communication*, p. 153.

should occur. If he introduces the suggestion too early, many in the audience may not yet be convinced and he will lose a portion of their attention. If he has not prepared the way for the suggestion rather carefully, his chances of success will be diminished considerably. To decide on the best place, the speaker must recall what he knows about audiences in general and his audience in particular. He must also know something about the nature of suggestion as it effects attitude change. Schramm suggests the following basic facts about suggestion and attitude change:[7]

1. *"To accomplish attitude change, a suggestion for change must first be received and accepted."* This fact gives the speaker the first clue about where to place his most direct suggestion for change. It is generally accepted that people will try to avoid any communication which is unsympathetic to their existing attitudes. They tend to forget an unsympathetic communication or attempt to recast it to fit the existing frame of reference. So if the suggestion comes too soon, it will likely meet one of these fates. Where the direct suggestion occurs within a speech depends basically on the attitudes of the audience toward the direction of the change and how strongly the audience feels about the objects, ideas, or emotions involved in the change.

2. *"The suggestion will be more likely to be accepted if it meets existing personality needs and drives."* Generally this is self-explanatory. It should be noted, however, that some people are more suggestible than others, and that some attitudes are more easily changed than others. The speaker should allow the members of the audience time to clarify their own thinking so that they are fully aware of their attitudes on the topic. He should also point out that a shift in attitude will be to their favor, that it will fulfill their needs. The degree of change involved and the force of existing attitudes help determine where the suggestion for change should occur.

3. *"The suggestion will be more likely to be accepted if it is in harmony with valued group norms and loyalties."* Almost every study on the subject stresses the importance of group relationships to individual attitude change. Members of a group will more quickly reject standards opposed to group norms than those opposed

[7]Wilbur Schramm, ed., *The Process and Effects of Mass Communication* (Urbana: University of Illinois Press, 1954), pp. 210–12.

to their individual norms. The speaker must consider which set of norms he is attacking and determine which needs more time to prepare the way for his suggestion for change.

4. *"The suggestion is more likely to be accepted if the source is perceived as trustworthy or expert."* We have already discussed the influence of ethical proof on evidence. Here the question the speaker must ask is, "How long will it take me to establish my 'trustworthiness,' my 'expertness,' concerning my topic?" "When group norms are in conflict with expert opinion, they may win out, unless the matter is very technical or the expert unusually prestigeful or the matter relatively unrelated to the group norms." The speaker should consider this feature of attitude change in determining where direct suggestion should occur.

summary

To separate the act of arrangement from the act of invention is misleading. As the speaker selects his material, as he eliminates some materials, he is shaping his materials. As he explains one point, expands it, reconstructs it, he is proportioning material. When he explores the associations which exist between his ideas, he is beginning to determine the way in which they can be ordered for his audience. In short, he is already performing the first stages of arrangement.

As the materials and proofs are selected, they may suggest in themselves the order and proportion to fit a particular audience. The speaker's most important task is to make sure that he molds the organization of his speech; otherwise the audience may mold its own and it may or may not coincide with the speaker's way of handling his topic. Worse yet, the audience may perceive no direction at all. For complete understanding, the audience must be able to apprehend the speaker's method of thinking, his method of searching for the most pertinent and useful thoughts about his subject.

The importance of arrangement to the success of a speech can best be emphasized by relating a story of two of the greatest political antagonists of all times, Demosthenes and Aeschines, as they debated

whether or not Demosthenes should receive an award from the
Athenian Assembly. Aeschines, in his speech opposing the award,
urged the judges to require Demosthenes to follow the same order
in the reply to the charges which Aeschines had leveled against him.
Demosthenes turned the tables very neatly with the following approach. He asked the judges to give him an impartial hearing and
to demonstrate their openmindedness by permitting him to use
whatever arrangement of arguments he thought best for his defense.
Demosthenes then chose a very different arrangement from that of
Aeschines, because he knew as well as his antagonist that the arrangement of materials which is appropriate for fulfilling one speaker's purpose may not be appropriate for another's purpose. This
story also illustrates one very basic point for the beginning speaker
to keep in mind. Arrangement, when efficiently performed, becomes
as much a means of persuasion as the speaker's proofs.

rhetorical exercises

1. Deliver a ten to fifteen minute speech from a complete sentence
   outline. In this speech analyze the cause(s) of some international
   or national problem.
2. Below is a rhetorical jigsaw puzzle*—a dissected speech. Can you
   reassemble and label the parts of this speech?
   Directions: Each paragraph below is a separate unit of a speech.
   When put together in the right order, the units make up a complete speech. Put the parts together to make the best possible
   speech.

   Finally, think of the ordinary door-to-door salesman.

   Have you ever noticed how easy it is to do something else when
   the TV announcer is droning out his commercial? But what happens when he stills that golden tongue? You know that the set is
   on, but you don't hear the announcer's voice extolling the virtues

*From Theodore Clevenger, Jr., "A Rhetorical Jigsaw Puzzle: A Device
for Teaching Certain Aspects of Speech Composition," *The Speech
Teacher*, Vol. XII, No. 2 (March 1963), 141. Reprinted by permission of
The Speech Communication Association and the author.

of "lavish Camay Soap." So what do you do? You look at the TV screen, of course, to see what is going on.

Well, one way is by a brief interval of silence before and after the name of the product or sponsor.

The next time someone says to you, "Silence is golden," just smile and think to yourself, "Brother, you don't know how right you are."

Secondly, let us consider television.

Are you aware of the methods radio announcers use to call attention to their sponsor or product?

Such a salesman is one who has learned that silence is golden.

So you see, people in the field of selling are indeed aware that silence is golden, for they know it can mean dollars and cents in radio, in TV, and even in door-to-door selling.

As you see, the announcer puts a parenthesis of silence around the name of the product in order to catch your attention.

Silence is golden. That's an old cliché which you have heard many times, especially when your parents wanted to impress upon you another cliché—namely, that children should be seen and not heard.

First of all, take radio selling.

Thus you can see that the TV salesman has also discovered that silence can be golden.

The announcer doesn't say: Women-all-over-the-world-are-learning-that-delicious-Wrigley-spearmint-gum-is-a-grand-wholesome-family-treat. Instead he says: Women-all over the world-are learning that delicious-Wrigley's Spearmint gum-is a grand-wholesome-family treat.

I contend, however, that silence really IS golden.

If he's really good, he knows better than to just reel off his pitch —he knows how to listen to you.

And I would like to present three instances in the field of selling to prove my contention.

If you doubt the effectiveness of silence in TV, you just try not looking at the picture and notice how irresistibly your eyes will be pulled to the screen by a few moments of silence.

He is willing, if necessary, to listen to all of your troubles. If you want to raise a question, he will be quiet while you do. He will ask you a question, then be silent while you answer.

Construct similar jigsaw puzzles for use in class.

3. Listen carefully to the other speeches in class. Try to outline them. Can you perceive easily the speaker's purpose? Is the subject sentence a direct assertion? Is there a clear suggestion of structural progression to be followed in the speech development? Are the main ideas and subdivisions cast in a definite pattern and made clear through the use of transitions? Were the main ideas summarized and used as the basis for a future line of discussion?

4. Select a topic and outline it according to different patterns. Which one do you think is best? Why?

5. Outline the following speeches. First inquire into the speech situation for which each was designed. Then evaluate the appropriateness of each organizational pattern:

a. Abraham Lincoln's "Address at Cooper Union"

b. Thomas Jefferson's "First Inaugural Address"

c. John F. Kennedy's "Address before the Greater Houston Ministerial Association"

d. Any of Richard Nixon's televised speeches on the Southeast Asia Conflict.

collateral readings

Cathcart, Robert S., "An Experimental Study of the Relative Effectiveness of Four Methods of Presenting Evidence," *Speech Monographs*, Vol. XXII, No. 3 (1955), 227–33.

Ellingsworth, Huber W., and Theodore Clevenger, Jr., *Speech and Social Action: A Strategy of Oral Communication* (Englewood Cliffs, N.J.: Prentice-Hall, Inc., 1967). See especially Chapter 4, "The Macrostructure of Spoken Messages."

Frandsen, Kenneth D., "Effect of Threat Appeals and Media of Transmission," *Speech Monographs*, Vol. XXX, No. 2 (1963), 101–4.

Gilkinson, Howard, Stanley F. Paulson, and Donald E. Sikkink, "Effects of Order and Authority in an Argumentative Speech," *Quarterly Journal of Speech*, Vol. XL, No. 2 (1954), 183–92.

Goldstein, M. J., "The Relationship Between Coping and Avoiding Behavior and Response to Fear-Arousing Propaganda," *Journal of Abnormal and Social Psychology*, Vol. 58, No. 2 (1959), 247–52.

Hovland, Carl I., Irving L. Janis, and Harold H. Kelley, *Communication and Persuasion* (New Haven: Yale University Press, 1953). See especially Chapter 4, "Organization of Persuasive Arguments."

Insko, Chester, "Primacy Versus Recency in Persuasion as a Function of the Timing of Arguments and Measures," *Journal of Abnormal and Social Psychology*, Vol. 69, No. 4 (1964), 381–91.

Janis, I.L., and H. C. Milholland, "The Influence of Threat Appeals on Selective Learning of the Content of a Persuasive Communication," *Journal of Psychology* (1954), 75–81.

Krech, David, and Richard S. Crutchfield, "Perceiving the World," in *The Process and Effects of Mass Communication*, ed. Wilbur Schramm (Urbana: University of Illinois Press, 1954), pp. 116–37.

Mills, Glen E., *Message Preparation: Analysis and Structure* (Indianapolis: The Bobbs-Merrill Co., Inc., 1966). See particularly Chapter 5, "Outlining and Patterns of Arrangement," and Chapter 6, "Introductions, Conclusions, and Transitions."

Sharp, Harry, Jr., and Thomas McClung, "Effects of Organization on the Speaker's Ethos," *Speech Monographs*, Vol. XXXIII, No. 4 (1966), 182–83.

Smith, Raymond G., "An Experimental Study of the Effects of Speech Organization Upon the Attitudes of College Students," *Speech Monographs*, Vol. XVIII, No. 4 (1951), 292–301.

Sponberg, Harold, "The Relative Effectiveness of Climax and Anti-Climax Order in an Argumentative Speech," *Speech Monographs*, Vol. XIII, No. 1 (1946), 35–44.

Wilson, Warner, and Howard Miller, "Repetition, Order of Presentation, and Timing of Arguments and Measures as Determinants of Opinion Change," *Journal of Personality and Social Psychology*, Vol. 9, No. 2 (1968), 184–88.

The very many decisions that add up to a style
are decisions about what to say, as well as
how to say it. They reflect the [speaker's] organization
of experience, his sense of life, so that the most
general of his attitudes and ideas find
expression just as characteristically in his
style as in his matter . . .

Richard Ohmann

6

STYLE: SOME
THEORETICAL
CONSIDERATIONS

When Bergen and Cornelia Evans prepared their *Dictionary of Contemporary American Usage*, they stated that most people say, "None of them are coming," rather than saying, "None of them is coming." The *Chicago Tribune* saw fit to honor the Evanses with no fewer than ten attacks concerning this usage. Even though the Evanses had not said either one was right, the *Tribune* remained incensed with this license taken with "the language." Finally, Evans wrote a letter pointing out that Shakespeare had used "none" with the plural and that, in fact, God used "none" with the plural in the First Commandment, as found in Deuteronomy 5:5.[1] History does

---

[1]Bergen Evans recounts this story in "Editor's Choise—You Couldn't Do Woise," a speech reprinted in pamphlet form by the G. and C. Merriam Company.

not record whether the *Tribune* was impressed with such authority. The point of this story is not whether "none is" is more acceptable than "none are," but that usage often reveals a good many things about the person speaking, such as occupation, and often his relationship with his audience. For example, the use of "pad," "cool," and "far out" provokes visions of a very definite sort of person. Such terms as "median," "mean," "frequency polygon," and "asymmetrical distributions" indicate that the man speaking is a statistician, while such terms as "ozone," "endothermic compounds," and "dicyanocetylenes" indicate that the speaker is a specific kind of scientist.

language in use

Usage often reveals the nature of the interpersonal relationship between speaker and listener. For example, in French, a speaker may select "tu" or "vous"; in Spanish, he may select "tu" or "usted." English usage often reveals whether the one addressed is older than the speaker, or the parent of the speaker or his employer, whether the speaker and his audience share the same profession, attend the same schools, or have the same parents. For example, a father says "Jim" to his son, but doesn't ordinarily expect to be called "Jack" in reply. On a college campus, what the student refers to as "the libe" to other students, becomes "the library" when he is speaking to someone not connected with the college, "the P.O." becomes "the post office," "sike" and "sosh" become "psychology" and "sociology," and a "bluebook" becomes "an hour exam." The terms "phoneme," "taxeme," "morpheme," "allotax," and "allograph" generally indicate not only that the speaker is a linguist but also that he is speaking to another linguist.

Only in church, for example, would we hear this kind of language:

> Eternal God, Who dost call all men into unity with Thy Son, Jesus Christ our Lord, we pray Thee to pour Thy spirit upon the students of all nations, that they may consecrate themselves to Thy service; that being joined together by their common faith and obedience, they may come more perfectly to love and understand one another, that the world may know that Thou didst send Thy Son to be the

Saviour and the Lord of all men; through the same Jesus Christ our Lord Who with Thee and the Holy Spirit liveth and reigneth one God world without end. Amen.[2]

Stylistically, what has happened in this passage which makes it different from ordinary everyday speech? Without going into a detailed analysis, we might note these features: Direct address employing adjective plus noun is almost entirely restricted to religious usage, although occasionally in a formal letter one might say, "My dear Sir." In this passage, the noun is postmodified by a relative clause, "Who dost call." It would be unusual to find this construction elsewhere. Probably the most apparent characteristic is the speaker's use of the distinctive second person pronoun "Thee" and its adjectival form "Thy" together with the distinctive second and third person singular verb forms "dost," "didst," and "reigneth." Occasionally we find such passages in poetry and in a few dialects, but rarely in standard American English.

The following selection is part of a bill designed to authorize the Secretary of Agriculture to permit certain properties to be used for forestry work:

Be it enacted by the Senate and House of Representatives of the United States of America in Congress assembled, That the Congress recognize that for many years the United States and certain States have cooperated in the production of tree planting stock for use in the reforestation of the public and private lands of the Nation; that the program of production of tree planting stock which was initiated and pursued under the Soil Bank Act (7 U.S.C. 1801 et seq.) was carried on under written agreements which provided for (a) cooperation between the Forest Service, on behalf of the United States, and the States which participated in the program, (b) payments to said States for costs and expenses incurred in the development of nursery facilities, (c) the holding of such funds by the States in trust for the purpose of carrying out the provisions of said agreements, and (d) restoration to the trust fund of an amount equal to the residual value of any supplies, materials, equipment, or improvements acquired or constructed with trust funds and transferred to State forestry work other than the soil bank program; that such program under said Soil Bank Act has been discontinued, but the need for trees continues to be great; that the States and Federal Govern-

[2]Randolph Quirk, *The Use of English* (New York: St. Martin's Press, Inc., 1962), p. 156.

ment are cooperating in the procurement, production, and distribution of forest-tree seeds and plants under section 4 of the Clarke-McNary Act of June 7, 1924 (16 U.S.C. 567), and in the reforestation of lands under title IV of the Agricultural Act of 1956 (16 U.S.C. 568e–g); and that said supplies, materials, equipment, or improvements for use in connection with their respective forestry programs, and it is in the public interest to permit these States to use said property without the requirement that payment be made for the residual value thereof.[3]

Government language, like legal language, needs to weave the stipulations of bills into unbroken chains of grammatical constructions to lessen the probability of deliberate misinterpretation or some kind of fraudulent manipulation. Like the language of the law, business language, scientific language, or journalistic language, it contains certain characteristics which set it apart from the other uses of language. In all these instances, word choice and syntax reveal important features of the professions which use them and about the audience for which they are intended.

the users of language

Just as the various professional styles reveal something about the profession, so the style of an individual tells us something about him. It would be useful to distinguish between two types of style. The features of the English language that everyone shares may be termed the style of the language; the way in which one man uniquely uses the resources of the English language may be termed the style of the individual. Thus, style can be characterized in terms of a contrast between the variable and the constant, and a speaker's style may be said to be his unique relationship with the language. Contrast these two versions of the "Gettysburg Address":[4]

[3]*United States Statutes at Large, 1962* (Washington, D.C.: U.S. Government Printing Office, 1963), p. 107.

[4]Version One is printed by permission of the author and copyright owner, Oliver Jensen, *American Heritage.* Version Two, the Lincoln text, is taken from *American Speeches*, ed. Wayland Maxfield Parrish and Marie Hochmuth (New York: Longmans, Green and Co., 1954), pp. 306–7.

1. I haven't checked these figures but eighty-seven years ago, I think it was, a number of individuals organized a governmental setup here in this country, I believe it covered certain eastern areas, with this idea they were following up, based on a sort of national independence arrangement and the program that every individual is just as good as every other individual.

Well, now of course we are dealing with this big difference of opinion, civil disturbance you might say, although I don't like to appear to take sides or name any individuals, and the point is naturally to check up, by actual experience in the field—see whether any governmental setup with a basis like the one I was mentioning has any validity—whether that dedication, you might say, by those early individuals has any lasting values.

Well, here we are, you might put it that way, all together at the scene where one of these disturbances between different sides got going. We want to pay our tribute to those loved ones, those departed individuals who made the supreme sacrifice here on the basis of their opinions about how this setup ought to be handled. It is absolutely in order and 100 percent O.K. to do this.

But if you look at the overall picture of this, we can't pay any tribute—we can't sanctify this area—we can't hallow, according to whatever individual creeds or faiths or sort of religious outlooks are involved, like I said about this particular area. It was those individuals themselves, including the enlisted men—very brave individuals—who have given this religious character to the area. The way I see it, the rest of the world will not remember any statements issued here, but it will never forget how these men put their shoulders to the wheel and carried this idea down the fairway.

Our job, the living individuals' job here is to pick up the burden and sink the putt they made these big efforts here for. It is our job to get on with the assignment and from these deceased, fine individuals to take extra inspiration, you could call it, for the same theories about which they did such a lot.

We have to make up our minds right here and now as I see it, they didn't put out all that blood, perspiration and—well—that they didn't just make a dry run here, that all of us, under God, that is, the God of our choice, shall beef up this idea about freedom and liberty and those kind of arrangements, and that government of all individuals, by all individuals, and for all individuals shall not pass out of the world picture.

2. Four score and seven years ago our fathers brought forth on this continent, a new nation, conceived in Liberty, and dedicated to the proposition that all men are created equal.

Now we are engaged in a great civil war, testing whether that nation, or any nation so conceived and so dedicated, can long endure. We are met on a great battle-field of that war. We have come to dedicate a portion of that field, as a final resting place for those who here gave their lives that that nation might live. It is altogether fitting and proper that we should do this.

But, in a larger sense, we can not dedicate—we can not consecrate—we can not hallow—this ground. The brave men, living and dead, who struggled here, have consecrated it, far above our poor power to add or detract. The world will little note, nor long remember what we say here, but it can never forget what they did here. It is for us the living, rather, to be dedicated here to the unfinished work which they who fought here have thus far so nobly advanced. It is rather for us to be here dedicated to the great task remaining before us—that from these honored dead we take increased devotion to that cause for which they gave the last full measure of devotion—that we here highly resolve that these dead shall not have died in vain—that this nation, under God, shall have a new birth of freedom—and that government of the people, by the people, for the people, shall not perish from the earth.

You may want to analyze these two versions of the "Gettysburg Address" carefully, trying to point to differences between them. But let us briefly notice certain *dimensions* of style.

Impersonal/Personal
1. A number of individuals organized a governmental setup
2. Our fathers brought forth on this continent

Colloquial/Formal
1. I haven't checked these figures but eighty-seven years ago I think it was
2. Four score and seven years ago

Emphasis on Speaker/on Audience
1. The way *I* see it, the rest of the world will not remember any statement issued here
2. The *world* will little note, nor long remember what we say here

Prosaic/Poetic
1. to see whether any governmental set up with a basis like I was mentioning has any validity
2. testing whether that nation, or any nation so conceived, and so dedicated, can long endure

Nonrhythmic/Rhythmic
1. shall beef up this idea about freedom and liberty and those

> kinds of arrangements, and that government of all individuals by all individuals and for all individuals, shall not pass out of the world picture.
>
> 2. that we here highly resolve that these dead shall not have died in vain—that this nation, under God, shall have a new birth of freedom—and that government of the people, by the people, for the people, shall not perish from the earth.

Loose Parallel Structure/Stricter Parallel Structure

> 1. if you look at the overall picture of this, we can't pay any tribute—we can't sanctify this area—we can't hallow, according to whatever individual creeds or Faiths or sort of religious outlooks are involved
>
> 2. But, in a larger sense, we can not dedicate—we can not consecrate—we can not hallow—this ground.

When read carefully, these versions are not only different in style, but in a very real sense they do not say the same things. For example, Lincoln asks the audience to be "dedicated to the great task remaining before [them]." "Great task" is replaced in the other version by "big effort." The point of the Address is that the living must finish the work the dead had started and had, in effect, handed on to the living. "Task" suggests something that is imposed on one by duty; the other phrases do not. "Great" means not only "big," it also suggests "eminent" and "noble." *In short, style and content are inextricably associated, and to talk about one is to talk about the other.*

The speaker's task as he starts developing his own style is not easy. He must be fully aware of the resources of language before he can learn to manipulate them as a means of persuasion. Consequently, we shall divide our discussion of style into two chapters, exploring the resources of language here, and discussing the characteristics of effective oral style in Chapter 7.

the meaning of meaning

Language may be defined as *systematic verbal symbolism.* Thus, we may say that language has to do with verbal symbolism (words) and system (pattern and order), and that oral language has to do with sound. When someone speaks he uses symbols, system, and sound to say something, to convey some meaning. To say that language has meaning causes some confusion, for even the term "meaning" has a number of meanings. Consider the various uses of the word illustrated by the following sentences:

1. He doesn't exactly understand what you mean when you use that term.
2. I saw a flash of lightning. That usually means rain.
3. Winning that game means a lot to the team.
4. "S" at the end of a noun usually means that the noun is plural.
5. In tone languages such as Chinese, pitch serves to distinguish the difference in meaning among four or five forms which would otherwise be identical.

The term "meaning" in these sentences may be defined in these ways:

1. He doesn't know exactly what object or event you are referring to when you use that term.
2. Lightning is a sign which usually indicates that is going to rain.
3. Winning that game has a certain value to the team.
4. The *formal* meaning of an "s" on the end of a noun is "plural."
5. Pitch (a characteristic of *sound*) helps us to distinguish among four or five forms which are otherwise the same.

In these sentences, meaning has at least three different aspects: (1) meaning *signifies* something (an object, an event, a value); (2) form has meaning; and (3) sound has meaning. To say that language has meaning is to suggest that there are three basic resources of language: (1) semantic (significant) meaning; (2) formal meaning; and (3) sound (as it operates conjointly with semantic and significant meaning) meaning.

semantic meaning

Since words, as such, are merely scratches on a piece of paper or acoustic phenomena, where does their meaning come from? Meaning resides in the *relationship* between a word and the object (event or value) which it represents or re-presents. It also resides in the associations we have for those objects, events, and values.

Why does "table" represent what we think of as table and not what we think of as chair? There is nothing in the nature of a table which makes it a "table"; somebody labeled it "table," and *by agreement* it became "table." The arbitrary nature of meaning requires us to consider carefully the ways in which semantic meaning is developed: through (1) denotation; (2) connotation; and (3) context.

DENOTATION

The relationship between the word and the object it stands for is called the word's *denotative meaning*. Words come to represent the objects and events in our environment in much the same way as do the pictures of objects in a mail order catalogue. Just as there is a very real difference between the pictures (visual symbols) and the objects they represent, so there is a difference between words (verbal symbols) and things. Words represent things because they produce some replica of our actual behavior toward them.[5] But to think about a thing is not the same as to see it and react overtly toward it. So a word does not directly represent a thing, but our conception of that thing.

The denotative, or *literal*, meaning of a word is purely informative. For example, consider the language of the following passage:

> The hardness of metal can be measured in one of two ways, either by denting the metal with a ball of steel dropped from a known height or by using a diamond point, held in a testing machine to scratch the metal. Both the size of the scratch and the size of the dent can be examined with the aid of a microscope.[6]

This kind of language would "move" a person no more than the simple equation "two plus two equals four." Here, language serves only to assert, to state an objective fact, to convey information.

[5]Charles E. Osgood, *Method and Theory in Experimental Psychology* (New York: Oxford University Press, 1953), p. 695.

[6]F.A. Philbrick, *Language and the Law* (New York: The Macmillan Company, 1949), p. 5.

The scientist especially makes use of predominantly informative, referential "meanings." He works to eliminate all emotional colorings, associations, and implications of judgment. Denotative meanings, would not be described in terms of aesthetic adjectives such as "pretty" or "lovely." Denotative meanings do not elicit such emotions as anger, fear, or joy. In fact, the scientist is trying *not* to influence the hearer's attitude toward what he is saying.

CONNOTATION

It cannot be too strongly stressed that total context (the situation, the person involved) finally determines the point at which a meaning is no longer purely denotative, but connotative as well. Almost any word can have personal meanings as well as strictly denotative or referential ones. On a very elementary level, the sentence "Look! There is a spider!" can illustrate this point. To the scientist used to dealing every day in an impersonal, objective way with arachnids, the word "spider" holds no emotive connotations. To the young child who has been frightened by a spider prankishly put on his bed, "spider" becomes an emotive word, carrying with it a fear response. Thus, although denotative meaning resides in the relationship between the object and the word which represents it, *connotative meaning* resides in the relationship among the object, the words, and the speaker/listener.

Recall our discussion of how communication takes place. If the experiences of the speaker do not at least partially coincide with those of his listener, then communication is very difficult, if not altogether impossible. Mr. A (speaker) views each word in the context of all the psychophysiological events which he associates with it. So does Mr. B (listener). These may be referred to as each one's personal or connotative meanings. Where these associations overlap, communicated meaning occurs. Although it is relatively easy to agree on denotative meaning, it is much more difficult to agree on a word's connotative meaning.

One class constructed the following Semantic Differential to test the likenesses and differences found in a word's meaning by the members of the class:

good	— — — — — — —	bad
beautiful	— — — — — — —	ugly
soft	— — — — — — —	hard
weak	— — — — — — —	strong
quick	— — — — — — —	slow
unpleasant	— — — — — — —	pleasant
masculine	— — — — — — —	feminine
active	— — — — — — —	passive
small	— — — — — — —	large
negative	— — — — — — —	positive
honest	— — — — — — —	dishonest
peaceful	— — — — — — —	warlike
tall	— — — — — — —	short
slow	— — — — — — —	fast
hot	— — — — — — —	cold
young	— — — — — — —	old
dynamic	— — — — — — —	lethargic
devious	— — — — — — —	straightforward
intelligent	— — — — — — —	stupid
unconcerned	— — — — — — —	concerned
unjust	— — — — — — —	just
closed	— — — — — — —	open
optimistic	— — — — — — —	pessimistic
impatient	— — — — — — —	patient
creative	— — — — — — —	pedestrian

Charles E. Osgood and his associates have designed a way to check how well we agree on, how well we are able to share, the meaning of any one word. He calls this method the Semantic Differential.[7] The Semantic Differential consists of a scale which permits people to indicate the meaning they attach to a word by making a series of binary decisions: It is beautiful (not ugly), soft (not hard), quick (not slow), and so forth. If asked to rate the word "tornado" on a seven point scale from slow ⟶ fast, a person would prob-

[7]Charles E. Osgood, George J. Suci, and Percy Tannenbaum, *The Measurement of Meaning* (Urbana: University of Illinois Press, 1957).

ably rate it "extremely fast." On the other hand, someone rating the same word in terms of honest ——→ dishonest would probably be neutral. Osgood and his colleagues determined that there were three dominant factors or dimensions: (1) a Potency Factor (represented by scales such as strong ——→ weak, heavy ——→ light, hard ——→ soft); (2) an Evaluation Factor (represented by scales such as good ——→ bad, pleasant ——→ unpleasant, positive ——→ negative); and (3) an Activity Factor (represented by such scales as fast ——→ slow, active ——→ passive, excitable ——→ calm). Of course, some words have a greater variety of connotative meanings than others, and words often prove to have slightly variable referential meanings as well.

CONTEXT

Single words do not comprise the bulk of our communication or literature. Rather, most communication consists of groups of words such as phrases, clauses, and sentences. Placing a word in context stabilizes meaning somewhat. For example, the word "Robert" might not have any meaning for a person, because too many meanings are possible; it could refer to any one of many Roberts. On the other hand, if "Robert E. Lee" or "Robert Burns" were specified, who Robert is—that is, what the word "Robert" means—becomes more obvious.

"Joan Hollins, Sellersburg, Indiana," may be sufficient for an address, or "Mary Dodd, 22220 Grand Concourse, Apartment 2C, Chicago, Illinois," may be necessary. With enough additions to the context, however, one person can be identified among several billion people. The same kind of consideration must be given to identifying a word's meaning. Abstract words generally need more context than concrete ones to establish their meanings.

structural meaning

Vocabulary comes and goes. New words are invented, such as "sputnik," "hippie," and "fallout," and old words acquire new meanings; for example, "clean" now refers to air free from radioactivity and "cool" to something that is unusually nice. Vocabulary and vocabulary meanings are the least stable elements of language; structure is the most stable.

SIGNALS

Spoken language may be viewed as a series of physical or acoustical events. When they are intelligble, these events are not random; rather, they succeed each other in characteristic sequences and within strictly limited possibilities. These patterns of the English language are often complex, but because they are recurring, they are at least partially predictable. To help the listener predict what is coming next in a message, all languages are full of *signals*. A signal is something in one word that tells us something about another one. Consider the following four sentences:

> *The* children go home.
> *Die* Kinder gehen nach Hause.
> *Les* enfants vont chez eux.
> *Los* chicos van a casa.

Although the languages are different and contain different signals, the articles maintain a certain relationship with the nouns. In French, for example, the article tells us the number of the noun and, if it is in the singular, also the gender.

'In English, the verb "sing" reflects the *number* ("sings" would tell us that the subject of the sentence was singular), and the *tense* of the action ("sang" would tell us the action was past). The verb also reflects the *voice*, active or passive ("is sung" would tell us that the verb is passive) and the *mood* ("that the children sing" would tell us that the mood is subjunctive).

To further illustrate how form tells us something—that structure has meaning—consider the following sentence:[8]

> Most zaps have lak.

[8]This treatment follows one suggested by David K. Berlo, *The Process of Communication* (New York: Holt, Rinehart and Winston, Inc., 1960), pp. 196–206.

Do we know what the word "zaps" means? Or the word "lak"? Yet not knowing these two terms does not mean that the sentence has no meaning. Where does the meaning reside? To discover that, we shall have to compare two more sentences with the first one:

One zaps have lak.

and

Most zap has lak.

Both sentences make us uncomfortable. Why? First of all, when we say "one" we usually say "has" rather than "have," and when we say "most" we say "have" rather than "has." Plural noun forms are generally followed by plural verb forms. Also, nouns which end in "s" rarely follow the adjective "one," just as the adjective "most" is rarely followed by a noun without an "s" ending. Thus, the form or structure of language sequences means something, not in the semantic sense—it does not *denote* anything, refer us to any object— but it does help us to communicate more efficiently. Signals help reduce uncertainty for the listener.

WORD-WORD RELATIONSHIPS

Note how the relationship between words changes the meaning of these two sentences:

The football coach said, "The halfback is stupid."
"The football coach," said the halfback, "is stupid."

Here, the same words were used; the same semantic meanings involved. The word-object relationships (denotative meaning of each word) remained stable, but the word-word relationships were changed and thus meaning of the sentences also changed.

WORD ORDER

To change word order is also to change sentence meaning. Consider these two sentences:

    John hit Bill.
    Bill hit John.

The same words are used and the same semantic meanings are employed. But the order is different and thus the meaning is also different.

sound meaning

    Perhaps much of your past thinking about language has been almost exclusively concerned with written English. In reality, written language is a reflection of spoken language and it is perhaps inevitable that, as a copy of actual speech, it should be imperfect and incomplete. Note the different overtones of meanings this sentence can have, depending upon emphasis:

    What do you think?   What *do* you think?
    What do *you* think?   What do you *think?*

Although printed language can use varying type faces and different sizes and colors of type, it has not yet duplicated the speaker's tone of voice or the subtleties of inflection and rate which give us clues to his feelings.

    Now let us discuss certain ways in which sound is organically related to sense and the way in which, at the same time, sound operates as an independent aspect of language separable from sense.

CHARACTERISTICS OF SOUND

    All vocal sounds have four fundamental attributes: loudness, pitch, duration, and quality. The neuromuscular controls of the human vocal mechanism are subtle and complex enough to allow a wide range of variation for each sound attribute. Although we shall consider each of them separately, they operate simultaneously.

    loudness. Assume that the speaker has no problem in making himself heard and is now concerned with the use of loudness or force to give color and meaning to what he is saying. Force is the way in English by which we establish syllable stress in polysyllabic words. Differences in the meaning of words occur when the syllable stress is shifted from one syllable to the other. Consider, for example:

ob*ject*	*ob*ject
con*vict*	*con*vict
*con*duct	con*duct*

When we change the stress from one word in the sentence to another, the emphasis in the sentence shifts and so, to some extent, do the various shades of meaning. Change the stress from the first word of these sentences to the succeeding words and you will agree:

Mary can do anything.

You and I must go.

Or try to change the stress emphasis in this line of a Churchill speech:

Never in the field of human conflict was so much owed by so many to so few.

Or in Patrick Henry's:

I know not what course others may take; but as for me, give me liberty or give me death.

pitch. Although changes of pitch in speaking are not so wide or distinct as they can be in singing, pitch often reveals subtleties of meaning. We often associate a rise in pitch with anger, fear, or excitement. Variations in pitch in English are most closely associated with conventions that have arisen concerning sentence types and formations. For example, we generally use a downward or falling inflection to indicate that we have completed our thought. The upward or rising inflection we associate with uncertainty, incompleteness, or a question. Between these two extremes we would somehow have to account for the vast spectrum of inflections which express sarcasm, cynicism, innuendo, irony, and so on. Although most of us would employ one of the three circumflex inflections (down-up, up-down, or down-up-down), each individual use is likely to call for more subtle differences than we can chart here. Consider the variety of inflections one would normally use when saying "Yes" to indicate absolute certainty, some doubt, real indecision, or a bit of sarcasm. Or the way in which one says "No" to indicate "Absolutely not"; "Well, perhaps"; "I'm a bit surprised to hear that"; "That certainly annoys me"; and, "I am glad to hear that."

duration. Changes in both the time intervals between words and phrases and the time involved in the production of speech sounds allow us to emphasize or subordinate meanings and to express our feelings more vividly. The simple fact is that some sounds take longer than others to articulate. Quite often sorrow or sadness are expressed by a slow rate of utterance and joy and gladness by a faster rate.

One way of emphasizing key words is by slowing the rate. *Pause,* or silence, however, is the feature which requires the most discussion. Occasionally, we must stop to ask whether a friend has said he will meet us on East Eighth Street or East State Street. One of the differences between the two is where the silence occurs. Silence indicates the end of structural units such as sentences or phrases. Silence in speech often operates much as the pause or rest in a musical composition. It is an integral part of the meaning. In fact, we often talk about the "meaningful pause." When the speaker pauses, the listener must wait, and he tends to fill the silence with the last bit of information he has heard. This kind of inner repetition of what the speaker has said emphasizes the idea. Franklin D. Roosevelt quite often used the pause in this way:

> We Americans of today, together with our allies, are passing through a period of supreme test.//It is a test of our courage// of our resolve// of our wisdom// of our essential decency.//
>
> If we meet that test// successfully and honorably// we shall perform a service of historic importance which men and women and children will honor throughout all time.//
>
> As I stand here today, having taken the solemn oath of office in the presence of my fellow countrymen// in the presence of our God // I know that it is America's purpose that we shall not fail.//[9]

Consider Dwight D. Eisenhower's use of the pause in his "Second Inaugural Address":

[9]In *A History and Criticism of American Public Address,* Vol. III, ed. Marie Hochmuth (New York: Longmans, Green and Co., 1955), p. 510. Parallel lines are added.

May we pursue the right//without self-righteousness.//May we know unity//without conformity.//May we grow in strength// without pride of self.//[10]

quality. We are not concerned here with such quality as "breathiness" or "nasality," but rather with quality as related to the speaker's feeling or mood. There is no real way to capture the quality of a speaker's voice in written language. The best way to study variations in voice quality is to listen to records of distinguished speakers giving speeches on a variety of topics under different circumstances. The quality of Franklin Roosevelt's voice as he delivered the United States' declaration of war in 1941 is very much different from the voice quality of campaigner Roosevelt delivering a cutting attack against a political opponent or the President talking about domestic matters in one of his fireside chats. Churchill managed to convey by voice quality, as well as by what he said, his deep and abiding hatred of Hitler and Mussolini. Contrast with this the quality of his voice when he spoke of his beloved Britain.

ELEMENTARY SOUND DEVICES

On a somewhat different level, the speaker must consider other sound devices of language which affect meaning. Onomatopoeia and specific speech sounds are often somehow related to various emotions and moods.

onomatopoeia. Onomatopoeia means quite literally "name-making." Onomatopoeic words are imitative of their own literal meanings; onomatopoeia refers to the use of words to suggest, by their sounds, the objects they represent. It has even occasioned a theory of the way language originated. While such a theory is open to question, the sounds of such words as "crash," "buzz," "swish," "whiz," "roar," "rumble," "flop," "sniffle," "flash," and "thump" are highly suggestive of their meanings. Onomatopoeic effects are most likely to occur in either descriptions or narrative passages to intensify the actions being talked about.

sound suggestion. Although onomatopoeia depends upon

[10]In Ernest J. Wrage and Barnet Baskerville, eds., *Contemporary Forum: American Speeches on Twentieth-Century Issues* (Harper & Row, Publishers, 1962), p. 314. Parallel lines are added.

direct imitation, vowel and consonant sounds can be related to meaning in a more sophisticated way in which sound does not imitate but suggests. Review for a minute the sounds of the English language: Some are harsh and short, some are long and fluid. We often associate harsh sounds with harsh meanings. Winston Churchill, for example, called Mussolini a "jackal" and Hitler a "bloodthirsty guttersnipe."

Although a speaker need not analyze speech sounds in detail, certain elementary facts are helpful to him. First, consider some of the vowels as they progress along a continuum, from those placed high and toward the front of the mouth to those pronounced high and toward the back of the mouth. One writer[11] has suggested that this progression is from "thin, bright, shrill" vowels to "richer, darker, more resonant" ones:

*e*at	h*o*t
*i*t	l*a*w
*a*te[12]	h*o*me
m*e*t	g*oo*d
c*a*t	f*oo*d
*a*rt	

He suggests that there are four more with a "muffled" quality:

c*u*t	fath*e*r
h*u*rt	sof*a*

There are also diphthongs or combinations of two vowels. Because they are composite sounds, the pace with which they are said tends to be slowed:

r*i*ght	th*ere*
b*oy*	d*ear*
*ou*t	p*oor*
*u*se	

Consonant sounds may be either voiced or voiceless. A consonant is voiced when the vocal cords vibrate; a voiced consonant

---

[11]This follows a treatment by Chad Walsh, *Doors into Poetry* (Englewood Cliffs, N.J.: Prentice-Hall, Inc., 1962), pp. 87–88.

[12]This sound may be pronounced either as a vowel [e] or as a diphthong [ei].

tends to have a fuller sound than a voiceless one. One group are the stop plosives, those consonants made by abruptly stopping the flow of air from the mouth. They tend to have "an explosive, staccato effect":

unvoiced	*voiced*
p	b
t	d
k	g

Another group of consonants are called fricatives, or sounds made with only a partial closure of the articulating organs. They are characterized, as the name indicates, by the sound of friction:

unvoiced	*voiced*
f	v
s	z
th(in)	th(en)
sh	zh
h	

Another group of consonants are smoother in sound. They are all voiced:

l	n
r	ng (single sound)
m	

Two consonants are often termed "semivowels." Speak them and you will see why: w, y.

One can suggest certain general effects with certain sounds. For example, we associate heaviness with the sonority of the long back vowel sounds such as oh, ah, aw, oo. A good way to appreciate how sound helps convey an idea is to list words designed to describe the emotions. Recall Atlanta newspaperman Henry Grady's speech in 1886, describing the Confederate soldier after the Civil War. He pictures the soldier as making a "slow" and "painful" journey home. The long *o* and *a* sounds help to emphasize the point the speaker was trying to make. One ought to note, however, that this kind of relationship between sound and meaning holds true only when sound operates in conjunction with the other resources of language.

SOUND REPETITION

Now consider how the speaker may organize sounds, especially through repetition, to achieve effects. We shall discuss three devices, varying in complexity from the relatively simple forms of repetition known as alliteration and assonance to the highly complex level of organization known as rhythm.

alliteration. The repetition of consonant sounds beginning neighboring words or accented syllables is perhaps one of the best known sound effects of oral language. Notice how Lincoln used alliteration simply but effectively in his "Farewell Address" to the citizens of Springfield, Illinois, as he left there to assume the Presidency:

> No one, not in my situation, can appreciate my feeling of sadness at this parting. To this place, and the kindness of these people, I owe everything. Here I have lived a quarter of a century, and have passed from a young to an old man. Here my children have been born, and one is buried.[13]

There are whole chains of alliterated words: "appreciate . . . parting . . . place . . . people . . . passed." Especially effective is the alliteration in "been born . . . buried."

Effective alliteration does not call attention to itself. Recall the effects manifested in the opening words of the "Gettysburg Address": "Four score and seven years ago our fathers brought forth . . ."

assonance. Assonance can be defined as repetition of the same stressed vowel sound; for example, dream . . . beach. Again recall examples from the "Gettysburg Address":

[f]our	score
in	liberty
testing	whether

---

[13]Parrish and Hochmuth, *American Speeches*, p. 305.

final   lives
on   continent
not   consecrate
our   power
so   nobly
will   little

rhythm. Degrees of formality in rhythm vary from ordinary prose to strict verse forms such as the sonnet. Any language, however prosaic or poetic, is capable of possessing rhythm. Rhythm may be defined as a regularity in the occurrence of accents. It possesses a far more highly developed level of organization than alliteration and assonance. We can think of rhythm in terms of repetition and expectancy. It is this very combination which allows rhythm to animate and bring emphasis to ideas. Consider this line from Edmund Burke's "Speech on Conciliation," urging England to attempt to reconcile the breach between herself and her American colonies:

> It will take /its perpet/ual ten/or, it
> will receive /its fi/nal impress/sion, from the
> stamp of this very hour.[14]

Basically, there are three kinds of rhythm: (1) the metrical rhythm of verse, in regular feet. Although sometimes used in prose, this is rarely used for more than three or four continuous feet; (2) syllabic stress-rhythm. Here the syllables which are most heavily stressed occur at regular time intervals, generally with a varying number of either unstressed or lightly stressed syllables in between; (3) rhythm of grammatical units. Here, the recurring phrase patterns or sentence patterns give the effect of regularity. Note how this speech by Churchill before the House of Commons on June 18, 1940, combines all three of these rhythmic types (primarily the first two):

[14]For a discussion of prose rhythm see Wayland Maxfield Parrish, "The Rhythm of Oratorical Prose," in *Studies in Rhetoric and Public Speaking in Honor of James Albert Winans* (New York: Russell and Russell, Inc., 1962), pp. 217–32.

The Battle of Britain is about to begin. On this battle depends the survival of Christian civilization.

Upon it depends our own British life and the long continuity of our institutions and our empire. The whole fury and might of the enemy must very soon be turned upon us. Hitler knows he will have to break us in this island or lose the war.

If we can stand up to him all Europe may be freed and the life of the world may move forward into broad sunlit uplands; but if we fail, the whole world, including the United States, and all that we have known and cared for, will sink into the abyss of a new dark age made more sinister and perhaps more prolonged by the lights of a perverted science.

Let us therefore brace ourselves to our duty and so bear ourselves that if the British Commonwealth and Empire last for a thousand years, men will still say "This was their finest hour."[15]

Just as alliteration and assonance do not operate fully by themselves, rhythm cannot produce its total effect without meaning and form. Ultimately, language is not composed only of semantic meanings, structural meanings, or sound effects. Rather, language = semantic meanings + structural meanings + sound.

summary

All the resources of language are available to the speaker. Every speech is a *selection* from the English language. Just as the speaker has selected his topic, proofs, and pattern of organization, so he selects from all possible resources of the language those which compose the style of his speech. Therefore, he must become aware of the vast array of potentialities which language holds for him: semantic meaning, structural meaning, and sound. As Weaver puts it: "Using a language may be compared to riding a horse; much of one's success depends upon an understanding of what it *can* and *will* do."[16] To know the resources of language is to find "an inex-

[15]From *The World's Great Speeches*, ed. Lewis Copeland and Lawrence Lamm (2nd rev. ed.; New York: Dover Publications, Inc., 1958), p. 446.
[16]Richard Weaver, *The Ethics of Rhetoric* (Chicago: Henry Regnery Co., 1953), p. 117.

haustible abundance of manifold treasures." We have mentioned only a few of them. As "the instrument with which man forms thought and feeling, mood, aspiration, will and act," and as "the instrument by whose means he influences and is influenced," language and its resources may surely be said to be "the ultimate and deepest foundation of human society."[17]

rhetorical exercises

1. Write a ten to fifteen minute speech and deliver it from manuscript. Thus, you will be able to "polish" the language of your speech more carefully.

2. Design your own Semantic Differential to test how well your own class agrees on the meaning of words they often use. Discuss the points of disagreement to see why they have arisen.

3. Find examples where the context of a word helps stabilize word meaning. What kinds of words need more of a context for their meanings to be clear?

4. Select a prose passage and look for all of the possible structural signals or meanings which you can find. How did you go about discovering these signals?

5. Select passages to read aloud which you feel illustrate the close relationship between sound and meaning.

collateral readings

Berlo, David K., *The Process of Communication: An Introduction to Theory and Practice*. New York: Holt, Rinehart and Winston, Inc., 1960. See especially Chapter 7, "Meaning and Communication," and Chapter 8, "Dimensions of Meaning."

[17]Louis Hjelmslev, *Prolegomena to a Theory of Language*, rev. Eng. ed., trans. Francis J. Whitfield (Madison: The University of Wisconsin Press, 1963), p. 3.

Black, Max, ed., *The Importance of Language*. Englewood Cliffs, N.J.: Prentice-Hall, Inc., 1962. See especially "Words and their Meanings" by Aldous Huxley.

Blankenship, Jane, *A Sense of Style: An Introduction to Style for the Public Speaker*. Belmont, Calif.: Dickenson Publishing Co., Inc., 1968. See Chapter 1, "Toward a Definition of Style."

Carroll, John B., *Language and Thought*. Englewood Cliffs, N.J.: Prentice-Hall, Inc., 1964.

Clark, Ruth Anne, Frederick Williams, and Percy H. Tannenbaum, "Effects of Shared Referential Experience upon Encoder-Decoder Agreement," *Language and Speech*, Vol. 41 (1965), 253–59.

Heise, David R., "Semantic Differential Profiles for 1,000 Most Frequent English Words," *Psychological Monographs*, Vol. 79, No. 8 (1965), 1–31.

Langer, Suzanne K., *Philosophy in a New Key*. Cambridge, Mass.: Harvard University Press, 1942. See especially Chapter 5, "Language."

Ohmann, Richard M., *Shaw: The Style and the Man*. Middletown, Conn.: Wesleyan University Press, 1962.

Osgood, Charles E., George J. Suci, and Percy Tannenbaum, *The Measurement of Meaning*. Urbana: University of Illinois Press, 1957.

Quirk, Randolph, *The Use of English*. New York: St. Martin's Press, Inc., 1962. See especially Chapter 10, "Looking at English in Use."

Richards, I. A., *The Philosophy of Rhetoric*. New York: Oxford University Press, 1936. See especially "The Interinanimation of Words" and "Metaphor."

Sebeok, Thomas A., ed., *Style in Language*. Cambridge, Mass.: The M.I.T. Press, 1960.

Vygotsky, Lev, *Thought and Language*, trans. Eugenia Hanfmann and Gertrude Vokar. Cambridge, Mass.: The M.I.T. Press, 1962.

Weaver, Richard, "Language is Semonic," in *Dimensions of Rhetorical Scholarship*, ed. Roger Nebergall. Norman, Okla.: University of Oklahoma Speech Department, 1963.

Whatmough, Joshua, *Language: A Modern Synthesis*. New York: New American Library, 1957.

*Style, in its finest sense, is the last acquirement
of the educated mind; it is also the most useful.*

Alfred North Whitehead

7

STYLE:
SOME
PRACTICAL APPLICATIONS

Effective oral style is not magic. The decisions the speaker makes
about what to say, as well as how to say it, determine his style. Both
reflect the speaker's way of viewing objects, events, and people, so
that the most general of his attitudes and the most general of his
ideas find expression as characteristically in his style as they have
in the content of his speech. The beginning speaker cannot immediately become a William Pitt or a Winston Churchill, an Adlai
Stevenson or a John Kennedy, but he can recognize, as they did,
that our language is capable of stating ideas with vitality and drama,
of conveying information concisely and accurately, and of sensitively
conveying attitudes and relationships. Basically, there are three steps
in becoming an effective stylist: (1) the speaker must determine what
the qualities of effective style are; (2) he must learn how to achieve

them; and (3) he must practice constantly to use them at every opportunity.

Aristotle described three qualities of effective style,[1] and while many other authors have since divided those qualities into lists of eight or ten or twenty-five, they generally can still be placed under a threefold division. To be effective, style should be clear, appropriate, and vivid. We shall consider each of these three qualities briefly, suggesting how you may achieve them.

clarity

The first prerequisite of effective oral style is clarity. Without clarity of statement, there is no meaning, or the meaning is ambiguous and perhaps misleading.[2] For example, when Calvin Coolidge announced "I do not choose to run," one might have questioned, "Do you mean that you do not intend to run under any circumstance; that is, that you *will* not run? Or do you mean that you do not really want to run, though duty may require it; that is, that you will bow to pressure for you to run?" "Choose," in the Coolidge statement, is ambiguous. An ambiguous word is any word whose meaning is uncertain, a word which is capable of being understood in either of two or more possible ways. From time to time, ambiguity may be semihumorous, as in the following example:

> *Professor*: When you turn in your mid-term papers, I shall lose no time in reading them.
>
> *Students*: (to themselves, of course): Good, then we shall lose no time in writing them.

However, in the language of diplomacy or of political concealment, ambiguity may have far-reaching consequences.

According to one dictionary, the word "run" has over two

---

[1]Aristotle, *Rhetoric*, trans. W. Rhys Roberts (New York: Random House, Inc., 1954). Book Three, Chapters 2, 6, and 7.

[2]See Monroe C. Beardsley's discussion of ambiguity in *Thinking Straight: Principles of Reasoning for Readers and Writers* (2nd ed.; Englewood Cliffs, N.J.: Prentice-Hall, Inc., 1956), pp. 151–59.

hundred fifty verbal meanings which are clearly distinguishable only if they are given a context. Ambiguity can often be avoided by giving a word enough context to clarify its intended meaning. From the statement, "Max rented the house yesterday," a listener would not know whether Max rented the house *to* somebody or *from* somebody. The context is not complete enough to give the listener an accurate picture of what "rented" means.

Because of the difficulty in defining them, certain words are in and of themselves ambiguous. They are meaningless, not in the sense that they have no meaning, but because they may have a great variety of subtly different meanings. For example, the "truth" of a scientific principle is a very different "truth" from a Biblical one. The meaning of "believe" in the sentence, "I don't believe in coddling children," is not the same "believe" as in the sentence, "I don't believe in sea monsters." Even a word such as "case" in the sentence, "I was reading an interesting police case in the newspaper this morning," is a very different "case" from the one used in the sentence, "I think we should buy a case of cokes for the party."

Ambiguity may also arise when the parts of a phrase or of a clause are not clearly related, as in "A moment after Miss Baker christened the ship, the S.S. Goldenrod, she was afloat in the river." Or, "The diamond pin was a present for Mrs. Donahue, when she married Mr. Donahue in 1964, at a cost of $50,000." We will consider syntactical ambiguity after we have completed our discussion of clarity in word choice. Words are said to be clear when they are accurate, concrete, and familiar. Let us discuss each of these qualities briefly.

ACCURACY

In one of the two versions of the "Gettysburg Address" discussed earlier, Lincoln asked his audience "to be dedicated to the great task remaining before [them]." The other version used "big effort." It is not really synonymous with "great task" because, to be accurate, it simply does not mean the same thing.

Accuracy comes from the Latin *ad-cura*, to care. Note the care with which Thomas DeQuincey, the nineteenth century English essayist, once wrote in "On Knocking at the Gate of *Macbeth*": ". . .

I had always felt a great perplexity on one point in *Macbeth*."[3] Why is "perplexity" a better word than "interest" or "curiosity" or "bewilderment" or "confusion"? It is better because the other words convey only one portion of DeQuincey's feeling. "Perplexity," however, suggests that DeQuincey's interest was aroused and that he was puzzled as well; thus, it accurately states his mood.

Each person has three vocabularies: (1) the vocabulary of his ordinary conversation; (2) the vocabulary of his more formal conversation and of his writings; and (3) his recognition vocabulary of the words he reads or hears. The beginning speaker must constantly and systematically work to unite his speaking vocabulary and his recognition vocabulary. Although a large vocabulary does not mean that a speaker will be good, it does provide him with a larger choice of words and more materials with which to be precise.

The use of specific rather than general words helps the speaker achieve accuracy. "Our old black cat" carries more meaning than "an animal we once owned." Specific words name individual objects or events. For example, "move" is a general verb; "stride," "amble," "glide," "run," "trot," are specific verbs and give a more accurate picture of the kind of movement involved. General words are, of course, a very important part of the language, but too frequent and unnecessary use of them is risky. How old is a "middle-aged" man? What is the temperature when it is "cold" outside? How wealthy is a "rich" man? In each case, the wide variety of possible answers would make the key words in those sentences all but useless.

CONCRETENESS

Accuracy and concreteness are closely related. For example, Joe X meets Bill Y on the street and says: "I've just come from a good lecture!" The word "good" may mean that the lecture was instructive, witty, stimulating, or eloquent. The lack of accuracy is compounded by the use of the word "good," which on an abstract ——→ concrete continuum tends to be abstract.

Concrete words tend to yield more information than do

[3]Thomas DeQuincey, "On Knocking at the Gate in *Macbeth*," in John F. Genung, *Handbook of Rhetorical Analysis: Studies in Style and Invention* (Boston: Ginn and Company, Publishers, 1892), p. 8.

abstract ones. A concrete word stands for an observable thing, for something perceived through the senses; for example, "tree," "robin," "coffee aroma," "noise."

FAMILIARITY

Unless a word is familiar (or made familiar through definition), it contains no information at all. If a zoologist says to his nonzoologist friend, "I met a very interesting copepodologist today," the nonzoologist probably would not understand whom his friend had met.

Audiences are critical of a speaker who uses words they don't understand. During one class session five students were asked to write a critique of another student who gave a speech on the Latin poet Virgil. Here are some of the comments: "I don't think you paid enough attention to whether or not anybody in the class knew what you were talking about. Many words without definitions." "You tended to throw around names without telling us who they were." "What *is* an eclogue?" "Audience interest was rather good considering we often did not know what you were talking about." "You used a lot of terms unknown to the listeners. Why?" Another student gave a speech using terms familiar to a debater but not to a class of nondebaters: "flow sheet," "prima facie case," "canned rebuttal," and "causal warrants." Both speakers might just as well have been speaking Russian or Serbo-Croatian.

SYNTACTICAL AMBIGUITY

After the speaker decides that his words are accurate, concrete, and familiar, he must not destroy the clearness of his message by the improper arrangement of words. We shall discuss some typical kinds of syntactic ambiguity and show how they may be corrected.

modifiers. There are two simple rules to remember when using modifiers: (1) place all modifiers, whether they are words, phrases, or clauses, as close as possible to the words they modify; and (2) do not place these elements close to other words they might be taken to modify.

Clauses:

Unclear: When you were young do your remember all the good
              times you had? (The clause could refer to "remember"
              or "good times you had.")
Clear: Do you remember all the good times you had when you
              were young?

Phrases:

Unclear: Mary began to lose her desire to finish the project after
              a time. (The phrase could refer to "to finish" or "began
              to lose.")
Clear: After a time Mary began to lose her desire to finish the
              project.

Words:

Unclear: She merely goes because she has nothing else to do.
Clear: She goes merely because she has nothing else to do.

Squinting modifiers (modifiers placed so they could be understood with either the following or the preceding words):

Unclear: As Jack and Bill walked along occasionally they slipped
              on the ice. (The speaker could place a long pause after
              "along," but that may not eliminate the confusion.)
Clear: As Jack and Bill walked along, they occasionally slipped
              on the ice.

It is also good practice not to separate words that usually belong
close together, such as subject and verb.

Unclear: The scientists had after many years of work and a num-
              ber of setbacks successfully completed their experiment.
Clear: After many years of work and a number of setbacks, the
              scientists successfully completed their experiment.

correlatives. Remember to use correlatives such as "both . . .
and," "not only . . . but also," "whether . . . or," "either . . . or,"

"neither . . . nor," only before sentence elements that actually are parallel in form.

> *Incorrect*:   You are either wrong or I am.
> *Correct*:   Either you are wrong or I am.

parallels. Avoid parallel structure when your ideas are not parallel.

> *Unclear*:   Joan has brown hair, grey eyes and is very tanned.
> *Clear*:   Joan has brown hair, grey eyes, and tanned skin.

shift in point of view. Avoid any unnecessary shift in point of view.

In subject:

> *Unclear*:   Jack was a good scholar, but athletics were not his strong point.
> *Clear*:   Jack was a good scholar but a poor athlete.

In pronoun person and number:

> *Unclear*:   If one's ears pop while driving in high altitudes, chew a stick of gum.
> *Clear*:   One should chew a stick of gum, if his ears pop when driving in high altitudes.

In verb tense:

> *Unclear*:   Terry asked the teacher about his mistakes, but gets little help.
> *Clear*:   Terry asked the teacher about his mistakes, but got little help.

In verb voice:

> *Unclear*:   We dusted our room meticulously, and the floors were also swept.
> *Clear*:   We meticulously dusted the room and swept the floors.

pronoun references. Avoid letting a pronoun refer to an antecedent that is remote or vague.

> *Unclear*: I can recall that Mary and I spoke with many people that day, but I did not enjoy it at all.
>
> *Clear*: I can recall that Mary and I spoke with many people that day, but I did not enjoy speaking with any of them.

transitions. When it is possible, use transitions to connect thoughts within a sentence or in a group of sentences. You might use conjunctions and transitional expressions:

at the same time	in addition
for example	on the other hand
conversely	next
in particular	to sum up
of course	finally
moreover	indeed
after all	on the contrary

Repeat key words:

> Four score and seven years ago our fathers brought forth on this continent, a new *nation, conceived* in Liberty, and *dedicated* to the proposition that all men are created equal.
>
> Now we are engaged in a *great* civil *war,* testing whether that *nation,* or any *nation* so *conceived* and so *dedicated,* can long endure. We are met on a *great* battle-*field* of that *war.* We have come to *dedicate* a portion of that field . . .[4]

Use parallel structure and repetition of key words conjointly:

> Our Constitution, the foundation of our Republic forbids it [depriving "millions" of the "blessings of liberty"]. The principles of our freedom forbid it. Morality forbids it. And the Law I will sign tonight forbids it. (President Lyndon Johnson on the Civil Rights Bill)[5]

length. Now that we have suggested some ways to achieve syntactical clarity, we might consider how many words are necessary for clarity. The answer is, of course, as many as it takes to accomplish whatever purpose the speaker has in mind. Let us again pro-

---

[4]Wayland Maxfield Parrish and Marie Hochmuth, eds., *American Speeches*
[5]*The New York Times,* July 3, 1964.
(New York: Longmans, Green and Co., 1954), p. 306. Italics added.

ceed through examples. One critic said about the novelist Thomas Wolfe: "For a moment, but a moment only, there is a sudden release of compassion. . . . Then the moment passes, and compassion fails."[6] He could have said this in fewer words and still have retained clarity, but not without limiting the effect. Instead of saying "For a moment, but a moment only," he could have said, "For only a moment," hence deleting three words. Why is the first more effective than the second? Because it better emphasizes the point the critic is trying to make—the fleeting nature of the compassion.

Length, however, is no guarantee of clearness or effectiveness. Lincoln used five words to say, "all men are created equal" and another version of the "Gettysburg Address" used ten words to say, "every individual is just as good as every other individual."

Rather than talking about sentence length in absolute terms, the speaker should consider: How many words are necessary for the adequate expression of my thoughts? Why are the words being used: that is, for what effect? How can I best achieve my specific purpose? Nikos Kazantzakis was once criticized for using too many adjectives with each noun. He replied:

> I love adjectives but not simply as decoration. I feel the necessity of expressing my emotion from all sides, spherically; and because my emotion is never simple, never positive or negative only, but both together and something even more. . . . One such adjective, whatever it might be, would cripple my emotion, and I am obliged, in order to remain faithful to my emotion and not betray it, to invite another adjective, often opposed to the previous one, always with a different meaning, in order that I may see the noun from its other equally lawful and existent side.[7]

Length, as such, is not wordiness. The speaker should use only as many words as he needs. He should make sure every word is doing its job and never hesitate to eliminate all the "loafers." Economy should not be achieved at the expense of clarity and effect. Fuzziness often results not so much from long sentences as from awkward,

[6] As cited in Maurice Natanson, "The Privileged Moment: A Study in the Rhetoric of Thomas Wolfe," *Quarterly Journal of Speech*, Vol. XLII, No. 2 (April 1957), 148.

[7] Nikos Kazantzakis, *The Odyssey: A Modern Sequel*, trans. Kimon Friar (New York: Simon and Schuster, Inc., 1958), p. xxxii.

confused, and illogical sentence structure, which often just reflect carelessness and/or lazy thinking.

appropriateness

Effective style is not only clear, it must also be appropriate to the speaker, his audience, the topic, and the occasion. A speech that is clear to the audience is most likely to be appropriate. As previously suggested, the speaker should use words which are familiar to his audience, or he risks having them misunderstood or not understood at all. The speaker would do well to remember these words from Shakespeare's *Richard II*: "Uncle . . . speak comfortable words!"[8] The audience must feel at home with the language of the speech, either because they know the words and precisely how they are meant, or because the words are explained to them during the speech itself.

The language of the speech should be appropriate not only to the audience, but also to the speaker. He should avoid the use of unfamiliar technical terms and infrequently used words. Bergen Evans, in his book, *Comfortable Words*, argues against the use of elegant words by a speaker who is not really used to them:

> The cheapest form of decoration is the unfamiliar word, which the speaker thinks must be elegant merely because it is unfamiliar to him. But since no one can use a word effectively unless he is so familiar with it that he has no awareness of its being strange or in any way unusual, the *un*familiarity is the thing that stands out.[9]

One cannot make a poor choice of words better by decorating it with unnecessarily complex or elegant adornment. Ornament is fairly tricky in any field, and if the ornament is wrongly used, the result may be disastrous.

The language of the speech should also be appropriate to the

[8] *The Complete Plays and Poems of William Shakespeare*, ed. William A. Neilson and Charles J. Hill (Boston: Houghton Mifflin Company, 1942), p. 611.

[9] Bergen Evans, *Comfortable Words* (New York: Random House, Inc., 1962), pp. 8–9.

topic and to the occasion. Just as you do not attend a formal dinner in jeans, sweater, and sneakers, so a speaker's good sense is his best gauge in degree of formality. For example, colloquialisms are not wrong in themselves. They may be correct in informal speeches or in conversation, but they are not appropriate to a more formal speech. On the other hand, the speaker should avoid at all times stiff, formal language that is not natural to him.

The language of formal speech is not measured by the number of syllables per word, but by choice of words and sentence structure. Let us examine three examples: (1) the formal language of a presidential inaugural; (2) the less formal language of a public man bidding farewell to the public at the end of his tenure of office; and (3) the informal language of an everyday conversation.

Formal language is marked by its lack of colloquial style. It is direct, but not chatty. Here is an excerpt from the "Inaugural Address" John F. Kennedy delivered on January 20, 1961:

> So let us begin anew—remembering on both sides that civility is not a sign of weakness, and sincerity is always subject to proof. Let us never negotiate out of fear. But let us never fear to negotiate.
>
> Let both sides explore what problems unite us instead of belaboring those problems which divide us.
>
> Let both sides, for the first time, formulate serious and precise proposals for the inspection and control of arms—and bring the absolute power to destroy other nations under the absolute control of all nations.
>
> Let both sides seek to invoke the wonders of science instead of its terrors. Together let us explore the stars, conquer the deserts, eradicate disease, tap the ocean depths and encourage the arts and commerce.
>
> Let both sides unite to heed in all corners of the earth the command of Isaiah—to "undo the heavy burdens . . . (and) let the oppressed go free."[10]

Now consider a somewhat less formal, but nevertheless not casual, passage from President Harry Truman's "Valedictory," a radio broadcast at the end of his Presidency:

[10]Ernest J. Wrage and Barnet Baskerville, eds., *Contemporary Forum: American Speeches on Twentieth Century Issues* (New York: Harper & Row, Publishers, 1962), p. 319.

I suppose that history will remember my term in office as the years when the "cold war" began to overshadow our lives. I have had hardly a day in office that has not been dominated by this all-embracing struggle—this conflict between those who love freedom and those who would lead the world back into slavery and darkness. And always in the background there has been the atomic bomb.

But when history says that my term of office saw the beginning of the "cold war," it will also say that in those eight years we have set the course that can win it. We have succeeded in carving out a new set of policies to attain peace—positive policies, policies of world leadership, policies that express faith in other free people.[11]

"I suppose that history will" is measurably more informal than "History will." "I have had hardly a day in office" is measurably more personal even than "Hardly a day in office." Yet, phrases such as "this conflict between those who love freedom and those who would lead the world back into slavery and darkness" mark the speech as something other than casual conversation.

Consider this example of conversation between two students:

I don't know if I should use a term like "marginal propensity" in my speech on inflation. Of course, I could just not use it, but then the speech might be pretty superficial. I suppose if I clarified it, it might be all right. Still, it would probably take too much of my time to explain it. Ten minutes is not a lot of time to get anything said in. I'll probably just end up changing my subject.

To be really accurate, we would probably have to consider the same conversation, this time between student and teacher:

I'm not sure if it is possible to deal with a topic like inflation in a ten minute speech. So many terms such as "marginal propensity" would have to be explained that it might be best to select another subject. I find it very difficult to get much said in a ten minute speech.

So, even within our conversational style, there are varying degrees of formality. Contrast "just end up changing my subject" with "might be best to select another subject." In all four examples, the

[11]*Ibid.*, p. 308.

speakers have let the occasion and the audience determine the appropriate style.

impressiveness

Style should not only be clear and appropriate, it should also be vivid and impressive. Impressive language depends on a frame of mind. It depends on a fresh, incisive way of viewing the objects one is speaking about. New relationships are seen and explored, made clear and vivid. One critic suggests that image-making (one of the elements of impressiveness which we shall discuss in detail later) is synonymous with imagination. Imagination may be the key to all the elements of impressiveness. Two examples serve to demonstrate this point. They are both from Wendell Phillips' speech, "The Scholar in a Republic," delivered in 1881.[12] At one point he mentions Ralph Waldo Emerson, suggesting that Emerson's characteristically quiet words were powerful explosives against the prejudices of his time. He terms Emerson "[t]hat earthquake scholar at Concord, whose serene word, like a whisper among the avalanches, topples down superstitions and prejudices. . . ." We are a bit startled by two such disparate objects as an earthquake and a scholar placed side by side. We are impressed with the newness of the comparison.

Consider Phillips' fresh way of viewing the naturalness of the growth and development of the American Republic and the great power inherent in that naturalness:

> English common-sense and those municipal institutions born of the common law, and which had saved and sheltered it, grew inevitably too large for the eggshell of English dependence, and allowed it to drop off as naturally as the chick does when she is ready. There was no change of law, no thing that could properly be called revolution, only noiseless growth, the seed bursting into flower, infancy becoming manhood. It was life, in its omnipotence, rending whatever dead matter confined it. So have I seen the tiny weeds of a luxuriant Italian spring upheave the colossal foundations of Caesars' palace, and leave it a mass of ruins.

[12]Parrish and Hochmuth, *American Speeches*, pp. 349, 335.

Impressiveness of word choice may be obtained through the use of: (1) concrete language; (2) imagery; and (3) metaphor and simile.

CONCRETE LANGUAGE

Concreteness is closely linked to accuracy. Specific verbs, rather than general ones, not only name an action, but they describe concretely the manner of the action; for example, "spoke" is a general verb, "whispered," "shouted," "muttered," "mumbled" are more specific. When possible, it is effective to use a verb that carries within itself the force of a descriptive, adverbial modifier; for example, instead of "ran quickly," say "fled," "rushed," "sprinted."

Concrete nouns tend to evoke a more specific image: "bird" is general; "robin," "crow," "sparrow" are specific. They tend to present a definite picture to the listener's mind. Concrete adjectives function in the same way. Precise adjectives such as "friendly," "generous," and "sympathetic" are more effective than "nice." The more clues the speaker can give his audience about his exact meaning, the greater his chance of making his point.

IMAGERY

Imagery may be defined as the use of words designed to make the listener respond with his sensory apparatus as he would if he were actually around the objects to which the speaker refers. As we noted earlier, the word "imagined" contains the central key to the term "image," for the response to an image is a replica of an actual sense impression. Check your responses to the following images: "cold as ice," "quick as lightning," "smooth as silk."

Through verbal images we can capture the representation of seven general types of sense impressions: (1) those we see (visual); (2) those we hear (auditory); (3) those we smell (olfactory); (4) those we taste (gustatory); (5) those we feel through the sense of touch (tactile); (6) those we feel through bodily movements (motor); and, (7) those we feel through muscle sense (kinesthetic).

Both the speaker and the listener participate in the use of imagery. The listener's understanding of what the speaker says is strengthened by his own activity in responding to the image. The speaker is creative when he uses an image and asks the listener to be creative also, to be an active participant in the speech. Consider these images:

1. We will not be stampeded into the dark night of tyranny.
2. . . . our political parties must never founder on the rocks of moral equivocation.
3. . . . we must take care not to burn down the barn to kill the rats.
4. The road we travel is long, but at the end lies the grail of peace. And in the valley of peace we see the faint outlines of a new world, fertile and strong. It is odd that one of the keys of abundance should have been handed to civilization on a platter of destruction.
5. No nation can longer be a fortress, lone and strong and safe. And any people, seeking such shelter for themselves, can now build only their own prison.
6. From Stettin in the Baltic to Trieste in the Adriatic, an iron curtain has descended across the Continent.[13]

What happens when you read these passages? Let us consider only the first example. "Dark night" suggests primarily a visual image, although one would also have to account for all other associations the hearer might have. "Stampede" suggests a visual image (running cattle), an auditory image (sounds of pounding hoofs), an olfactory image (the smells associated with running cattle, dust), and a sense of movement. In fact, "dark night" and "stampede" operate together, not as separate images; a stampede in the daytime would not have precisely the same associations.

[13]The first four examples are from *The Major Campaign Speeches of Adlai E. Stevenson, 1952* (New York: Random House, Inc., 1953), pp. 226, 104, 20, 22. By permission. The fifth example is from Wrage and Baskerville, *Contemporary Forum*, p. 316. The last example is from Lewis Copeland and Lawrence Lamm, eds., *The World's Great Speeches* (2nd rev. ed.; New York: Dover Publications, Inc., 1958), p. 615.

METAPHORS AND SIMILES

Imagery and metaphor are closely related in that both are creative forces in language. Imagery seeks to *re*create, or to *create a replica*, of a sense impression. Metaphor, on the other hand, *creates* a new idea by finding a similarity in two essentially disparate ideas or objects. For example, consider some relatively simple metaphors:

> My roots are deep in our prairies
>
> this portal to the Golden Age
>
> we want no shackles on the mind or the spirit[14]

The first metaphor involves a comparison of a plant's roots with a person's basic beliefs: both bring nourishment and sustain. The second metaphor involves a comparison of an impressive, grand doorway with a way of entering into a historical period of great promise and fulfillment: each is an entryway. The third compares physical chains which bind man with ideological restraints which limit man's potential: both are restrictions. Yet, it is difficult to say that the meaning of each of these metaphors comes from either of the things compared. Rather, the metaphor's meaning is a result of the interaction of both.

Metaphor is not some trick with words, but rather a basic animating force of the language. Its animating power comes from the interaction just described. Our everyday language is deeply metaphorical: "the sun is trying to come out," "a snow-capped mountain," "table leg," "party platform," jump on the bandwagon," "tied up in knots," "don't try to pin me down to an exact meaning." Metaphors which have become so common are often called dead metaphors, because the implied comparison no longer offers new ideas.

A metaphor consists of two parts, as we have already suggested: the underlying idea, the *tenor,* and the figure of speech, the *vehicle.* The principle on which metaphor is founded is the formal principle

[14]From *The Major Campaign Speeches of Adlai E. Stevenson, 1952,* pp. 14, 10, 3. By permission.

of analogy. A metaphor is often called a compressed comparison.
One way of checking the soundness of a metaphor can also be used
to check the soundness of an analogy: break it down into a ratio
of at least four terms which could be stated in much the same way
as 2:4::6:12. If the relationship between the two sets of terms is the
same, the analogy or the metaphor is correct. How can we apply
this system to language? Recall the example we gave earlier by
Wendell Phillips:

> English common-sense and those municipal institutions born of the
> common law, and which had saved and sheltered it, grew inevitably
> too large for the eggshell of English dependence, and allowed it to
> drop off as naturally as the chick does when she is ready.

It can be broken down into the following ratio:

> sustenance which the chick draws from within the eggshell : growth
> and independence of the chick as she emerges from the shell ::
> sustenance which the early United States drew from her British
> heritage of laws and institutions : the growth and emergence of the
> new nation as an independent force.

Patrick Henry's cry: "Our chains are forged! Their clanking
may be heard on the plains of Boston!"[15] can be broken down into
the following ratio:

> chains : individual for whom they are forged :: tax on tea and
> housing militia in private homes : colonies

In metaphor, the comparison is implied; in a simile, the comparison is expressed. "She is an angel" is a metaphor, but "She is
like an angel" is a simile. Consider these examples of similes:

> [Ralph Flanders speaking of the Army-McCarthy hearings] There
> are new synthetic and irrelevant mysteries served up each day, like
> the baker's breakfast buns, delivered to the door hot out of the
> oven.[16]

> [Jonathan Edwards, the great Puritan preacher, exhorting his colo-
> nial parishioners] They [the efforts of man to help himself] are as

[15]Parrish and Hochmuth, *American Speeches*, p. 94.
[16]Wrage and Baskerville, *Contemporary Forum*, p. 303.

great heaps of light chaff before the whirlwind; or large quantities of dry stubble before devouring flames.[17]

Similes may be tested for soundness in much the same way as metaphors. Like metaphors, they are among the basic forces animating the language.

STRUCTURAL IMPRESSIVENESS

We have already suggested that order gives meaning, and that through order we see the relationships the speaker draws between his words. Now let us discuss some of the ways a speaker can develop an impressive effect through manipulation of order. We shall discuss briefly the techniques of emphasis, contrast and antithesis, suspense, and variety.

emphasis. If the speaker wants to emphasize a word, he generally places it either toward the beginning or at the end of a sentence. He may construct a sentence involving a hierarchy of clauses, or he may invert the usual order of construction. Consider G. Lowes Dickinson's summary of the Greek view of life: "The beauty, the singleness, and the freedom which attracts us in the consciousness of the Greek was the result of a poetical view of the world. . . .[18] Why didn't he say: "In the consciousness of the Greeks, the beauty, the singleness, the freedom . . . ?" Because the key words are "the beauty, the singleness, the freedom"; that is, the qualities of the Greek view constitute the most important piece of information. They come before the prepositional phrase for emphasis.

Not only position helps determine emphasis—parallel structure is also a key means for emphasizing, especially through repetition. A good example comes from Franklin D. Roosevelt's 1937 speech on the urgency of domestic problems:

> Here is one-third of a Nation ill-nourished, ill-clad, ill-housed—NOW!
>
> Here are thousands upon thousands of farmers wondering whether next year's prices will meet their mortgage interest—NOW!

[17]Parrish and Hochmuth, *American Speeches*, p. 75.

[18]G. Lowes Dickinson, *The Greek View of Life* (Ann Arbor: University of Michigan Press, 1958), p. 67.

Here are thousands upon thousands of men and women laboring for long hours in factories for inadequate pay—NOW!

Here are thousands upon thousands of children who should be at school, working in mines and mills—NOW!

Here are strikes more far-reaching than we have ever known, costing millions of dollars—NOW!

Here are Spring floods threatening to roll again down our river valleys—NOW!

Here is the Dust Bowl beginning to blow again—NOW!

If we would keep faith with those who had faith in us, if we would make democracy succeed, I say we must act—NOW![19]

Here both the same word and the same type of construction are repeated for maximum effect.

contrast and antithesis. To stress the contrast between two ideas or objects, the speaker might place them close together by means of antithesis. Technically speaking, antithesis may be defined as an opposition of ideas which is brought out by means of a parallelism in expression. Edmund Burke, in his speech "On Conciliation with America," says at one point: ". . . a great empire and little minds go ill together."[20] How much more effective that is than "a great empire does not go well with little minds." Another case in point is La Bruyère's comment on the court of Louis XIV:" . . . its joys are visible, but artificial, and its sorrows hidden, but real."[21] Or G. Lowes Dickinson's "The eating of the tree of knowledge drove the Greeks from their paradise; but the vision of that Eden continues to haunt the mind of man. . . ."[22] In each example, the opposition of ideas is brought out more clearly by placing the ideas close together.

suspense. Notice the suspense that is involved when the key

[19]Cited in Marie K. Hochmuth, ed., *A History and Criticism of American Public Address*, Vol. III (New York: Longmans, Green and Co., 1955), p. 511.

[20]Chauncey A. Goodrich, *Select British Eloquence* (Indianapolis: The Bobbs-Merrill Co., Inc., 1963), p. 291.

[21]As quoted in Adlai E. Stevenson, *Putting First Things First* (New York: Random House, Inc., 1960), p. 35.

[22]Dickinson, *The Greek View of Life*, p. 68.

ideas are placed at the end of a sentence. Churchill, in speaking to the House of Commons in 1955, said: "It may well be that we shall by a process of sublime irony have reached a stage in this story where safety will be the sturdy child of terror, and survival the twin brother of annihilation."[23]

The speaker may also heighten suspense even more through the use of a somewhat longer and more complex periodic sentence structure. Notice how the audience has to wait for John Bright's full meaning until the end of this sentence.

> By adopting that course [negotiation] he would have the satisfaction of reflecting that, having obtained the object of his laudable ambi-tion—having become the foremost subject of the Crown, the director of, it may be, the destinies of his country, and the presiding genius in her councils—he had achieved a still higher and nobler ambition: that he had restored the sword to the scabbard—that at his word torrents of blood had ceased to flow—that he had restored tranquility to Europe, and saved his country from the indescribable calamities of war.[24]

variety. The law of change is one of the laws governing atten-tion. Sentence variety, both in type and in length, appeals to at-tention. Recall the sentences of conversation. We do not always think in sentences of six words in length, nor do we always think in declarative sentences. We question. We use imperatives. Note the variety in length of sentence in this passage from Adlai Steven-son's speech "Ordeal of the Mid-Century":

> History has not stood still for us. Instead it has moved faster than ever before, and with the development of the H-bomb and the ferment of revolution spreading from Asia to Africa, history's dizzy pace shows no signs of moderating.
>
> *   *   *
>
> There was a time, and it was only yesterday, when the United States could and did stand aloof. In the days of our national youth Wash-ington warned against "entangling alliances," John Adams spoke of that "system of neutrality and impartiality" which was to serve

[23]*The Eloquence of Winston Churchill*, ed. F.B. Czarnomski (New York: The New American Library of World Literature, Inc., 1957), p. 190.

[24]As cited in J.A.K. Thompson, *Classical Influences on English Prose* (New York: Collier Books, 1962), p. 122.

us long and well, and Jefferson enumerated among our blessings
that we were "kindly separated by nature and a wide ocean from
the exterminating havoc of one quarter of the globe." But those
days are gone forever.[25]

For variety in both length and type, recall this portion of
Daniel Webster's reply to Hayne. Hayne argued in 1829 that the
states had a right to nullify acts of Congress that they deemed uncon-
stitutional. Webster argued that, on the contrary, the Constitution
established itself as the supreme law of the land:

> The Constitution has itself pointed out, ordained, and established
> that authority. How has it accomplished this great and essential end?
> By declaring, Sir, that *"the Constitution, and the laws of the United
> States made in pursuance thereof, shall be the supreme law of the
> land, any thing in the constitution or laws of any State to the con-
> trary notwithstanding."*
>
> This, Sir, was the first great step. By this the supremacy of the Con-
> stitution and laws of the United States is declared. The people so will
> it. No State law is to be valid which comes into conflict with the
> Constitution, or any law of the United States passed in pursuance of
> it. But who shall decide this question of interference? To whom
> lies the last appeal? This, Sir, the Constitution itself decides also,
> by declaring, *"that the judicial power shall extend to all cases arising
> under the Constitution and laws of the United States."* These two
> provisions cover the whole ground. They are, in truth, the keystone
> of the arch! With these it is a government; without them it is a
> confederation.[26]

To separate style from thought would be virtually impossible here,
because thought is revealed through style.

style and purpose

Now that we have discussed the characteristics of effective oral
style and have suggested ways by which the speaker can develop his
own style, let us determine how style can be utilized as a means of

[25]Adlai E. Stevenson, *Call to Greatness* (New York: Harper & Row, Publishers, 1954), p. 3.

[26]Parrish and Hochmuth, *American Speeches*, p. 221.

persuasion through which the speaker can achieve his purpose. We must explore four interrelated aspects of language: sense, feeling, tone, and intention.[27]

Sense. The speaker speaks to say something.

Feeling. The speaker has some attitude, some feeling for what he is saying.

Tone. The speaker recognizes his relationship to his audience in what he says.

Intention. The speaker sets up certain effects he is endeavoring to promote.

For the speaker, intention governs the other aspects. Notice the difference in intent evidenced in the word choice of what Cerf terms "conjugating irregular verbs":[28]

a. I look younger.
   You are well preserved.
   She must have had her face lifted.
b. I am stimulated by talking to successful people.
   You are a celebrity chaser.
   He is a snob.

Let us explore more closely three examples from British philosopher Bertrand Russell. Notice the tone and intention of the following passages.

1. Here he is discussing the philosophical tenet that there can be nothing real, or, at any rate, nothing known to be real, except minds and their thoughts:

Such an argument, in my opinion, is fallacious; and of course those who advance it do not put it so shortly or so crudely. But whether valid or not, the argument has been very widely advanced in one form or another; and very many philosophers, perhaps a majority, have held that there is nothing real except minds and their ideas. Such philosophers are called "idealists." When they come to explaining matter, they either say, like Berkeley, that matter is really noth-

[27]I.A. Richards, *Speculative Instruments* (Chicago: University of Chicago Press, 1955).

[28]Bennett Cerf, "Trade Winds," *Saturday Review of Literature* (September 4, 1948), p. 4.

ing but a collection of ideas, or they say, like Leibnitz . . . that what appears as matter is really a collection of more or less rudimentary minds.[29]

2. Here he is reminiscing about a friend, novelist Joseph Conrad. He is telling of their first meeting:

> At our very first meeting, we talked with continually increasing intimacy. We seemed to sink through layer after layer of what was superficial, till gradually both reached the central fire. It was an experience unlike any other that I have known. We looked into each other's eyes, half appalled and half intoxicated to find ourselves together in such a region. The emotion was as intense as passionate love, and at the same time all-embracing. I came away bewildered, and hardly able to find my way among ordinary affairs.[30]

3. Here he warns of the dangers of nuclear armaments:

> Is all this to end in trivial horror because so few are able to think of Man rather than of this or that group of men? Is our race so destitute of wisdom, so incapable of impartial love, so blind even to the simplest dictates of self-preservation, that the last proof of its silly cleverness is to be the extermination of all life on our planet? . . . I cannot believe that this is to be the end. I would have men forget their quarrels for a moment and reflect that, if they will allow themselves to survive, there is every reason to expect the triumphs of the future to exceed immeasurably the triumphs of the past. There lies before us, if we choose, continual progress in happiness, knowledge, and wisdom. Shall we, instead, choose death, because we cannot forget our quarrels? I appeal, as a human being to human beings: remember your humanity, and forget the rest. If you can do so, the way lies open to a new Paradise; if you cannot, nothing lies before you but universal death.[31]

About each passage let us ask a question: In the first, do we have an elementary knowledge of one view of what is real? Yes, because the

---

[29]Bertrand Russell, *The Problems of Philosophy* (New York: Oxford University Press, 1959), pp. 14–15. First published 1912.

[30]Bertrand Russell, *Portraits from Memory* (New York: Simon and Schuster, Inc., 1956), p. 89. © 1951, 1952, 1953, 1956 by Bertrand Russell. By permission. Permission for rights outside the U.S. granted by George Allen & Unwin Ltd.

[31]*Ibid.*, p. 238.

language *accurately* conveys that information. Do we sense in the second, the depth of the friendship between Russell and Conrad? Yes, because the language *sensitively* conveys Russell's attitude. In the third, do we grasp the importance of the decision we are urged to make? Yes, because the language states it with *vitality* and *force*. In each instance, we have a sense of fitness, of appropriateness of language. Each statement has a different intention. To be sure, all three have the same basic function—to convey information. The first states the facts of the matter. The second not only states the facts, but also demonstrates Russell's feeling toward the subject of his discourse. The third states a case, reveals what Russell thinks about what he says and, at the same time, indicates how the listener (or hearer) should respond.

To demonstrate more fully the relationship between purpose and style, consider the "War Message" delivered by President Franklin D. Roosevelt on December 8, 1941. He was speaking to a joint session of Congress, asking for recognition of a state of war, when he said:

To the Congress of the United States:

Yesterday, December 7, 1941—a date which will live in infamy— the United States of America was suddenly and deliberately attacked by naval and air forces of the Empire of Japan.

The United States was at peace with that nation and, at the solicitude of Japan, was still in conversation with its government and its Emperor looking toward the maintenance of peace in the Pacific. Indeed, one hour after Japanese air squadrons had commenced bombing in Oahu, the Japanese Ambassador to the United States and his colleague delivered to the Secretary of State a formal reply to a recent American message. While this reply stated that it seemed useless to continue the existing diplomatic negotiations, it contained no threat or hint of war or armed attack.

It will be recorded that the distance of Hawaii from Japan makes it obvious that the attack was deliberately planned many days or even weeks ago. During the intervening time the Japanese government had deliberately sought to deceive the United States by false statements and expressions of hope for continued peace.

The attack yesterday on the Hawaiian Islands has caused severe damage to American naval and military forces. Very many American lives have been lost. In addition American ships have been reported torpedoed on the high seas between San Francisco and Honolulu.

Yesterday the Japanese government also launched an attack against Malaya.

Last night Japanese forces attacked Hong Kong.

Last night Japanese forces attacked Guam.

Last night Japanese forces attacked the Philippine Islands.

Last night the Japanese attacked Wake Island.

This morning the Japanese attacked Midway Island.

Japan has, therefore, undertaken a surprise offensive extending throughout the Pacific area. The facts of yesterday speak for themselves. The people of the United States have already formed their opinions and well understand the implications to the very life and safety of our nation.

As Commander in Chief of the Army and Navy I have directed that all measures be taken for our defense.

Always will we remember the character of the onslaught against us.

No matter how long it may take us to overcome the premeditated invasion, the American people in their righteous might will win through to absolute victory.

I believe I interpret the will of the Congress and of the people when I assert that we will not only defend ourselves to the uttermost but will make very certain that this form of treachery shall never endanger us again.

Hostilities exist. There is no blinking at the fact that our people, our territory, and our interests are in grave danger.

With confidence in our armed forces—with the unbounded determination of our people—we will gain the inevitable triumph—so help us God.

I ask that the Congress declare that since the unprovoked and dastardly attack by Japan on Sunday, December 7, a state of war has existed between the United States and the Japanese Empire.[32]

Three "actors" emerge from the speech:

Japan (air squadrons, government, ambassador)

United States of America (we the people, our people, American ships, Congress of)

I (the President)

Notice how each of the actors performs certain specific actions and in specific orders:

Japan squadrons had commenced bombing
attacked (repeated six times)

[32]Parrish and Hochmuth, *American Speeches*, pp. 507–9.

United States *was* attacked, *was* (at peace), *was* (in conversation),
    and so on.
      (lives) *have been* lost
      will remember, *will* defend, *will* make very certain,
        will gain (the inevitable triumph)

I   believe
    assert
    ask
    declare

Note especially the progression: the President believes, asserts, stops
to ask, and only then declares. What kinds of adverbs are used; that
is, how is the action described?

Japanese actions	in infamy
	deliberately
	suddenly
United States actions	at peace
	in conversation
	always (will remember)
	very certainly
	well (understand)
	(have) already (formed)
President's action	(no adverbial modifiers)

The emphasis in this speech is on different kinds of action. Heavy
reliance on adverbial modifiers lends significance to the precise
nature of the action performed by each actor and tends to charac-
terize two very sharply defined opposite groupings—exactly what the
President needed to achieve when speaking to a nation suddenly
and unexpectedly involved in war.

    The key word is "attack." After picturing the United States in
conversation, trying to negotiate, he reinforces his central idea (the
key word) by constantly repeating it. Instead of saying "Last night
Japanese forces attacked Hong Kong, Guam, the Philippine Islands,
Wake Island, and Midway Island," he chooses to say:

Last night Japanese forces attacked Hong Kong.
Last night Japanese forces attacked Guam.
Last night Japanese forces attacked the Philippine Islands.
Last night the Japanese attacked Wake Island.
This morning the Japanese attacked Midway Island.

The repetition, the stylistic strategy helped Roosevelt make it abundantly clear that this declaration of war was necessitated by a widespread attack "extending throughout the Pacific Area." Reread the speech to determine other ways in which the President prepared the nation for war, how he worked to fulfill his purpose in delivering the speech.

Let us discuss briefly one more example of the way in which a speaker worked to achieve his purpose. Abraham Lincoln, in the closing portion of his "First Inaugural Address," wanted to be concise, simple, and affectionate.[33] He wanted to be understood distinctly by all the people and to present himself as a peacemaker rather than a troublemaker, one who wanted to save the Union, not destroy it. Let us compare Secretary of State Seward's original suggestion with Lincoln's text as it was actually delivered. Through this comparison we can see more clearly how Lincoln directly tried, through word choice, to accomplish his purpose.

Secretary Seward's suggestion:

> I close. We are not we must not be aliens or enemies but countrym fellow countrymen and brethren. Although passion has strained our bonds of affection too hardly they must not be broken they will not I am sure they will not be broken. The mystic chords of memory which proceeding from every ba so many battle fields and patriot so many patriot graves br pass through all the hearts and hearths all the hearths in this broad continent of ours will yet harmo again harmonize in their ancient music when touched as they surely breathed upon again by the better angel guardian angel of the nation.[34]

Lincoln's final draft:

> I am loath to close. We are not enemies, but friends. We must not be enemies. Though passion may have strained, it must not break our bonds of affection. The mystic chords of memory, stretching from every battle-field, and patriot grave, to every living heart and hearth-stone, all over this broad land, will yet swell the chorus of the Union, when again touched, as surely they will be, by the better angels of our nature.

"I close" is abrupt and states an obvious fact. "I am loath to close" reveals a frame of mind; he is sorry that he can not continue

[33]*Ibid.*, p. 69.

[34]*Ibid.* Facsimile of the original suggestion of Seward.

speaking with his audience. "We are not enemies, but friends" is positive, simple, direct, and kind. "We are not, we must not be aliens or
enemies but fellow countrymen" is more negative, and "aliens" and
"countrymen" are less direct. "Though passion may have strained,
it must not break the bonds of affection" places "strain" and "break"
close together to heighten the contrast. The Seward version allows
them to be further apart. Seward says "Passion has strained" but
Lincoln tempers his language to "passion may have strained."
Seward's "I am sure they will not be broken" interjects the speaker
as an asserter; Lincoln is talking with, not at, his audience. "Every
battlefield, and patriot grave" is stronger than "so many battle
fields." Lincoln places "patriot grave" close to "every living heart
and hearthstone" to provide a more direct contrast than Seward's
"from . . . so many battle fields and . . . so many patriot graves . . .
pass through all the hearts and all the hearths in this broad continent." The more concise statement more directly links the living
and the dead. "Will yet again harmonize" is a shade more negative
than Lincoln's "will yet swell the chorus . . ." "[B]y the better angels
of our nature" is much more personal than "by the . . . guardian
angel of the nation." And so Lincoln worked through personal tone,
unifying imagery, word choice, and syntax to achieve directness,
simplicity, and warmth; that is, to fulfill his purpose.

style and the three modes of proof

One of the best ways the speaker can work to achieve his purpose through style is to become aware of the dimensions of language. When we discussed connotative and denotative meaning we
began to discuss these dimensions. Recall our discussion of the
relationship between words and things. Words act as a means of
cataloguing the things, events, and processes in our environment.
The key word is "catalogue." As Leighton puts it: "Language is a
means of categorizing experience."[35] The ways in which we categorize experience through language shape our ideas, beliefs, prejudices, and aspirations. Roughly speaking, the ways we categorize

---

[35]Clyde Kluckhohn and Dorothea Leighton, "Language and the Categorizing of Experience," in *The Language of Wisdom and Folly*, ed. Irving
J. Lee (New York: Harper & Row, Publishers, 1949), p. 266.

experience correspond to the ways we offer proof. Just as, ultimately, one cannot separate the modes of proof one from the other, we cannot, in the end, separate the dimensions of language and response.

Because of the complex nature of human response, it is not accurate to say, "When I think, I think, and when I feel, I feel." We conceive of ideas, have feelings toward them, and pass value judgments on them—often all at the same time. Recognizing then the limitation of what we are about to say, let us discuss the ways in which the speaker works to choose language suitable to the types of proof he uses by exploiting the logical, ethical, and emotional dimensions of language.

Before we look at some specific examples of referential words used in substantive proof, it cannot be too strongly emphasized that total context (the situation, the persons involved, and so on) determines how a word functions; context determines, in the long run, the point at which a referential meaning becomes emotive. Recall the language used in the examples we gave of logical proof: "On December 20, 1606, the Susan Constant, Godspeed, and Discovery set sail from London for Virginia under the command of Captain Christopher Newport." Contrast that version with the following: "On December 20, 1606, that glorious year in American history, three gallant ships set sail from London filled with fearless men seeking new lives in Virginia under the command of that courageous seaman, Captain Christopher Newport." Or contrast, "Talleyrand was born at Paris on February 2, 1754 into a family well known in the court," with "The clever and completely unscrupulous Talleyrand . . ." or with "Talleyrand was born on February 2, 1754 into a family who, for several generations, had been sound but undistinguished servants of the king." Or contrast "Dylan Thomas was twenty years old when he published his first book of poems," with "Dylan Thomas was only twenty years old when he published his first book . . . ," or with "Dylan Thomas was twenty when he published what he termed 'the record of [his] individual struggle from darkness towards some measure of light.' " In each instance, we would say that the meanings are largely denotative because they are predominantly referential in function. They refer the listner to substantive things.

Almost any word can be used to express our emotions, but we have, by convention, set certain words aside for that purpose.

When the speaker deals with motivational proof he becomes more concerned with this specific class of words. A good example of emotive words is in the speech by Marc Antony in Act Three of *Julius Caesar:*

> He was my friend, faithful and just to me;
> But Brutus says he was ambitious,
> And Brutus is an honourable man.
> He hath brought many captives home to Rome,
> Whose ransoms did the general coffers fill;
> Did this in Caesar seem ambitious?
> When that the poor have cried, Caesar hath wept;
> Ambition should be made of sterner stuff:
> Yet Brutus says he was ambitious,
> And Brutus is an honourable man.
> You all did see that on the Lupercal
> I thrice presented him a kingly crown,
> Which he did thrice refuse. Was this ambition?
> Yet Brutus says he was ambitious,
> And, sure he is an honourable man.
> I speak not to disprove what Brutus spoke,
> But here I am to speak what I do know.
> You all did love him once, not without cause;
> What cause withholds you then to mourn for him?
> O judgement! thou art fled to brutish beasts,
> And men have lost their reason. Bear with me;
> My heart is in the coffin there with Caesar,
> And I must pause till it come back to me.[36]

Emotive words are deliberately used to excite feelings. Antony, here the persuasive speaker, appeals to the basic interests and instincts of his hearers. He appeals to the audience's indignation. Indignation is generally aroused when we think someone hasn't gotten "what's coming to him." Caesar, according to Antony, did not deserve to be killed. He was not "ambitious." He was "faithful" and "just" to his "friends." He "wept" for the "poor." Most of the words have rather specific emotive connotations.

Recall the words deliberately designed to excite feelings in Henry Grady's word picture of the Confederate soldier returning to his home after the Civil War. Because of Grady's conscious effort,

[36]Neilson and Hill, eds., *The Complete Plays and Poems of William Shakespeare*, p. 1031.

his audience, which was Yankee to the core and included Northern generals, was moved to make favorable responses:

> Think of him as ragged, half-starved, heavy-hearted, enfeebled by want and wounds; having fought to exhaustion, he surrenders his gun, wrings the hands of his comrades in silence . . . and begins the slow and painful journey.[37]

Just as some words elicit specific emotions, others, by convention, represent ethical values and judgment. It should be noted that although valuative words are often emotive, not all emotive words are valuative. Evaluative words generally claim a greater degree of objectivity than do emotive utterances. Recall the words of Henry Clay in 1850 when, as Nichols puts it, "he came out of retirement to add his prestige and his wisdom to a cause more important than himself—and in minimizing man, he elevated him":[38]

> . . . what is an individual man? An atom, almost invisible without a magnifying glass—a mere speck upon the surface of the immense universe—not a second in time, compared to immeasurable, never-beginning, and never-ending eternity. . . . Shall a being so small . . . so fleeting, so evanescent, oppose itself to the onward march of a great nation, to subsist for ages and ages to come—oppose itself to that long line of posterity which, issuing from our loins, will endure during the existence of the world? Forbid it God! Let us look to our country and our cause, elevate ourselves to the dignity of pure and disinterested patriots, wise and enlightened statesmen, and save our country from all impending dangers. What if, in the march of this nation to greatness and power, we should be buried beneath the wheels that propel it onward. What are we—what is any man worth who is not ready and willing to sacrifice himself for the benefit of his country when it is necessary?[39]

As the speaker works to clarify his reason for speaking, he realizes that certain words help him achieve that purpose more directly and efficiently than others. As he becomes aware of the

[37]Parrish and Hochmuth, *American Speeches*, p. 454.

[38]Marie Hochmuth Nichols, *Rhetoric and Criticism* (Baton Rouge: Louisiana State University Press, 1963), p. 9.

[39]*Ibid.*, pp. 9–10.

dimensions and resources of language as means of persuasion, he has progressed substantially toward acquiring an effective oral style.

oral and written style

Generally, when we have talked about style in this chapter, we have specifically mentioned oral style, and for a very good reason. When we are reading a book or an article, we may choose our own pace. If we find a word that we do not understand, we can stop, look it up in a dictionary, and then go on reading. If a whole passage is not clear, we can reread it a number of times until we understand it more fully. When we are listening, however, we cannot go back to rehear, we cannot hurry away to a dictionary and then come back to the speech. We cannot pause at our own leisure to reflect on what the speaker is saying. Thus, although the writer need not be concerned with making his ideas *instantly intelligible*, this must be the speaker's vital concern.

Because of this necessity, several features of oral style make it somewhat different from written style. We shall discuss four: (1) oral style must be quickly comprehensible; (2) it must be more direct than written style; (3) it must contain more restatement; and (4) it must be easily spoken. We have already suggested why oral style must be quickly comprehensible—mainly because of the temporal nature of the speech act. This is not to suggest that the speaker use only simple, monosyllabic words. However, the speaker should carefully analyze his audience to determine what words its members are likely to know. If he thinks they may not be readily aware of a word's meaning, he must, either by context or by definition, work to ensure their understanding of it. Thus, there need be no difference between oral and written style in the selection of words. But, because his audience is listening rather than reading, the speaker must doubly ensure that he is easily comprehended.

The speaker confronts his audience; thus, quite often there is more direct reference to time, place, and occasion than there is in writing. He speaks directly to its members; they listen to him *while* he is speaking. He sees his audience most of the time unless he is speaking on radio or television, and even then, an audience of some kind is often present; for example, the reporters at the Nixon-Kennedy debates of 1960, or a small group of office workers, colleagues, and others when Franklin Roosevelt gave his fireside chats. Because the speaker is addressing his audience directly, he tends to use more personal pronouns than he would when writing (except personal essays or letters). Here, of course, degree of formality would determine, both in oral and in written style, the directness of the words chosen.

Because of the temporal aspect of speech, oral style often contains more repetitions than does written style. Avoiding repetitiousness requires a high degree of originality on the part of the speaker. Although his main idea should be repeated to ensure comprehension, it must not be repeated verbatim or it may become monotonous. Ideas must be *restated*, rather than simply repeated.

Since the speaker is saying his words aloud, they should be easily speakable. A formal speech is no place to experiment with tongue twisters or words the speaker is not thoroughly used to saying. Mispronounced words may impede the flow of ideas—they certainly will not help it.

It would be misleading to suggest that good oral and good written style are antithetical. It may be true that oral style is not "abstract," that it is not "fuzzy," but all this suggests, as one critic points out, is that ". . . good oral style differs from bad written style."[40] Basically, it is not whether language is spoken or written that determines word choice and syntax, but the degree of formality/informality based on the interpersonal relationship between the speaker and his audience.

summary

Effective oral style possesses three characteristics. It must be clear. It must be appropriate. It must be impressive. To develop all

[40]Richard Murphy, "The Speech as Literary Genre," *Quarterly Journal of Speech*, Vol. XLIV, No. 2 (April 1958), 124. For an extended treatment of the differences between oral and written style, see Chapter 5, "Oral Style," in Jane Blankenship, *A Sense of Style* (Belmont, Calif.: Dickenson Publishing Co., Inc., 1968), pp. 112–25.

three characteristics the speaker must understand and utilize all the resources of language as he seeks to fulfill his purpose for speaking. Intention (purpose) determines style just as it determines all other means of persuasion which comprise his speech.

rhetorical exercises

1. Prepare a ten to fifteen minute speech in which you attempt to define an abstract concept. Pay particular attention to making your language not only clear and appropriate, but impressive as well.

2. Select some speeches in class for everyone to read and analyze in terms of style. Compare your analyses. What features did you discuss? Were there disagreements in evaluating the stylistic effectiveness of any given speech? Consider this question: How effective was the style in relation to the audience and occasion on which it was given?

3. Find a speech you think particularly vivid in style. Analyze the text of the speech carefully. Then, discuss what particular word choices and what particular sentence constructions led you to your overall impression.

4. Bring to class passages from magazines, books, newspapers, which strike you as unclear. What specific elements in the passage contribute to the lack of clarity? Then, select passages which strike you as very clear. What elements of style contribute to the clarity?

5. Select a prose passage which you feel lacks vividness and accuracy. Rewrite the passage so that it is both animated and precise. What changes did you make? Discuss each change.

6. For information concerning the fine points of style keep available a booklet on the elements of style. Which ones are in your library?

7. Discuss style as "a means of persuasion." Review the section of this chapter entitled "Style and Purpose." Then, explore the following statements of Kenneth Burke:
   a. *It* [rhetoric] *is rooted in an essential function of language itself, a function that is wholly realistic, and is continually born anew; the use of language as a symbolic means of inducing co-*

operation in beings that by nature respond to symbols. (From: *The Rhetoric of Motives*)

b. Style is a mode of "ingratiation." (From: *Permanence and Change*)

collateral readings

Blankenship, Jane, *A Sense of Style: An Introduction to Style for the Public Speaker.* Belmont, Calif.: Dickenson Publishing, Inc., 1968. See especially "Word Choice" and "Rhetorically Effective Sentences."

Joos, Martin, *The Five Clocks.* Bloomington: Publication 22 of the Indiana University Research Center in Anthropology, Folklore, and Linguistics. Also Part V of the *International Journal of Linguistics*, Vol. 28, No. 2 (1962). See especially the first two sections discussing five sorts of style.

Lee, Irving, J., ed., *The Language of Wisdom and Folly.* New York: Harper & Row, Publishers, 1949. See especially "Language and the Categorizing of Experience" by Clyde Kluckhohn and Dorothea Leighton, and "Language and the Communication of Thought" by Jean Piaget.

Nebergall, Roger, "An Experimental Investigation of Rhetorical Clarity," *Speech Monographs*, Vol. XXV, No. 4 (November 1958), 243–54.

Osborn, Michael, "Archetypal Metaphor in Rhetoric: The Light-Dark Family," *Quarterly Journal of Speech*, Vol. LIII, No. 2 (April 1967), 115–26.

————, and Douglas Ehninger, "The Metaphor in Public Address," *Speech Monographs*, Vol. XLII, No. 2 (August 1962), 223–34.

Stelzner, Hermann G., "Analysis by Metaphor," *Quarterly Journal of Speech*, Vol. LI, No. 1 (February 1965), 52–61.

Thomas, Gordon, L., "Oral Style and Intelligibility," *Speech Monographs*, Vol. XXIII, No. 1 (March 1956), 46–54.

Ullman, Stephen, *Language and Style.* New York: Barnes and Noble, Inc., 1964.

. . . all the study of [rhetoric] is ineffective
unless the other department of it be held together
by memory as an animating principle.

Quintilian

8

REMEMBERING
YOUR
SPEECH

When one speaks of memory in relationship to speechmaking, it usually refers to word-by-word memorization. The memory we are discussing here is not the relatively simple matter of short-term rote memorization. Few situations necessitate a memorized speech instead of an extemporaneous or manuscript speech. Rather, memory as it will be talked about in this brief chapter is inextricably associated with the learning process itself. It has to do with the "knowing" of one's materials and proofs, with the understanding of the relationships those materials bear to each other, and with the use of those materials and relationships in a rhetorical event.

The point of this chapter is not to provide a series of memory aids. Neither is it meant to provide a psychological or philosophical account of memory. Those who will want to explore the psychological and philosophical bases of memory will find relevant materials listed at the end of the chapter. Rather, the intention here is to point out the intimate relationship of this aspect of the speech act to all the other aspects.

Cicero told the story of Simonides,[1] who "invented" the art of memory, and it is worth recalling, for it has many useful implications. Once, at a banquet, Simonides was called from the room to receive an urgent message. While he was gone, the roof of the banquet hall collapsed and crushed all the guests beyond identification. However, when Simonides returned, he could identify each guest for burial because he could remember where each person sat at the table. Cicero comments that this led to the discovery that memory is assisted by the impression of places or localities on a person's mind. A man could remember if he could recall where things were in relationship to other things, that is, if he could recall their "places." Thus, one of the ancients taught memory through the concepts of place and relationships.

There are at least five major reasons why people have trouble with memory while giving a speech. Let us explore each of these reasons briefly:

1. The invention process has not been handled adequately.
2. The speaker has failed to prepare a clear, well-organized outline of his materials.
3. Speakers often use general, rather than specific, materials.
4. Speakers sometimes fail to select concrete, descriptive language which vividly expresses their ideas.
5. Delivery assumes too much importance to the speaker and in his stage fright he cannot concentrate properly on the materials of his speech.

relation to invention

The interdependence of an idea and its recall cannot be over-emphasized. If the speaker's ideas are strong and vital, they can be remembered more easily. It is simple to remember the ideas which

[1]Cicero, *De Oratore*, trans. E. W. Sutton and H. Rackham, 2 vols., The Loeb Classical Library (London: W. Heinemann Ltd., 1948), Book II, lxxxvi.

interest us, which we know about, which we can relate directly to ourselves and the other things we know. That is why we have stressed selection of the proper topic. If the speaker chooses a topic he is familiar with and has considered at length, he is relaxed and can recall it more easily.

A second aspect of invention is especially closely related to memory. The speaker should take extra care to omit nonpertinent materials. All proofs selected should have a definite relationship to one another. On the other hand, the speaker must include all pertinent material necessary to the full and clear explanation of each of his points.

When ideas are sharply defined, when they have been carefully developed and well explained, they are easier to remember because they are sharp and clear in the mind. The speaker has, in effect, explained his ideas, examined them, explored them until he is familiar with them; he *knows* them thoroughly.

A speaker should dwell on each idea when preparing a speech until it becomes distinct from all other ideas. Principal and subordinate ideas should then be distinguished so that it is obvious how one idea supports another. The speaker must consider each specific support to determine how his evidence operates to prove the principal idea or ideas.

relation to arrangement

If the act of arrangement has been performed efficiently, memory will be still easier. As the famous Roman schoolmaster Quintilian observed, order and arrangement are strong adjuncts to memory: ". . . if your structure be what it should, the artistic sequence will serve to guide the memory."[2]

In building a brick house, the wall supports the roof, and the foundation supports them both; the roof makes the top wall of the enclosure and serves to keep out sun and rain. The windows of the house let in air and light. All components have a definite purpose which is clearly conceived as the house is built. Each part of the house is in relation to, or, indeed, in many relations to every other

---

[2]Quintilian, *Institutio Oratoria*, trans. H. E. Butler, 4 vols., The Loeb Classical Library (London: W. Heinemann Ltd., 1920–22), Book XI, 2, 39.

part; each has a definite and planned place in the whole, and serves the whole.

Every building is erected for a purpose: to serve as a home, a gas station, an office building, and so on. Sometimes a building doubles as both home and grocery, but predominantly it fulfills one major purpose. In the same way, the speech is concentrated on a definite purpose. All materials in the speech are unified around the purpose and serve to activate it.

To create a speech, one takes a few elements from many and creates a unified, organic whole, centered around a single idea. The whole and all its parts are devoted to the function of developing and presenting that one idea.

Through reading about a speech topic, a conscious awareness should be formed of the associations between ideas and perceived patterns of organization. Read the following statements, then close the text and try writing the points down.

1. Many advantages are to be gained from increasing federal support to higher education.
2. Loan funds that exist for students often charge a high rate of interest.
3. The total of above-average students kept from college by a lack of finances is about 150,000 per year.
4. Corporations, although extending their gifts to higher education, are not increasing them rapidly enough and their gifts are often highly restrictive.
5. About half of the top 24 percent of high school graduates do not enter college.
6. Current scholarships are often too small and many times are restrictive. Moreover, a small percentage of colleges offers the bulk of scholarship funds.
7. Only the federal government can provide a stable financial base.
8. The states themselves do not have adequate finances to handle this problem.
9. Of those who do not enter college, most give financial problems as the reason.
10. Alumni gifts, although increasing, represent only a small portion of the sum needed.

Could you remember most of them? Probably not. Now, try reading the ideas in this order:

1. About half of the top 24 percent of high school graduates do not enter college.
2. Of those who do not enter college, most give financial problems as the reason.
3. The total of above-average students kept from college by a lack of finances is about 150,000 per year.
4. Current scholarships are often too small and many times are restrictive. Moreover, a small percentage of colleges offers the bulk of scholarship funds.
5. Loan funds that exist for students often charge a high rate of interest.
6. The states themselves do not have adequate finances to handle this problem.
7. Corporations, although extending their gifts to higher education, are not increasing them rapidly enough and their gifts are often highly restrictive.
8. Alumni gifts, although increasing, represent only a small portion of the sum needed.
9. Only the federal government can provide a stable financial base.
10. Many advantages are to be gained from increasing federal support to higher education.

Now close the text and see how many you can write down. Probably more, not only because you have now read the list twice, but also because there is a more readily grasped sequence to follow. That is, in effect, what memory is—the mastery of material in an orderly sequence.

relation to detail

Many times, speakers are general in their preparation rather than specific. Concrete specific details are often easier to remember because they bring a particular image to mind. Compare the following lists:

a large midwestern city	Cleveland, Ohio
a house	a red brick, two-storied house
a famous statesman	John Adams

about ten years ago	in 1962
Yellowstone National Park is very large.	Yellowstone National Park is as large as the states of Delaware and Rhode Island put together.
writers of western novels	writers of western novels such as Luke Short and Ernest Haycox

Specific names, dates, and places should be used when feasible so that both the speaker and his audience know exactly what he is talking about. Both concreteness and specificity help the speaker to "center" and clarify an idea. The use of an example is often helpful for the same reason. The speaker and the audience can remember the specific illustration more easily.

Amplification of an idea, describing a point in more detail to make it vivid, enlarging upon an idea for emphasis—all tend to make the point more memorable, mainly because they force the speaker to clarify.

relation to style

We have already used the word's "memorable language" in the chapters on style. The two main qualities of easily remembered language, clarity and vividness, are achieved largely through precision. The speaker must be sure he is saying exactly what he wants to say and that, in fact, he is "saying" all he can say. Every speaker, if he is earnest, is constantly learning and practicing so that his words will become precise, effective tools.

One of the techniques a speaker can develop is the *reiterative pattern*. The repetitive technique makes it easier for him to remember his speech and will tend to make it more memorable for his audience. The reiterative pattern can be developed in a number of ways: parallel structure, repetition of key words, alliteration, assonance, and rhyme-sound repetition. One of the speeches which almost every one remembers is the "Gettysburg Address." Why is it so easily remembered? In large part, because Lincoln was a master of the reiterative technique. Note just this short passage from that speech:

> *Four score* and *seven* years ago our *fathers* brought *forth* on this *continent*, a *new nation, conceived* in liberty, and dedicated to the *proposition* that all men are *created* equal.
>
> Now we are *engaged* in a great *civil war*, testing whether that (nation), or any (nation) so (conceived) and so (dedicated), can long *endure*. We are met on a (great) battle-*field* of that (war). We have come to (dedicate) a *portion* of that (field), as a *final* resting *place* for those who here gave their *lives* that that (nation) might *live*. It is altogether *fitting* and *proper* that we should do this.[3]

Key words which have been repeated are in parentheses. Examples of alliteration and assonance have been italicized. The reiterative pattern provides clarity and emphasis which aid both the speaker and the listener.

The reiterative pattern requires willingness to spend time on one's speeches, and patience to work painstakingly with language. It is not easily achieved, but its effectiveness is unmistakable.

relation to delivery

Although we will discuss effective delivery at some length in the following chapter, mention should be made here of stage fright and memory. Although the beginning speaker may have prepared adequately, he sometimes becomes so conscious that he is giving a speech that he cannot remember all he wants to say.

Recall one of the early concepts of Chapter 1—that of the speech as a dialogue. The speaker is speaking *with* his audience, not *at* them. As he is speaking, members of the audience are responding, sometimes by nodding agreement or smiling, sometimes by frowning when they disagree. This is exactly what happens in a conversation. The speaker and the person or persons he is talking with are actively sharing a common experience; they are thinking about the same information, sharing the same ideas, trying to decide on a course of action. In short, the speaker is not alone with

[3]Wayland Maxfield Parrish and Marie Hochmuth, eds., *American Speeches* (New York: Longmans, Green and Co., 1954), p. 306. Italics and parentheses added.

his materials. He is sharing them. As the beginning speaker develops this concept of dialogue in his own mind, as he begins to concentrate solely on the *ideas* he is is trying to get across, stage fright diminishes. The speaker then has more time to remember what he wants to say because he is concentrating on his ideas—not on overcoming nervousness.

summary

From the moment the speaker selects his topic and begins his preliminary planning, he has started memorizing his speech. As he seeks to clarify his ideas, draw relationships between them, and set them forth in vivid language, he is storing the facts and materials of his speech for use when it is delivered. Memory is, quite literally, the storehouse of knowledge. The storehouse is only as sturdy as the materials that have gone into it. In the end, the best advice for the beginning speaker is, in Cato's words: "Hold to your matter and the words will come."[4]

rhetorical exercises

1. Prepare a ten minute speech on any topic of your choice and deliver it with the aid of only one note card. How did you and the other members of the class go about preparing for the assignment? What methods seemed to work? Which ones did not work?

2. For those of you who would like to explore the basis of short-term memory, check through the following journals for a variety of articles: *Journal of Verbal Learning and Verbal Behavior, Perceptual and Motor Skills, Quarterly Journal of Experimental Psychology, Psychonomic Science, Psychological Bulletin, Canadian Journal of Psychology,* and other journals recommended by your teacher.

[4]As cited in Donald Lemen Clark, *Rhetoric in Greco-Roman Education* (New York: Columbia University Press, 1957), p. 67.

3. Devise lists similar to the one given in the chapter and test them in class to see which kinds can best be remembered.

4. Try to recall how you learn new materials. Compile a list of ways in a class discussion. Why are some more effective than others?

5. Read Cicero's *De Oratore*, Book II. What is to be gained by recalling the traditional incident which supposedly prompted Simonides to invent the art of memory?

6. Recall your last speech. Did you have trouble trying to remember it? If you did, analyze your process of invention, arrangement, and style. Was part of the problem caused by a lack of planning during the early stages of preparation? Or did a problem of delivery interfere with your remembering what you wanted to say? Once the source of the problem has been determined, concentrate on trying to correct it in your next speech.

7. After your next speech, test the audience's recall of your subject. How much of it did they remember? Would they have liked more details? More examples? A clearer outline? More amplification? More sharply focused ideas? More precise choice of words?

8. As you listen to the speeches in class, how carefully do you pay attention to what you hear? A good listener is one who gives his full and undivided attention to what he is hearing. Frequently the best listeners are also the best speakers, because they pay attention, they concentrate more fully on what they are doing. Are you a good listener?

collateral readings

Benjamin, B.S., "Remembering," *Mind*, Vol. LXV, No. 259 (July 1956), 312–31.

Bilodeau, Edward, *et al.*, "Long-term Memory as a Function of Retention Time and Repeated Recalling," *Journal of Experimental Psychology*, Vol. 67, No. 4 (1964), 303–9.

Furlong, E.J., "Memory," *Mind*, Vol. LVII, No. 255 (January 1948), 16–44.

Hargis, Donald E., "Memory in Rhetoric," *Southern Speech Journal*, Vol. 17 (1951), 114–124.

Harrod, R.F., "Memory," *Mind*, Vol. LI, No. 201 (January 1942), 47–68.

Holland, R.F., "The Empiricist Theory of Memory," *Mind*, Vol. LIV, No. 216 (October 1945), 464–86.

Hoogestraat, Wayne E., "Memory: The Lost Canon?" *Quarterly Journal of Speech*, Vol. XLVI, No. 2 (April 1960), 141–47.

Malcolm, Norman, *Knowledge and Certainty*. Englewood Cliffs, N.J.: Prentice-Hall, Inc., 1963.

Martin, C.B., and Max Deutscher, "Remembering," *Philosophical Review*, Vol. LXXV, No. 2 (April 1966), 161–96.

Munsat, Stanley, *The Concept of Memory*. New York: Random House, Inc., 1967.

Peterson, Lloyd R., "Short-term Memory," *Scientific American*, Vol. 215, No. 1 (1966), 90–95.

———, "Short-term Verbal Memory and Learning," *Psychological Review*, Vol. 73, No. 3 (1966), 193–207.

Scandura, Joseph M., and William Roughead, Jr., "Conceptual Organizers in Short-term Memory," *Proceedings of the 74th Annual Convention of the American Psychological Association* (1966), pp. 33–34.

Schwartz, Fred, and Patricia M. Perkins, "Structure and Uncertainty in Immediate Memory," *Psychological Reports*, Vol. 18, No. 2 (1966), 561–65.

Winans, James A., *Speech-Making*. New York: Appleton-Century-Crofts, 1938. See especially Chapter 20, "Further Study of Delivery," pp. 404–22.

. . . one speaks not merely to express himself,
but to accomplish some purpose with relation
to a given audience, and this conception
must determine the nature of the speaker's delivery.

Wayland Maxfield Parrish

9

DELIVERY

Delivery can be regarded as the culminating feature of the rhetorical act. During delivery the communicator's preparatory experience becomes actualized. The speaker is engaging in dialogue with some listener, about some idea, in certain language, with some purpose in mind, and in answer to some situation that called for a public response.

The physical basis of delivery—vocal and bodily behavior—is dominated by the meaning of what the speaker says and why he says it. His overt physical behavior reveals something of his total inner experience, since the communicative need prompted him to initiate a speech act. It is modified and shaped by that experience. Delivery, then, is not a separate act, but *one aspect of the whole speech act.* Thus, as with all other aspects of the speech act, "meaning must be regarded as an integral feature of delivery."[1]

Observe what goes on in conversation. People are animated.

[1] Karl R. Wallace, "A Modern View of Delivery," in *Essays in Honor of Claude M. Wise,* ed. Cj Stevens (Hannibal, Mo.: Standard Printing Co., 1970), p. 165.

They punctuate and emphasize their points with gestures. They look directly at the people they are talking to. The whole body is responsive. They are constantly alert to what they are saying. In short, they feel a lively sense of communication.[2]

In conversation, attention is focused on the ideas under discussion, not on the way in which they are delivered. The animation and directness of a speaker are taken for granted; they are not a feature overlaid on his material, but rather grow out of the vitality of his ideas and his eagerness to express them to his audience. He is responsive to his ideas, to his audience, and to himself.

Have you ever seen a conversation conducted between two people reading their speeches aloud from manuscript? Or between two people who have memorized word-for-word what they want to say to each other? Very probably not, because in conversation we talk about the things we are interested in, the things we know about, the things we think other people should know about. The speaker's mind is constantly alert to his subject. His "speech" is not something copied down or memorized and then spewed back like a tape recording. His mind deals directly and vigorously with his ideas as he discusses them with his audience. Further, he is physically direct. He looks at the people he is talking to. How else can he know whether or not they are dealing with his ideas, and responding to what he is saying? This kind of physical directness is termed eye contact.

The speaker's mental alertness, reflected in his eyes and in his face, gives the audience the cue that he wants to communicate, that he is interested in his topic, that he is concerned with what he is saying. In conversation, we let our audience know what we think and feel about our topic, what we think they should be feeling—anger, indignation, and so on.

The point of all talk is to convey ideas, and anything which impedes that is a barrier to communication. To say that delivery as such is good or bad is misleading. Delivery should not stand out; the ideas of the speech are foremost. However, if the speaker does not speak loudly enough, his ideas cannot be heard, no matter how important they are. If his pronunciation is not acceptable, his articulation not clear, if he mumbles, the ideas may be lost or misunder-

[2]James A. Winans, *Speech-Making* (New York: Appleton-Century-Crofts, 1938), p. 26.

stood. If he is speaking too rapidly, no one in his audience will have time to think about what he is saying. The "natural manner," as Whately terms it, is not spontaneously adopted.[3] It is developed by hard work and much practice and, in the final analysis, the natural manner is determined, as are all other rhetorical processes, by the subject, the audience, and the occasion.

If a speaker fully understands the concept of speech as a dialogue, that a speech is part of a circular pattern of stimulus ⟶ response ⟶ stimulus ⟶ response, he will begin to develop the natural manner, because he will no longer feel a sense of separateness from his audience. He will not feel separated from them because he is speaking *with*, not at, them. His listeners respond to what he says and he in turn responds to them. They are both constantly concentrating on the same idea, exploring it, moulding it, using it—together. They are experiencing a lively sense of communication.

Lest the problems connected with the process of delivery seem oversimplified, the speaker does need to recognize that he communicates his ideas through overt behavior of both an audible and visual nature. One recent experiment to determine the relationship of content and delivery to general effectiveness suggests that: ". . . delivery is almost twice as important as content in determining the general effectiveness of self-introductions and is almost three times as influential as content in determining the effectiveness of attempts to 'sell' an idea."[4] Another experiment attempted to check the effect of variations in nonfluency on audience rating of a speaker's credibility. It reports: "Generally . . . as the quantity of nonfluency presented by a speaker increases, audience ratings of perceived source credibility decrease."[5] The report goes on to clarify how it uses the term "source credibility." It involves three factors: competency, dynamism, and trustworthiness. While lack of fluency

[3]Richard Whately, *Elements of Rhetoric*, ed. Douglas Ehninger, *Landmarks in Rhetoric and Public Address* reprint edition (Carbondale: Southern Illinois University Press, 1963), p. 347. This work was first published in 1828.

[4]Paul Heinberg, "Relationships of Content and Delivery to General Effectiveness," *Speech Monographs*, Vol. xxx, No. 2 (June 1963), 107.

[5]Gerald R. Miller and Murray Hewgill, "The Effect of Variations in Nonfluency on Audience Ratings of Source Credibility," *Quarterly Journal of Speech*, Vol. l, No. 1 (February 1964), 42.

generally did not affect judgments of trustworthiness, it did affect the audience's judgment of both competency and dynamism. Much more experimentation is needed concerning the relation of delivery to content and general effectiveness. However, the kinds of experiments mentioned above indicate that, through delivery, the speaker gives a series of cues to the audience.

The speaker "tells" an audience that: (1) he is interested in his topic; and (2) he is dealing with the topic rigorously and dynamically; that is, that he knows his material, and is at ease discussing it. The end of public speaking is persuasion. To persuade others to believe any point, the speaker must seem firmly convinced of its truth himself. How can he persuade unless he delivers his speech in the manner used by persons who are speaking earnestly?

the basic elements of good delivery

In his effort to acquire effective delivery, the speaker should: (1) recognize what good delivery is; (2) observe and evaluate himself objectively; and (3) practice, first to eliminate large problems, then to refine his skill. Let us briefly discuss each stage.

RECOGNIZE GOOD DELIVERY

The main way to discover the elements of effective delivery is to observe both poor and good speakers. Try to suggest ways in which they vary. Among the many characteristics of effective delivery, the two major elements are probably directness and force.

directness. The quality of directness in conversation and in public speaking stems mainly from two sources: (1) a desire to communicate, to exchange opinions, to talk out ideas; and (2) a concentration on the ideas under discussion which allows the speaker to forget himself. Whately has commented: "The practical rule . . . to be adopted . . . is, not only to pay no studied attention to the Voice, but studiously to *withdraw* the thoughts from it, and to dwell as intently as possible on the Sense; trusting to nature to suggest spontaneously the proper emphases and tones."[6]

When the speaker has eliminated all distinct thought of himself, he can concentrate on what he has to say, on his audience, and on the relationship between himself and his audience. He can concentrate on the essential feature of communication, the sharing of an idea, attitude, or opinion. The delivery of most great speakers has been marked by their conversational powers. Consider this comment about the speaking of the great abolitionist orator, Wendell Phillips: "The *character* of his voice—the man in it—had the effect of 'finding' its auditor. It has an *intimate* tone, as if he were speaking to each one as an unknown friend. . . ."[7]

Most people manage, in everyday conversation, to convey their attitudes toward a subject in many ways—tone of voice, word choice, gesture. Why then, when we stand on a platform before an audience to give a speech, should there be a psychological compulsion to repress outward manifestations of interest in a subject we have presumably spent time and work preparing specifically for presentation?

force. Force is associated with the features often designated as "animation" and "vitality." It stems from a feeling of deep earnestness and communicates to the audience the excitement of a nervous system and a brain working at top form, stimulated by having to think rapidly and aloud, and responding with spontaneity, imagination, and vividness.

Force is motivated by deep interest in the subject. Unless ideas are animated, delivery must necessarily be dull and lifeless. A speaker can experiment with the mechanics of voice and gesture, but they represent no substitute for a strong belief in what one is saying. When beliefs are strong and clearly defined, when the speaker is confident of them, he can rely on them, just as he does in conversation, to convey his feelings and his attitudes about what he is saying. When the speaker has carried over into his public speaking the most desirable qualities of his conversational speaking, he will fully realize the content of his words as he utters them. The force of his ideas will be naturally manifested in forceful delivery.

[6]Whately, *Elements of Rhetoric*, p. 352.

[7]William Norwood Brigance, ed., *A History and Criticism of American Public Address*, Vol. I (New York: McGraw-Hill Book Company, 1943), p. 359.

OBSERVE AND EVALUATE
YOUR OWN DELIVERY

After the beginning speaker has watched and listened to the delivery of other speakers, he should evaluate himself by listening to himself as he speaks, by tape recordings of his own speech, through teacher criticism, and the criticisms of other students in the class. He should check especially for directness of communication (both intellectual directness and physical directness):

1. Is there "vivid-realization-of-idea-at-moment-of-utterance"?
2. Is there eye contact—direct and sustained?
3. Is there bodily responsiveness to what is said?
4. Does pronunciation meet acceptable standards? Is articulation clear?
5. Is there vocal variety in rate, inflection, and volume?

When the student knows what particular areas of delivery need work, he can, with the aid of his teacher, plan exercises designed specifically to help him.

PRACTICE TO ELIMINATE PROBLEMS AND REFINE SKILLS

The next step is to get as much practice as possible by speaking often and always objectively evaluating your own performance. The two basic prerequisites to effective delivery must be remembered: (1) preparedness, and (2) a genuine desire to communicate.

special problems of beginning speakers

Beginning public speakers face some special problems in delivering a speech. We shall discuss nine. By exploring the causes of the problems, their remedies will become clearer.

NERVOUSNESS

Nervousness should be viewed as a natural phenomenon, almost universally felt in the public speaking situation. The speaker's task is not easy, and some degree of tension serves to remind him of this. Insofar as stage fright is controlled, it is basically helpful. As Walter and Scott point out, certain physical changes take place during stage fright that can aid the speaker. They indicate that the body may obtain more than its usual *energy* under tension because of these changes:

1. More blood sugar, which furnishes energy, is available.
2. Insulin, which increases the permeability of the membrane surrounding the cells to the blood sugar, is secreted, with the result that more food can get inside the cells.
3. Thyroxin, a catalyst that speeds the burning of sugar inside the cells, is added to the blood stream.
4. Blood pressure increases.
5. Respiration increases.
6. The conductivity of nerves increases slightly.
7. More oxygen is available so that more fuel is burned.
8. The poisons from metabolism are removed more speedily so that toxicity and fatigue are reduced.[8]

Thus, the speaker can potentially think more rapidly about his subject when he is on his feet delivering the speech than he can when sitting quietly in an armchair.

Channeled tension can therefore help the speaker. In great part, uncontrolled stage fright is due to improper emotional conditioning. The beginning speaker often thinks of himself as apart from his audience. He is speaking and they are listening. We have stressed throughout this book the idea of a public speech as part of a dialogue, carried on between people engaged in *sharing* ideas. Both the speaker and his audience are thinking about the same

---

[8]Otis M. Walter and Robert L. Scott, *Thinking and Speaking: A Guide to Intelligent Oral Communication* (2nd ed.; New York: The Macmillan Company, 1968), p. 106.

topic at the same time: facing the same problems, trying to find new ways of action, evaluating both old and new ways of action. Thus, the speaker is talking *with* his audience. If he accepts this view of public speaking and is well prepared, then the undesirable features of stage fright can be controlled and the helpful and desirable features will remain.

LACK OF EYE CONTACT

The speaker fails to look at his audience mainly for two reasons: (1) he is confined to his notes because he lacks preparedness; or (2) he is suffering from stage fright. The remedy for the first problem is simply to prepare more fully and learn to use notes efficiently. We shall discuss the use of notes in detail later. The remedy for the second problem can be found in learning to accept the implications of a speech as part of a dialogue. In conversation we normally look at the people we are speaking with because we are sharing an idea, attitude, or opinion with them. We are speaking not at, but *with*, them.

When we look at people, it tells them that we are interested in them, that we are concentrating on them, that we are communicating directly with them. Eye contact is the speaker's most important means of knowing how, or whether, an audience is responding to him. The audience must be a part of the speaking situation. The very idea of communication, of moving another's mind, requires constant sharing of the speaker's ideas with those of the audience. One of the surest signs that the speaker wants to work with the members of his audience on a common problem is his direct eye contact with them.

RAPIDITY

The beginning speaker is likely to rush through the materials so he can sit down. You may have heard this question before: "Did the man run because he was frightened or was he frightened because he ran?" The point is that, by rushing, the speaker accentuates his own nervousness. When he is speaking too rapidly he has less time to think of what he wants to say, less time to consider his ideas and to perform the physical act of saying them.

The listener also needs time to discriminate between sounds, to listen, to hear and respond, to think about what has been said, to assimilate it, and to work with it. If the listener is not given the time he needs to consider the speaker's point, he may give up trying, and unless his audience is paying attention to what the speaker is saying, he has no reason to be speaking. In short, both the speaker and the audience need time to perform the communication act effectively.

HESITATION PHENOMENA

Most of our speech consists of well-learned sequences of words which make their utterance automatic. As children, most people begin to master the mechanics of speech utterance—the phrases and idioms, the conventionally used and grammatically prescribed sequences of words which soon become habits and roll off our tongues automatically. But at the same time, in near-spontaneous speech, each utterance is a creative act. Any utterance which we say for the first time and which is not an habitual response makes a great demand on our capacity for improvisation.

Speech, at the most elementary level, demands extensive mental effort. Before it takes form in speech, a meaning is something which is not yet defined. Its communication in speech requires that it be conveyed in some kind of order.

We rarely achieve a continuous flow of speech. The speaker and the listener cooperate. Listeners concentrate on the message, integrating elements of it and bridging the gaps which divide the groups of words. The speaker, on the other hand, cooperates by minimizing the gaps in the stream of words and making them coincide with semantic groups such as phrases. Pausing is as much a part of speaking as vocal utterance; it is a basic part of speech production.

Thus, pause has a specific function in public speaking. It permits delay—the time for the thought process to take place. There is no need to substitute ah, er, um, well, now, and the like. The listener will not find a pause unusual. Delay is simply a built-in feature of oral language. Most pauses go unnoticed, so there is no reason to have a continuous flow of sound while speaking. Concentrate on the ideas you are dealing with, gain confidence and a sense of rapport with your audience, and your hesitations will be no longer than the minimal delays which we have come to expect, and in fact need, in spontaneous speech.

LAZY ARTICULATION

Many beginning speakers suffer from lazy lips, tongue, and jaw; they fail to pay enough attention to manipulating the various parts of the articulatory mechanism. Most American-English speech sounds are articulated through activity of the lips and part of the tongue. These moving articulators touch fixed or relatively fixed portions of the roof of the mouth or the upper jaw. Quite often the lazy speaker has never become consciously aware of what happens physically when he speaks. Try to feel how these sounds are made: "p" as in pat; "t" as in tin; "c" as in cook; "f" as in fast; "l" as in let. Feel the various parts of the articulatory mechanism move.

However, overarticulation, an overly precise, affected way of speaking, should not be developed, because it calls attention to delivery and hense detracts from the substance of the speech. The best course of action to follow is this: simply do not become lazy about articulating sounds clearly. Make it easy for listeners to listen.

SPEAKING TOO SOFTLY

Common sense tells us that if we speak too softly, our ideas will be lost. Adequate loudness is one of the essential attributes of an effective speaker. Most problems in this respect are a result of the speaker failing to adjust to the size of room in which he is speaking and to the size of the audience in the room. Practice in speaking under different conditions will give the speaker a good sense of how loudly he must speak in any given situation.

If the speaker makes his audience work just to hear his physical sounds, it may well lose interest in trying to follow the ideas he is expressing. The same thing may happen to the speaker who lets his voice drop at the ends of sentences. Part of his message may be lost, and misunderstanding or lack of attention will surely follow.

LACK OF VOCAL VARIETY

Lack of vocal animation is also quite common among beginning speakers. If the speaker talks in a monotone, he gives no indication that one word, one idea, one point, is more important than others. When a point needs emphasis, a monotone not only fails to help establish degree of importance, but may actually conceal it altogether. The vocally unanimated speaker gives no cues that he is dealing with ideas that are interesting and dynamic.

Most people manage throughout their lives to convey vocal cues to the people they talk with. As we asked earlier, why should the speaker repress animation in the public speaking situation? There is no reason to believe that this problem cannot be cured with a little effort and concentration on the speaker's part.

Once again, the speaker can refer himself to conversation. He can listen to the animation of his own voice—to changes in volume, pitch, inflection, and length of pauses. He can become consciously aware of what he sounds like. A large portion of the problem is lack of awareness.

A student suggested a good technique to develop this awareness. He and his roommate had been practicing their speeches for class with the aid of a tape recorder. Between speeches the recorder continued to run. When the tape was played back, they were surprised to hear the contrast between the animated, dynamic way they spoke in the short conversations between speeches and the flat, unanimated way they delivered the speeches. The student was so enthusiastic about his discovery that we decided to try an experiment with the whole class, with the aid of the tape recorder. As each person stood ready to deliver his speech he was casually engaged in a short stretch of conversation. Then he gave his speech. In the following class session we played the tape back and asked each person to note the biggest difference he observed between the conversations and the speeches. Almost without exception, recognition of the problem proved to be the best way to alleviate it.

Just as a moving object generally attracts more attention than a still one, so an animated voice is a powerful attention-maintainer and an effective cue-provider.

A speaker must learn to use all his resources, among which is his voice. No amount of discovery and practice, however, will really aid a speaker who persistently selects topics for which he has no interest or enthusiasm. An animated voice and animated ideas usually go hand in hand.

LACK OF BODY MOVEMENT

Just as an animated voice proves to be an attention-getter, so a body that is responsive to what is being said shows the audience what the speaker thinks of his subject, and often demonstrates that he *is* thinking about it. An emphatic gesture underlines, emphasizes, and points to the idea being discussed. Gestures grow naturally from a desire to use all available means to communicate. They should grow out of the subject matter rather than being imposed mechanically from without.

Lack of body movement generally stems from a kind of self-consciousness that the beginning speaker sometimes feels before an audience. When he becomes at ease in his part of the dialogue, his body and voice are free to return to the totality of communication felt in the most stimulating conversations. That includes an animated voice and unconscious gestures.

Check to become aware of precisely what you do when speaking. For example, the speaker who walks up to the speaker's stand and places his hands on either side of it often never gets around to gesturing at all. If the hands are free, there is a much greater chance that the speaker will feel compelled to use them. The speaker who clutches his notes or manuscript also has less chance of gesturing naturally.

Since gestures grow out of the substance of the speech, the relationship between a responsive body and animated, dynamic ideas cannot be overemphasized. Speakers should respond not to a rule which says it is helpful if speakers gesture, but to the reality that communicating an important idea is hard work, and that the speaker must use all available means of persuasion. The responsiveness of the speaker to what he is saying is surely one such means.

INCORRECT USE OF NOTES

Some notes are generally necessary in extemporaneous speaking to insure accurate and complete statements of fact and opinion, but they should be used unobtrusively. Improperly used notes detract from the import of the speech. If they become a barrier between the speaker and the audience, encouraging him to speak to his notes rather than to communicate directly, then they will seriously impede efficient communication.

Notes may also facilitate spotty and/or jerky eye contact, and in this way also become a barrier to communication. A common sense rule is to use notes not as a crutch, but as an aid to facilitate the understanding of what you are saying. The speaker who has carefully prepared, who knows what he is talking about, can use them in this advantageous way.

Each speaker should develop his own method of using notes. However, several general suggestions can be made:

1. Make sure the notes are easy to read; otherwise, they are more hindrance than help. Type them if you can; write them legibly in ink if you do not type.
2. Many speakers find it helpful to underline, capitalize, or write in a different color ink the key words and ideas so that they stand out clearly.
3. Most speakers find it more helpful to put their notes on small note cards when they are giving an extemporaneous speech. They are less conspicuous and easier to handle than large sheets of paper.
4. Make sure you include only essential material in your notes. Either a sentence or a topic outline is helpful. Generally, materials quoted verbatim should be included unless they are very short quotes which are easily remembered.

5. When you practice, practice with your notes. Be very familiar with them before you give your speech.

6. Never spend most of your time looking at your notes. You are not speaking to them, but to your audience.

Following are examples to illustrate several different kinds of notes students have used when delivering speeches in the classroom.

The direct quote:

Carl N. Dengler. Out of Our Past: the Forces that

Shaped Modern America (N.Y.: Harper and Row,

Publishers, 1959), p. 154.

"The very act of being a reformer reveals something

of one's assumption about the world. To work for re-

form implies a belief in the efficacy of making the

world over, even if only in a small corner. To

Americans tomorrow always looked better than today,

not because today was so miserable, but because it

was so good."

The topic outline ("Capitalism in Early Modern Times"):

Card one

I. Commerce and a capitalism

   A. Geographical discovery and trade

   B. Mercantilism

   C. Money lending

II. Industry and capitalism

   A. Fading out of medieval craft guilds

   B. Domestic or putting-out system

   C. Factory system still lacking

III. Agriculture and capitalism

   A. Breaking down of manorial system

   B. Production for profit

   C. Enclosure movement

The complete sentence outline ("Four Aspects of the Puritan Tradition"):

I. The morality and religion of the Puritans was not based wholly on ignorance and superstition.

   A. Their fundamentalism can be viewed as intellectually respectable.

   B. Their fundamentalism did not have to reject biology, physics or historical criticism to maintain its dogma.

II. The Puritan belief in democracy and limited government was rather ambiguous.

   A. They were not really democrats, but they possessed an "irrepressible democratic dynamic."

   B. They supported constitutionalism and limited government, but they were sometimes tempted to claim almost unlimited power.

Card three

Card Three

III. The Puritan "business ethic" was a relatively

stable force in their economy.

   A. They believed in the moral dignity of work.

   B. They believed that leisure was to be dis-

trusted.

   C. They were suspicious that the poor were

ungodly.

Card four

IV. Education, from the beginning, held an important

place in Puritan life.

   A. They set up schools and colleges.

   B. They produced a variety of different kinds

of literature.

You may want to use more or different kinds of notes. However, keep in mind that they are for the purpose of facilitating, not impeding, communication.

summary

Public speaking is merely an extension of that most familiar act, conversation. Delivery of the speech is the natural culmination of all that has happened since some need in his environment caused the speaker to decide to speak. The physical aspects of delivery are shaped by the speaker's purpose, meaning, and all of the work that has gone before: the act of rhetorical invention, the arrangement of materials, the wording of those materials in appropriate language, and becoming thoroughly aware, through memory, of what he wants to say. At the same time, if the delivery is ineffective, the work that has preceded it has little chance of succeeding—for all aspects of the speech act are intimately bound together, and only as they operate efficiently together can the speaker participate in public dialogue with full effectiveness.

If the other steps in the rhetorical act have been handled successfully and the speaker fully understands the *nature* of the communicative act, then there should be few problems with delivery. If there *are* any, first carefully analyze the causes of the problem and then patiently practice to eliminate them and refine your skill in delivery.

When analyzing the causes of the problems, keep firmly in mind how most problems are related to other aspects of the rhetorical process, especially invention. Cicero's conception of delivery, written in the *De Inventione* when he was a young man, is still one of the most useful. By delivery, he meant "the control of the voice and body in a manner suitable to the subject matter and the style."[9]

rhetorical exercises

1. Give a ten minute extemporaneous speech on a topic which will necessitate the use of notes.

2. Listen to the speakers in class. Comment on their delivery. Are they direct, animated, conversational? Why or why not?

3. Listen to a tape of yourself. Check your own communicativeness according to these criteria:
   a. *Intellectual directness.* Is the speaker vividly aware of what he is saying? Is he trying to talk his ideas out directly with his audience?
   b. *Physical directness.* Can he easily be heard? Is he speaking at an understandable, pleasant rate of speed? Does he have vocal

[9]Ray Nadeau, "Delivery in Ancient Times: Homer to Quintilian," *Quarterly Journal of Speech*, Vol. 1, No. 1 (February 1964), 58.

variety? Does he have clear articulation? Is his pronunciation of an acceptable standard? Does he maintain eye contact? Is his body responsive?

Compare your own notes with those of the other members of the class and the teacher. Keep your own checksheet or, if the teacher uses a critique sheet, see if you are improving or if the same problems continue to occur.

4. Make another tape later in the class term. Compare the two tapes according to the criteria set forth above. Have you improved? Where do you still need work?

5. If you still find it difficult to gesture, to move freely when speaking, try giving a demonstration speech where you have to move; for example, explain badminton strokes or golf swings.

6. If you still have voice and articulation problems, ask your teacher for some additional reading materials. Several of the books listed in the collateral reading list will be especially helpful.

7. Whenever you can, consider the delivery habits of all the speakers you hear, both good and bad, to become aware of their practices and to gain insight into why some are effective and some are not.

collateral readings

Bronstein, Arthur J., and Beatrice F. Jacoby, *Your Speech and Voice*. New York: Random House, Inc., 1967.

Bryant, Donald C., and Karl R. Wallace, *Fundamentals of Public Speaking*, 4th ed. New York: Appleton-Century-Crofts, 1969. Part IV.

Clevenger, Theodore, Jr., A Synthesis of Experimental Research in Stage Fright," *Quarterly Journal of Speech*, Vol. XLV, No. 2 (April 1959), 134–45.

Ellingsworth, Huber, and Theodore Clevenger, Jr., *Speech and Social Action: A Strategy of Oral Communication*. Englewood Cliffs, N.J.: Prentice-Hall, Inc., 1967. See especially pp. 146–80.

Hildebrandt, Herbert W., and Walter W. Stevens, "Manuscript and Extemporaneous Delivery in Communicating Information," *Speech Monographs*, Vol. XXX, No. 4 (November 1963), 369–72.

Parrish, W.M., "The Concept of 'Naturalness,'" *Quarterly Journal of Speech*, Vol. XXXVII, No. 4 (December 1951), 448–54.

Walter, Otis M., and Robert Scott, *Thinking and Speaking*, 2nd ed. New York: The Macmillan Company, 1968. See especially Chapter 6, "Developing Confidence," and Chapter 7, "Delivering Ideas."

Winans, James A., *Speech-Making*. New York: Appleton-Century-Crofts, 1938. Chapters 2 and 20.

III

ANALYSIS
AND
CRITICISM

. . . things that are true and things that are just
have a natural tendency to prevail over their opposites,
so that if the decisions of judges are not what
they ought to be, the defeat must be due
to the speakers themselves and they
must be blamed accordingly.

Aristotle

10

EVALUATING
SPEECHES

We live in a world of speeches. We are literally surrounded by them
—by short ones when we listen to the opinions of our friends or to
television commercial announcements, by medium-length ones in
meetings and on radio and television, and sometimes by tediously
long ones by visiting lecturers, professors, and politicians at election
time. In each situation, we are confronted with statements and we
evaluate them. Are they fact or opinion? If opinion, whose opinion?
We listen carefully to those whom we respect and not so carefully
to those we do not. Sometimes we merely switch off a dial, if not a
physical dial on a television set, then the mental one in our mind.
When we do, we are criticizing a speech.

When the beginning speaker learns to evaluate consciously
the speeches he hears, he is progressing toward being an effective
speaker. When he understands *why* he likes or dislikes the speeches
he hears, he begins to know how to give a better speech. Thus,

prerequisites to becoming a good speaker are learning to listen carefully and developing a sense of critical awareness. In this chapter, let us first list guide questions which suggest criteria for evaluating a speech, then read a speech given by a student to two different audiences and evaluate it in terms of these criteria.

guide questions

First, questions are raised about all five parts of the rhetorical act: invention, arrangement, style, memory, and delivery. Then questions are asked about total effectiveness. Although, as a critic, you may have more specific points, these questions will serve as guidelines for your further analysis.

RHETORICAL INVENTION

1. Does the speaker proceed from assumptions and hypotheses which are reasonable and fair?
2. Is the speaker's analysis of his topic clear and comprehensive?
3. Does the speaker deal with a reliably established body of material? Is his supporting material accurate? Sufficient? Recent? Well-documented?
4. Does the speaker substitute emotional appeals for substantive proof?
5. Does the speaker examine the implications of his suggestions?
6. Does the speaker's reasoning meet appropriate tests of validity? Were the materials of the speech internally consistent?
7. Does the speaker reflect creativity in the suggestions he offers for consideration?
8. Did the speaker seek to establish identification with his audience?
9. Did he work effectively to gain and maintain the attention of his audience?
10. Was the speech appropriate for this particular audience?

ARRANGEMENT

1. Was the speaker's purpose either made explicit or clearly implied?
2. Was the speaker's thesis clear?
3. Was there a clear indication of the structural progression which the speaker intended to take?
4. Was the speech well-organized into a clearly definable pattern?
5. Were there clear transitions to aid in developing the points of relationship between ideas?

STYLE

1. Was the language clear?
2. Was the language appropriate to the speaker, audience, and occasion?
3. Was the language vivid? Did it animate the ideas of the speech?
4. Was the language persuasive?

MEMORY

1. Did the speaker appear to be at ease with his materials?
2. Did he appear to know his subject matter?

DELIVERY

1. Was the speaker alert to what he was saying? Was there vivid-realization-at-moment-of-utterance?
2. Was the speaker responsive to his audience? Was there a lively sense of communication?
3. Was there directness of communication? Did the speaker have good eye contact with his audience?

4. Was the speaker animated? Was he facially animated? Vocally expressive? Bodily responsive?

5. Were the mechanical aspects of delivery satisfactory? Did the speaker speak loudly enough? Slowly enough? Were his voice and articulation adequate?

6. If notes or a manuscript were used, were they used effectively? Or did they present a barrier between speaker and audience?

TOTAL EFFECTIVENESS

1. Did the speaker exhibit a real desire to communicate? Did he show real interest in and knowledge of his subject?

2. Did the speaker use the best available resources to help him convey his point? Or were there better resources available?

3. Was the audience responsive to the speaker and what he had to say?

4. Would you like to hear the speaker again?

Although we have listed some guide questions to be used in evaluating a speech, in the end the most important questions are these: How well did the speaker carry out what he said or implied that he wanted to do? Did he use effective means of persuasion?

sample criticisms

Below are two versions of basically the same speech given by a college student in 1964. Her first audience was a group familiar with the topic, whose members had read a lot about it and had discussed it at length. They had some training in the use of evidence and argumentation. The second audience was much more general. Its members were not especially familiar with the topic and probably had no previous specific information on it. Some had taken the beginning course in public speaking.

After each paragraph of speech text there is commentary to explain what the student hoped to accomplish and how she hoped to accomplish it. Specific strategies are also criticized for strengths and weaknesses. It is best, in both cases, to read the entire speech and then reread it with specific criticisms. The criticisms are indented to set them apart from the speeches themselves.

FIRST VERSION

The Report of the U.S. Office of Education, which was meant to express the policy of the United States at the Twenty-second International Conference on Public Education said: "Education in the United States is based on two fundamental principles: (1) every person has an equal right to educational opportunities; and (2) an educated citizenry is essential to freedom and human welfare." However, as the House Committee on Education and Labor commented on this statement: "Opportunities for public education vary widely in the United States." Because there are these wide variations in educational opportunity, I believe that the Federal Government should guarantee an opportunity for higher education to all qualified high school graduates.

> [Here the speaker sets the stage for her topic. She pictures the differences between aims and actualities and orients the audience to her particular position. Next, she makes a clear statement of purpose and of her position on the topic. Because of the nature of her audience (they had come with the specific intention of working with the topic of her speech immediately after it was given), the speaker included no attention-getter as such. The opening for basically the same speech given to another audience (much more general and less attentive to the subject) is very different. This illustrates that, from the opening remarks, the materials of the speech must be adapted for the particular audience hearing it. Note that the speaker does not immediately begin with her thesis sentence, "I believe that the Federal Government should guarantee an opportunity for higher education to all qualified high school students." The reason for this is very simple. The audience needs a chance to begin thinking about the topic. Thus, it is seldom a good idea to have your thesis sentence as the *first* sentence of your speech. It is too important to be missed.]

I accept as rationale the statement of the Rockefeller Panel on Education that: "Federal programs in education now exist on a large scale and take a great many forms." Thus, it is not a question of whether or not the Federal Government should give aid to higher education, but what direction that aid should take.

[Notice how she begins to limit her topic by saying that she is not going to discuss the issue of whether or not the Federal Government *should* aid higher education, which is a topic in itself, but rather will discuss what *direction* the aid should take. The inclusion of an authority is probably a very wise move. The statement that "it is not a question of whether or not the Federal Government should give aid . . . but what direction that aid should take" is not one with which all her audience could agree. Given the added support of an important educational program, they might consider it more carefully.]

Before telling you why I think the Federal Government should *guarantee* an opportunity for higher education, I'd like to explain the way in which I'm using several terms. By "guarantee an opportunity," I mean a rather specific program to give formal assurance by means of federally underwritten loans. By "higher education," I don't mean just college, but post high school education at all institutions designated as institutions of higher education in the *Education Directory* published by the Department of Health, Education, and Welfare. This would, for example, include further work at trade and vocational institutions. By "qualified students," I mean simply those students who are competent to meet the entrance requirements of accredited institutions of higher education.

[Here she explains *how* she is using the key terms in her thesis sentence to clarify what she means for her audience. Consider the definition of "opportunity." It could have been rather ambiguously defined as "chance." That, in effect, is not a definition because it does not move the audience any further toward understanding the meaning of the term. Rather, the speaker is quite explicit about the meaning: "a formal assurance by means of federally underwritten loans." Again she limits her topic to more manageable proportions. She also takes care to point out that she is not just talking about college education when she says "higher education." On many topics and in many kinds of speeches, the speaker need not define so many terms, but whenever terms are being used in a specific way or may be unclear to the audience, they should be defined.]

I believe that there are three main reasons why you should agree with my position on this matter: (1) Many qualified high school graduates do not receive a higher education because they lack the necessary finances. (2) Existing sources cannot provide this needed financial assistance. (3) Only the Federal Government can provide a stable financial base for needy high school graduates.

[Here the speaker points out how she will support her thesis and indicates the structural progression of her ideas. The order of materials was dictated by the particular kind of speech she was giving and the particular motivational situation. In this case the speaker limited herself to three main points in order to make it easier for her audience to remember them and to allow herself sufficient time for each. Each speaker should include as few main points as possible in his material for those two reasons.]

Under the first reason, that many qualified high school graduates do not receive higher education because they lack the necessary finances, I'll show three things: First, a large proportion of high school graduates do not attend institutions of higher education. Second, this loss is serious enough to warrant immediate action. And, third, the primary cause of this nonattendance is lack of finances.

[The speaker continues to explain how she will handle her materials and points to her line of reasoning. In this particular instance, it was especially necessary because her audience was taking notes and would later discuss her method of handling the materials. The individual situation determines how much explanation of the use of materials must be included in the speech. In all events, the aim should be for clarity. The other "graces" can be developed later. The organization should be clear without being too obviously mechanical.]

Hurst R. Anderson of the American Council of Education, in testimony before the Senate Committee on Labor and Public Welfare in 1960 said, "About half of the top 24 per cent of high school graduates do not enter college."

[The speaker supports her first point with testimony which gives information. She documents her information with name, affiliation, and year. In this case no further documentation is necessary. She uses only one support because the statement is not particularly debatable. The speaker on any subject should determine the amount of supporting material by this criterion: "How much do I have to use to establish my point?"]

This loss is serious—serious both to the nation as a whole and to the individual. Each year the nation suffers a serious economic loss because of its failure to invest in its human capital. As Theodore Schultz of the University of Chicago states: "It is a simple economic fact that increases in goods and man hours combined appear to account for only a small fraction of the yearly increase in national income. Rather, it is the increase in capital formation by education which accounts for otherwise large, unexplained increases in output."

[Again she uses one support. Here she could have usefully indicated Mr. Schultz's special competence to speak on this subject.]

But in addition to talking about national output, let's see how the seriousness of this loss is reflected in each student's potential earning capacity. The *National Education Association Journal* of January 1963 showed what the monetary loss to a student is—that the expected average lifetime earnings of college graduates was $177,000 more, 42 per cent more, than the average of high school graduates. Thus, individual students also suffer serious economic loss.

[Note the transition phrase, ". . . in addition to talking about national output, let's see how the seriousness of this loss is reflected in each student's potential earning capacity." The use of flashback with preview is a particularly good transition type. She also gives one support and uses factual material, whereas she used testimony to support her "loss to the nation" point. There are two very good reasons for the difference: (1) variety, and (2) the nature of the material. There was no specific estimate of the relationship between increases in output and increases in capital formation by education. Thus, the *relationship* between the two was stressed. Since there *was* a specific dollar estimate, it was useful to use the estimate itself. When the factual material consists of monetary averages, it is relevant that she include the date in her documentation. This particular speaker avoided one of the pitfalls which can be distracting in the presentation of documentation. Note that she cited, not the *NEA Journal*, but the *National Education Association Journal*. Avoidance of letter names is important with an audience which may not know the journals in the particular field being discussed. Citing the *NEA Journal* to a general audience may be the same as or worse than using no citation at all.

> Some of the audience may pause to wonder what the letters
> stand for and miss the substance of the quotation. An audience
> should never be allowed to stray from the point being made
> in a speech. A lack of understanding or misunderstanding of
> the point may result.]

While we can talk in averages about economic loss, there is no way
to measure the loss of new ideas, of human fulfillment which occurs
when this tremendous potential is not realized.

> [Again the speaker uses flashback ("while we can talk in aver-
> ages about economic loss") plus moving forward ("there is
> no way to measure . . ."). Although the same type of transition
> device is used, the pattern of wording need not be the same.
> Here, the speaker deals with a generalization. While the state-
> ment in this case may well be self-evident, some good testimony
> would have strengthened it considerably. It is a telling point,
> not easily refuted, and should have been amplified and used
> to better advantage.]

The primary cause for these qualified students not attending college is lack of finances. According to the 1962 Office of Education
financed Project Talent, each year between 100 and 200,000 able
high school graduates who have high aptitude and interest in college
—that is they *are* motivated—fail to continue their education primarily because of the lack of money. Dr. Algo Henderson of the
American Council of Education substantiated this fact in his report.
Dr. Henderson stated that other studies he had seen, including those
by the American Youth Committee, the President's Committee on
Higher Education and the Commission on Financing Higher Education, concurred with this statement. The problem is not clearing
itself up, for a survey financed by the National Science Foundation
in 1958 reported almost the same total of above average students
kept from college by lack of finances—about 150,000 annually. Thus,
although the figures *do* vary somewhat, the consensus seems to be
that approximately 125,000 to 150,000 students do not continue
their education because of lack of finances.

> [Notice how the speaker keeps the language close to the lan-
> guage she used when explaining what she was going to do, both
> for clarity and for emphasis. Here she uses more than one
> piece of supporting material because of the controversial
> nature of the point; that is, some may deny the validity of a
> specific survey. The quoted material from Henderson very
> neatly adds a number of studies to the picture, without re-

quiring additional citations. It is also a short way to get enough material to support her point. In the Henderson citation note that the speaker gave his credentials rather than the specific source of the quotation. In this case the credentials did more to establish his authority (which is her point) than the name of the magazine containing the quotation would have done. The speaker should avoid cluttering his speech with unnecessary documentation by determining what part of the citation best establishes the worth of the particular support he is using. Observe how the speaker points out the obvious fact that the figures vary. The reason for this is twofold: (1) for accuracy; and (2) because some of the audience may be so concerned with the variance that they fail to move ahead with the speaker to her next point. The speaker should always tell the audience exactly *how* he arrived at his statement.]

Now, I realize there may be other reasons why students do not attend institutions of higher education and I am not denying that. However, existing evidence seems to indicate that the *primary* reason is financial.

[The speaker acknowledges a qualification to her material. If she hadn't, the thought would probably have occurred to her audience. Care in limiting the claim which she says her materials establish aids in establishing *ethos*, trustworthiness.]

Existing sources cannot provide this needed financial assistance. Here, I'd like to show you first, that they *are* not, and secondly, that they *can* not.

[She establishes her next major point, explaining again how she intends to handle her materials. She is careful to bring the audience along with her on every point. She makes certain that it is she who determines the method of handling the materials.]

During one five year period (1955–1960), according to the *World Almanac*, total scholarships issued increased only 10 per cent. Meanwhile, according to the Department of Health, Education, and Welfare, total enrollment increased 25 per cent over this same five year period. Because of this situation, it is not surprising that hearings before the House of Representatives in 1963 revealed that the percentage of undergraduates benefiting from college-administered assistance programs, the major source of student support, has declined in recent years.

[Here the speaker feels it is necessary to use three pieces of evidence. This passage is a bit overdocumented, but this was hard to avoid, since each bit of material did come from a different source. Try not to let the documentation, however brief, interfere with the flow of ideas. In this particular case, where the materials were to be examined in detail by the audience, it was hard to avoid. Use good judgment in other situations.]

Not only are scholarships too few and often too small, but also they are concentrated among a relatively small number of schools. The availability of scholarships, in other words, simply does not match the available room in colleges. Elmer D. West pointed this out in his book *Financial Aid to the Undergraduate* which was published in 1963. He states that besides the concentration of scholarship money in schools which may not be able to use it, only six states gave over 80 per cent of the financial assistance to higher education today, thus showing a concentration of scholarship funds geographically.

[Again the speaker uses the device of a summary of what has been said juxtaposed with a preview or moving forward. The date in the documentation is important here. The audience might like to know who Elmer D. West is. However, in this case, the speaker was presenting strictly factual material which could easily be checked in a variety of sources; she was not using West as an authority (although she could have) but as the source of factual material. Giving the size of the average scholarship would have helped support her statement that "not only are scholarships too few [which she did deal with] and often too small. . . ." The material is easily available and could have been inserted without seeming obtrusive; for example, "and the average scholarship of $_____, often too small. . . ." The second sentence of this passage is also not clear.]

Moreover, although some loan funds are available, they cannot hope to solve the problem because of restrictions, high interest rates, and the necessity, in some cases, to start repayment immediately. The *Congressional Digest* of October 1963 pointed out that although the American Medical Association, for instance, has loans for college students, these students must have completed their undergraduate education. Most other loans have some kind of "strings attached." The *Digest* also pointed out that most bank loans require either collateral or a co-signer who does have the collateral—both may be unavailable to a poor student. Even the United Student Aid Fund, the largest private organization designed to underwrite bank loans made to students, requires that colleges must match these funds; thus, if the college is not willing to match them, or cannot, then the student cannot use the loan.

> [There could have been a smoother transition between her point concerning scholarships and her point concerning loans, although as she gave the speech, she did *vocally* emphasize "loan funds" to emphasize the fact that she was no longer talking about scholarships. Her decision to use a series of examples to illustrate various limitations in three different kinds of loans was wise. Her use of specific names is good. A better example could have been found than the one using the American Medical Association, which would have been more representative of her undergraduate "strings attached" argument. There was no need to bring in graduate education at all. Also, there was no particular need to quote the *Digest* when saying that most bank loans require either collateral or a cosigner; it's a widely accepted fact. It was particularly good to use a variety of kinds of loan programs: (1) professionally based loan funds; (2) general bank loans; and (3) private loan funds designed specifically for loans to students. The use of the United Student Aid Fund was particularly good because it is "the largest" private organization of its sort.]

Thus, existing sources *are not* solving the problem. And, in fact, they *can not* solve it.

> [A summary with a preview used again as a transition device. The words *"are not"* and *"can not"* are italicized because the speaker was particularly careful to emphasize them vocally, both by saying them very forcefully and by pausing a little after them.]

The American Assembly at Columbia University pointed out the obvious variations in wealth among the fifty states, which are great, and that the poorer states are already making a tax effort out of proportion to their ability to pay. The House Committee on Education and Labor reported in 1960 that many states and localities have reached their fiscal limit. Thus, there is a great probability that many states have reached their fiscal limit, not only for higher education funds, but for funds of any kind. The American Assembly concluded that the states in recent years have had only from 13 to 15 per cent of the tax dollar.

[The statement that wealth varies among the states could have gone undocumented as a generally accepted fact. "The American Assembly at Columbia University pointed out the obvious variations in wealth among the fifty states, which are great . . ." is an awkward sentence in any event. It was, however, necessary to document the part of the statement: "the poorer states are already making a tax effort out of proportion to their ability to pay." It was also necessary to document the fact that "many states and localities have reached their fiscal limit." Examples might have helped, but the statement is adequate as it stands. The factual material could have been briefly interpreted for maximum effectiveness: "Thus, no matter how well intentioned the states may be, they simply have less to work with than the Federal Government." This amplification would have served two purposes: (1) to indicate very clearly that she is not blaming the states for laxity or ill will, but that they do not have sufficient tax revenues to alleviate the problem; and (2) to emphasize her point that since existing sources of income cannot take care of the program, the Federal Government should adopt the program she is advocating.]

State constitutions preclude some states from fully tapping certain tax sources, notably the property tax and personal income tax. An example is Illinois. And, since state tax systems are generally of the regressive variety, attempts to increase them are strongly resisted.

[Since these statements are based on easily checked facts, documentation was not necessary. A *brief* example was all that was necessary at this point, although possibly she could have described the practices of several other states for additional support.]

This excerpt constitutes about half the speech. The speaker went on to point out that, in addition to state revenues and the private sources of educational income she mentioned, corporations have provided funds. They represent, however, only a very small portion of the amount needed and cannot in the future be the stable bases needed to guarantee educational opportunity.

She concluded that since existing sources cannot meet the need, the Federal Government represents the most stable base on which to plan a long-range program. Federal underwriting of student loans would cost the government very little, since student borrowers have an excellent record of repaying loans. The program could operate through already existing agencies and would have the obvious advantages of increasing personal income and the gross national product, while at the same time affording personal fulfillment and producing a greater reservoir of new ideas.

> [Here are the rest of the speaker's main arguments to support her basic contention. By this time, her method of analysis, way of handling supporting material, type of outline, and simple functional style can be seen. Each speaker, of course, would handle the topic, materials, and presentation in a somewhat different way. The particular value of this speaker's method is that it is extremely clear. What lines of argument did this speaker use? What types of supporting material? As you answer these questions also consider: How would *you* have analyzed this speaker's topic? Would you have supported it in the same manner or can you think of other ways? Would you have used other lines of argument? A different method of presentation? A different sequence of materials within each main point?]

The final remarks were:

Since many qualified high school graduates do not receive a higher education because they lack the necessary finances, since existing sources cannot provide this needed financial assistance, and since only the Federal Government can provide a stable financial base for needy high school graduates, I urge you to agree with me: that the Federal Government should guarantee an opportunity for education to all qualified high school graduates.

> [In this version of the speech, since the speaker knows precisely *how* her audience will be using the materials, she closes by simply repeating her main lines of argument and by making a straightforward appeal for acceptance of the proposal. Note the difference between the summary of this speech and the summary of the other version which you will read. What type and how direct an appeal the speaker uses in closing is, of course, determined by the nature of the topic and the nature of the audience. In this instance, the speaker knew that her audience would be using the materials and arguments of her speech very directly and at length. Therefore, her appeal could be very direct and very short.]

We shall include and discuss only a small portion of what is basically the same speech as it was delivered to a *general* audience. The purpose is to demonstrate the concept of audience analysis and how it determines the speaker's way of handling his materials. Basic differences between the two speeches will be noted. Pay particular attention to the amount of amplification several of her ideas receive in the second speech and the care taken to bring her audience more directly into the speech. Also note the slightly more colloquial style and the attempts at attention-getting which were unnecessary with the first audience.

SECOND VERSION

Every year there are from 100,000 to 200,000 able, qualified students who are denied the opportunity to attend college because they lack the money to do so: from 100,000 to 200,000 students—enough students to fill ten universities with from 10,000 to 20,000 students for one year. Remember, I said able, qualified students—students who want to go to college, who are capable of going to college but who cannot. Why? Because they aren't as lucky as we are. Because their parents can't afford to send them. Because, for a variety of reasons, they can't get a scholarship or a loan. Because a part-time job often just doesn't pay for the expenses of college. Later I will show you how, if by some miraculous chance, they could get all three: the "average" loan, the "average" scholarship, and the "average" part-time job—most of them still would not be financially able to go to college.

[Here the speaker must work harder to get the audience interested and involved in the topic. She selects one of the most startling facts of the speech and begins to build around it. The figures 100,000–200,000 are impressive in themselves, but they are made still more impressive by the speaker's amplification that the students would fill ten universities of fairly large size. As soon as possible the speaker brings the members of her audience still more directly into the speech by saying that she is talking about students "who aren't as lucky" as they are. The orientation is longer because this audience needs more time to become adjusted to the topic. In addition the materials the speaker has selected for the orientation begin to orient the audience toward her particular position. Note also that the question, "Why?" calls again for the audience to participate rather directly in the speech. They must silently answer a question. In addition, by beginning three sentences with "because," she has the device of parallel structure. Repetition produces the piling up effect of the materials which support her position. Next, these three sentences are separated from the following point, which is that *even if* the students could have the advantages of all sources, they still wouldn't be able to attend college. The parallel structure is now effectively broken by interrupting the sequence of sentences beginning with "because."]

The irony of the situation is that these are students living in a country whose government stated these two fundamental principles as the basis for education in the United States at the 22nd International Conference on Public Education: "(1) Every person has an equal right to educational opportunities; and (2) An educated citizenry is essential to freedom and human welfare." Every person has an equal right to educational opportunities. Yet most of us would agree that in reality, as the House Committee on Education and Labor has commented, ". . . opportunities for public education vary widely in the United States."

[The word "irony" helps to prepare the audience, to put it into the right frame of mind for her next words. She prepares the way for the presentation of her position by contrasting the stated principles with the realities. The word "irony" also reinforces the point. Observe how the speaker works to suggest whenever she can the things most people in the audience would agree with: ". . . most of us would agree that . . . opportunities for public education vary widely." The speaker has anticipated that most of her audience would be *against* federal aid to higher education for a variety of reasons; thus, it became important for her to proceed more slowly than before, maximizing whatever points of agreement were possible at the outset.]

It is precisely because there *are* these wide variations in opportunities, and because existing programs have done all too little to lessen them, that I believe the Federal Government should guarantee an opportunity for higher education to all qualified high school graduates.

[Here the speaker makes a clear statement of purpose and of her position on the topic. She explains briefly what led her to her position.]

Before telling you in some detail why I think the Federal Government should guarantee an opportunity for higher education, I will explain several of the terms I will be using.

[The speaker begins to define terms. This is especially necessary when the audience is uninformed about the possible differences in meanings of the terms; for instance, that the Federal Government could "guarantee an opportunity" in a variety of ways. They may never have considered a federally underwritten loan program as one possibility. The definition not only functions to clarify the term, but also, given this early, eliminates a number of proposals toward which the audience is unfavorably disposed. Because she says precisely what program she is advocating, her listeners may not consider other proposals at all.]

The substance of the arguments used in the second version of the speech was basically the same as that used in the first version. So let us proceed to the conclusion of version two.

Recently we have heard a lot about television's "vast wasteland." But, we have heard practically nothing about the 100,000 to 200,000 people each year who inhabit higher education's vast wastelands of lost human potential, lost chance for economic improvement, lost new ideas which would benefit the national welfare.

[This conclusion is much different from the brief, simply stated summary of the other version. The topic of "television's vast wasteland" was, at the time the speech was given, much discussed and argued. She uses that fact to advantage, both because she has an effective metaphor (even though the analogy is somewhat strained) and also to prove her point; that is, that if people are hearing a lot about "television's vast wasteland" how much more they should be hearing about what she terms "higher education's vast wasteland."]

This failure to invest in the most basic resource the nation has, human potential, would in any time be serious. At a time when we are competing on every front with another economic-political system, it may prove to be disastrous.

[She adds the point that if the audience is unconcerned with the problem in general, then it should be concerned with it at this particular time. Note how she continues to suggest that the audience is directly concerned with the problem, thus preparing the way for her next question.]

What can we do about this problem? Several rather specific things. We can become very much aware of the problem. We can talk about it with the people we see and we can write about it to our representative in Congress who can do something about it directly. They have expressed their good faith in dealing with the problem by increasing the amount of money in the National Defense Education Loan Fund. But the lack of sufficient funds and the restrictions on how the loans are used make the NDEA Fund at best only a partial and temporary measure.

> [The speaker is no longer *suggesting* direct involvement; rather, she questions the audience very directly by using the word "we." She offers two possible ways in which the audience can use the speech and also suggests that the majority in Congress is willing to adopt a somewhat similar plan, thereby giving added authority to the reasonableness of her proposal. This mention of the National Defense Education Act was put into the speech after another student asked, when she heard the speech being practiced: "How do you know the members of Congress would really consider such a program?"]

The realities of our system of education must coincide with the aims of our system of education. Since they do not, since large numbers of qualified high school graduates do not receive a higher education because they can't afford it, since existing sources are not and cannot provide this needed financial assistance, since the Federal Government can provide a stable financial base for needy high school graduates, and since a federally underwritten loan program for students would cost the government almost nothing, but would reap great returns both for the nation and for the individual, I hope you will agree with me that the Federal Government should guarantee an opportunity for higher education to all qualified high school graduates.

> [Note that first the speaker repeats a fact with which most of her audience would agree. Then she repeats the line of thinking which led her to her original position that "the Federal Government should guarantee an opportunity for higher education to all qualified high school graduates." She again uses parallel construction with the word "since" to effect a building-up of arguments for added strength before asking for acceptance of her position. The conclusion to this version of the speech is three times longer than that to the other version. Follow her strategy:

1. She calls attention to a problem which most of her audience has been discussing.
2. She says the problem is more serious and calls for more attention than that of "television's vast wasteland."
3. She relates her problem to the general problem of the Cold War and tries to establish just how central it is to the general scheme of things.
4. Presuming that the members of her audience are now impressed by the magnitude and the immediacy of the problem, she offers ways in which they can help. The ways call for no great effort, but are *specific* "ways" that the audience can use the speech after they have left the room.
5. She closes first with a relatively noncontroversial statement, then moves instantly into her main line of argument including: (1) the noncontroversial statement that large numbers of students are not going on to higher education; (2) the statement for which she has offered most of her support; that is, that existing sources cannot provide the money; (3) her conclusion that only the Federal Government can handle the problem; (4) a "reply" to the most often heard objection to her kind of proposal; and (5) an indication of the possible rewards her proposal could bring. Only then does she restate her position.]

Before evaluating the two speeches, one more word must be said concerning version two. We have tried to show how it is possible to attempt identification with an audience that: (1) is general in nature, and (2) is somewhat opposed to the speaker's position. The speaker works to seek some agreement before moving into more controversial areas. She works to appeal to the audience without becoming so subservient to it that she weakens her original thesis. Her strategy has been outlined for you to follow. Strategy denotes movement based on careful analysis of the situation at hand. Thus, after surveying all the available means of persuasion, the speaker selects those which best aid his purpose. The quality of the speaker's choices determines the value of the speaker's rhetoric.

There are two additional points which should be made before starting an evaluation of these speeches: (1) the speaker's use of notes; and (2) her use of visual aids. This particular speaker chose to use a general outline and small cards with all the materials she wanted to quote verbatim written out. Although the speaker could easily remember most of the quoted material without referring to the cards, she decided to read from them, particularly her "testimony," for two reasons: (1) to give added authority to the speech; and (2) to provide a change in bodily movement. When the materials were read from the cards, she was particularly careful to maintain eye contact with her audience, especially at important words or key phrases.

This particular speaker generally feels no special stage fright, and, in fact, is used to speaking to audiences, large and small. However, a few notes do provide added assurance for any speaker and allay the fears of a beginning speaker.

During the speech the speaker used one visual aid, the blackboard. To the left, figures were added up to indicate the amount of money a student could get from all sources: average scholarship + average loan + average amount earned on a part-time job. To the right were the costs of an average year of college at both a private and a public institution. Although these figures could have been handled verbally, the use of visual aids at this point operated in two ways: (1) to call attention, to underline one of her more important points; and (2) to provide a change in bodily movement. Visual aids are effective only as they serve to underline points. They should not become objects of display in and of themselves.

In general, this speaker has done an effective job. In both speeches she explains what she is going to do and then proceeds to do it. Her organization is clear and she usually has careful transitions between major ideas to show the relationship between her chief points.

One of the speech's outstanding features is the speaker's good judgment about how much supporting material each point requires. When only one piece of support is necessary, she uses only one; when more are necessary, she uses two or three. She avoids using too much supporting material, and thereby filling up her speech time with unnecessary evidence at less strategic points, and avoids using too little evidence to support her major points. The speaker also uses a variety of types of supporting material: information, example, testimony, comparison, definition, and visual aids. Thus, she does not rely on any one type of support and at the same time provides a *variety* of supporting materials which maintain attention.

In both versions of the speech this speaker considers her audience. Her first audience came to hear the speech because it was especially interested in the topic and was, in general, fairly well-informed about it. The speaker did not have to spend so much time getting its attention as she did with the second group. The first group was particularly interested in sources, so the speaker gave more detailed documentation in her first version than in the second. In the summary, the first group did not have to be told directly *what* to do with the speech; they came to the speech with the intention of using it in very specific ways. On the other hand, the second group probably needed some prodding to do something about the speech after they left the room. The speeches could have been more impressive stylistically. A speaker should first work, however, to achieve clarity; he can then work for refinements of speaking. The style of these speeches is that of simple functional prose.

Two outstanding points about this particular speaker's delivery should be mentioned. First, the speaker enjoys giving speeches. She conveys this to her audience. Secondly, this particular speaker never speaks without a real feeling of confidence in her knowledge of the topic. She is never unprepared and this confidence allows her audience to relax, feeling that it is listening to somebody who knows what she is talking about. One reason for this confidence, in addition to the fact that she is always well-prepared, is that she speaks often in classes, meetings, and formal public speaking situations. Nothing can, in the end, replace practice in aiding a beginning speaker become a polished, adept public speaker. But practice without thorough knowledge of principles generally proceeds on a hit-or-miss basis. The more a speaker knows about what *should* be done and *why* it should be done, the more efficiently he can practice to achieve the skill which makes him a vigorous and effective speaker who actively participates in making his environment the kind he would like it to be.

summary

Throughout this chapter, and the text, we have tried to stress the interrelationships among the canons of rhetoric and the dependence of the last step, the actual giving of the speech, on all the preceding ones. As the speaker understands this, he begins to acquire a rhetorical perspective.

Only so well as the speaker has chosen the *best* available means of persuasion has he made an effective speech. The available means of persuasion include all the speaker's resources: his proof, his organization of those proofs, the use of clear and vigorous language to animate his ideas, and the fluent, communicative delivery of them. In the final analysis, the key question in evaluating speeches is this: "Has the speaker chosen, from *all* the available means of persuasion, the *best* ones for his purpose?" If the answer is yes, he has effectively seen the world through a rhetorical perspective.

rhetorical exercises

1. Design a critique sheet which would be useful in the criticism of speeches given in class. What items would you include? If you already use a critique sheet in class, discuss each item thoroughly. Now that you have had supervised experience in giving speeches, does the critique sheet become more useful? How effectively does the critique reveal the total impact of the speech?

2. Listen to a contemporary speech which you attend outside of class and try rhetorical criticism. Then try to evaluate a speech you have seen on television. What differences were there between your criticism of the first speech and your criticism of the latter? Some of the questions you might want to ask are:
   a. Who spoke? Did the audience know him? Did they know him well? Was he given an introduction? Do you think the audience listened in a certain way because of who was speaking? What did the speaker reveal about himself as he spoke?
   b. Who was in the audience? Were they likely to have preconceived ideas about the topic and the speaker? About his position on the topic?
   c. Where did the speech take place? In what kind of immediate environment? In what kind of ideological environment? Did the speaker refer to the place? How did place affect the speech?
   d. At what time was the speech given? Was the time of day relevant? Time in the "life" of the problem being discussed?
   e. What was the purpose of the speech? Was it implied or expressed? Did the speaker fulfill his purpose?

f. What did the speaker say? Were his main ideas clearly stated? Were they well supported? How would you evaluate the quality of the premises on which the speech was based? Was the content appropriate for the audience?

g. Was the speech clearly organized? Was it arranged for maximum effectiveness? Were there clear transitions between ideas and internal summaries when necessary? Did he spend enough time on each point to make it meaningful?

h. Was the style clear? Appropriate to the occasion, the audience, and the speaker? Was it vivid and animated? Was it impressive?

i. Was the speaker direct and communicative? Was he fluent?

j. What was your overall impression of the speech? Would you like to hear this speaker again?

3. What can the speaker gain by reading speeches of the past?

4. What insights can the critic gain from speaking experience? Discuss your answer in class.

5. Read several speeches given by the same speaker. Were the audience, the occasion, the time, and the place reflected in the speeches? In what ways?

6. Read some criticism of famous speeches of the past. See, for example, Marie Hochmuth's "Lincoln's First Inaugural" in *American Speeches*, pp. 21–71. You might also want to look at the criticisms of famous speakers in the three volumes of *History and Criticism of American Public Address*, and in the *Quarterly Journal of Speech*.

Following is a list of works on criticism and on the nature of criticism.

collateral readings

Andrews, James, "Confrontation at Columbia: A Case Study in Coercive Rhetoric," *Quarterly Journal of Speech*, Vol. LV, No. 1 (February 1969), 9–16.

Baskerville, Barnet, "The Cross and the Flag: Evangelists of the Far Right," *Western Speech*, Vol. XXV, No. 3 (Fall 1963), 197–206.

Black, Edwin, *Rhetorical Criticism: A Study in Method*. New York: The Macmillan Company, 1965.

Brandes, Paul D., *The Rhetoric of Revolt*. Englewood Cliffs, N.J.: Prentice-Hall, Inc., 1971.

Brockriede, Wayne, and Robert L. Scott, *Moments in the Rhetoric of the Cold War*. New York: Random House, Inc., 1970.

Burgess, Parke G., "The Rhetoric of Black Power: A Moral Demand," *Quarterly Journal of Speech*, Vol. LIV, No. 2 (April 1968), 122–33.

———, "The Rhetoric of Moral Conflict," *Quarterly Journal of Speech*, Vol. LVI, No. 2 (April 1970), 120–30.

Haiman, Franklyn S., "The Rhetoric of the Streets: Some Legal and Ethical Considerations," *Quarterly Journal of Speech*, Vol. LIII, No. 2 (April 1967), 99–114.

Heisey, D. Ray, "The Rhetoric of the Arab-Israeli Conflict," *Quarterly Journal of Speech*, Vol. XLVI, No. 1 (February 1970), 12–21.

Hendrix, Jerry, *et al.*, "Rhetorical Criticism: Prognoses for the Seventies— A Symposium," *Southern Speech Journal*, Vol. XXXVI, No. 2 (Winter 1970).

Hillbruner, Anthony, "Criticism as Persuasion," *Southern Speech Journal*, Vol. XXVIII, No. 4 (Summer 1963), 260–67.

———, *Critical Dimensions: The Art of Public Address Criticism*. New York: Random House, Inc., 1966.

Linsley, William A., *Speech Criticism: Methods and Materials*. Dubuque, Iowa: Wm. C. Brown Publishers, 1968.

Newman, Robert P., "Under the Veneer: Nixon's Vietnam Speech of November 3, 1969," *Quarterly Journal of Speech*, Vol. LVI, No. 2 (April 1970), 168–78.

Nichols, Marie H., *Rhetoric and Criticism*. Baton Rouge: Louisiana State University Press, 1963.

Nilsen, Thomas, "Criticism and Social Consequences," *Quarterly Journal of Speech*, Vol. XLII, No. 2 (April 1956), 173–78.

———, ed., *Essays on Rhetorical Criticism*. New York: Random House, Inc., 1968.

Rosenfield, Lawrence W., "George Wallace Plays Rosemary's Baby," *Quarterly Journal of Speech*, Vol. LV, No. 1 (February 1969), 36–44.

Scott, Robert L., and Wayne Brockriede, *The Rhetoric of Black Power*. New York: Harper & Row, Publishers, 1969.

———, and Donald K. Smith, "The Rhetoric of Confrontation," *Quarterly Journal of Speech*, Vol. LV, No. 1 (February 1969), 1–8.

Simons, Herbert, "Requirements, Problems, and Strategies: A Theory of Persuasion for Social Movements," *Quarterly Journal of Speech*, Vol. XLVI, No. 1 (February 1970), 1–11.

APPENDIX

william faulkner

NOBEL PRIZE SPEECH

I feel that this award was not made to me as a man, but to my work—a life's work in the agony and sweat of the human spirit, not for glory and least of all for profit, but to create out of the materials of the human spirit something which did not exist before. So this award is only mine in trust. It will not be difficult to find a dedication for the money part of it commensurate with the purpose and significance of its origin. But I would like to do the same with the acclaim too, by using this moment as a pinnacle from which I might be listened to by the young men and women already dedicated to the same anguish and travail, among whom is already that one who will someday stand here where I am standing.

Our tragedy today is a general and universal physical fear so long sustained by now that we can even bear it. There are no longer problems of the spirit. There is only the question: when will I be blown up? Because of this, the young man or woman writing today has forgotten the problems of the human heart in conflict with itself which alone can make good writing because only that is worth writing about, worth the agony and the sweat.

He must learn them again. He must teach himself that the

This speech was given on December 10, 1950. Reprinted with the permission of Random House. Text taken from *The Faulkner Reader*. Copyright © 1953.

basest of all things is to be afraid; and, teaching himself that, forget it forever, leaving no room in his workshop for anything but the old verities and truths of the heart, the old universal truths lacking which any story is ephemeral and doomed—love and honor and pity and pride and compassion and sacrifice. Until he does so, he labors under a curse. He writes not of love but of lust, of defeats in which nobody loses anything of value, of victories without hope, and worst of all, without pity or compassion. His griefs grieve on no universal bones, leaving no scars. He writes not of the heart but of the glands.

Until he relearns these things, he will write as though he stood among and watched the end of man. I decline to accept the end of man. It is easy enough to say that man is immortal simply because he will endure; that when the last ding-dong of doom has clanged and faded from the last worthless rock hanging tideless in the last red and dying evening, that even then there will still be one more sound: that of his puny inexhaustible voice, still talking. I refuse to accept this. I believe that man will not merely endure: he will prevail. He is immortal, not because he alone among creatures has an inexhaustible voice, but because he has a soul, a spirit capable of compassion and sacrifice and endurance. The poet's, the writer's duty is to write about these things. It is his privilege to help man endure by lifting his heart, by reminding him of the courage and honor and hope and pride and compassion and pity and sacrifice which have been the glory of his past. The poet's voice need not merely be the record of man; it can be one of the props, the pillars, to help him endure and prevail.

john f. kennedy

ADDRESS ON THE CUBAN MISSILE CRISIS

Good evening, my fellow citizens. This Government, as promised, has maintained the closest surveillance of the Soviet military build-up on the island of Cuba. Within the past week unmistakable evidence has established the fact that a series of offensive missile sites is now in preparation on that imprisoned island. The purposes of these bases can be none other than to provide a nuclear strike capability against the Western Hemisphere.

Upon receiving the first preliminary hard information of this nature last Tuesday morning (October 16) at 9:00 A.M., I directed that our surveillance be stepped up. And having now confirmed and completed our evaluation of the evidence and our decision on a course of action, this Government feels obliged to report this new crisis to you in fullest detail.

The characteristics of these new missile sites indicate two distinct types of installations. Several of them include medium-range ballistic missiles capable of carrying a nuclear warhead for a distance of more than 1,000 nautical miles. Each of these missiles, in short, is capable of striking Washington, D.C., the Panama Canal,

This text was taken directly from a tape of the speech delivered on October 22, 1962. It coincides with the text as it appeared in Robert F. Kennedy, *Thirteen Days* (New York: W. W. Norton & Company, Inc., 1969) and is reprinted with their permission.

Cape Canaveral, Mexico City, or any other city in the southeastern part of the United States, in Central America, or in the Caribbean area.

Additional sites not yet completed appear to be designed for intermediate-range ballistic missiles capable of traveling more than twice as far—and thus capable of striking most of the major cities in the Western Hemisphere, ranging as far north as Hudson Bay, Canada, and as far south as Lima, Peru. In addition, jet bombers, capable of carrying nuclear weapons, are now being uncrated and assembled in Cuba, while the necessary air bases are being prepared.

This urgent transformation of Cuba into an important strategic base—by the presence of these large, long-range, and clearly offensive weapons of sudden mass destruction—constitutes an explicit threat to the peace and security of all the Americas, in flagrant and deliberate defiance of the Rio Pact of 1947, the traditions of this nation and Hemisphere, the Joint Resolution of the 87th Congress, the Charter of the United Nations, and my own public warnings to the Soviets on September 4 and 13.

This action also contradicts the repeated assurances of Soviet spokesmen, both publicly and privately delivered, that the arms build-up in Cuba would retain its original defensive character and that the Soviet Union had no need or desire to station strategic missiles on the territory of any other nation.

The size of this undertaking makes clear that it has been planned for some months. Yet only last month, after I had made clear the distinction between any introduction of ground-to-ground missiles and the existence of defensive antiaircraft missiles, the Soviet Government publicly stated on September 11 that, and I quote, "The armaments and military equipment sent to Cuba are designed exclusively for defensive purposes," and, and I quote the Soviet Government, "There is no need for the Soviet Government to shift its weapons for a retaliatory blow to any other country, for instance Cuba," and that, and I quote the Government, "The Soviet Union has so powerful rockets to carry these nuclear warheads that there is no need to search for sites for them beyond the boundaries of the Soviet Union." That statement was false.

Only last Thursday, as evidence of this rapid offensive build-up was already in my hand, Soviet Foreign Minister Gromyko told me in my office that he was instructed to make it clear once again, as he said his Government had already done, that Soviet assistance to Cuba, and I quote, "pursued solely the purpose of contributing to the defense capabilities of Cuba," that, and I quote him, "training by Soviet specialists of Cuban nationals in handling defensive armaments was by no means offensive," and that "if it were otherwise," Mr. Gromyko went on, "the Soviet Government would never become involved in rendering such assistance." That statement also was false.

Neither the United States of America nor the world community of nations can tolerate deliberate deception and offensive threats on the part of any nation, large or small. We no longer live in a world where only the actual firing of weapons represents a sufficient challenge to a nation's security to constitute maximum peril. Nuclear weapons are so destructive and ballistic missiles are so swift that any substantially increased possibility of their use or any sudden change in their deployment may well be regarded as a definite threat to peace.

For many years both the Soviet Union and the United States, recognizing this fact, have deployed strategic nuclear weapons with great care, never upsetting the precarious status quo which insured that these weapons would not be used in the absence of some vital challenge. Our own strategic missiles have never been transferred to the territory of any other nation under a cloak of secrecy and deception; and our history, unlike that of the Soviets since the end of World War II, demonstrates that we have no desire to dominate or conquer any other nation or impose our system upon its people. Nevertheless, American citizens have become adjusted to living daily on the bull's eye of Soviet missiles located inside the U.S.S.R. or in submarines.

In that sense missiles in Cuba add to an already clear and present danger—although it should be noted the nations of Latin America have never previously been subjected to a potential nuclear threat.

But this secret, swift, and extraordinary build-up of Communist missiles—in an area well known to have a special and historical relationship to the United States and the nations of the Western Hemisphere, in violation of Soviet assurances, and in defiance of American and hemispheric policy—this sudden, clandestine decision to station strategic weapons for the first time outside of Soviet soil—is a deliberately provocative and unjustified change in the status quo which cannot be accepted by this country if our courage and our commitments are ever to be trusted again by either friend or foe.

The 1930's taught us a clear lesson: Aggressive conduct, if allowed to grow unchecked and unchallenged, ultimately leads to war. This nation is opposed to war. We are also true to our word. Our unswerving objective, therefore, must be to prevent the use of these missiles against this or any other country and to secure their withdrawal or elimination from the Western Hemisphere.

Our policy has been one of patience and restraint, as befits a peaceful and powerful nation, which leads a worldwide alliance. We have been determined not to be diverted from our central concerns by mere irritants and fanatics. But now further action is required—and it is underway; and these actions may only be the beginning. We will not prematurely or unnecessarily risk the costs of worldwide nuclear war in which even the fruits of victory would be ashes in our mouth—but neither will we shrink from that risk at any time it must be faced.

Acting, therefore, in the defense of our own security and of the entire Western Hemisphere, and under the authority entrusted to me by the Constitution as endorsed by the resolution of the Congress, I have directed that the following initial steps be taken immediately:

First: To halt this offensive build-up, a strict quarantine on all offensive military equipment under shipment to Cuba is being initiated. All ships of any kind bound for Cuba from whatever nation or port will, if found to contain cargoes of offensive weapons, be turned back. This quarantine will be extended, if needed, to other types of cargo and carriers. We are not at this time, however, denying the necessities of life as the Soviets attempted to do in their Berlin blockade of 1948.

Second: I have directed the continued and increased close surveillance of Cuba and its military build-up. The Foreign Ministers of the Organization of American States in their communiqué of October 3 rejected secrecy on such matters in this Hemisphere. Should these offensive military preparations continue, thus increasing the theat to the Hemisphere, further action will be justified. I have directed the Armed Forces to prepare for any eventualities; and I trust that in the interests of both the Cuban people and the Soviet technicians at the sites, the hazards to all concerned of continuing this threat will be recognized.

Third: It shall be the policy of this nation to regard any nuclear missile launched from Cuba against any nation in the Western Hemisphere as an attack by the Soviet Union on the United States, requiring a full retaliatory response upon the Soviet Union.

Fourth: As a necessary military precaution I have reinforced our base at Guantanamo, evacuated today the dependents of our personnel there, and ordered additional military units to be on a standby alert basis.

Fifth: We are calling tonight for an immediate meeting of the Organ of Consultation, under the Organization of American States, to consider this threat to hemispheric security and to invoke articles six and eight of the Rio Treaty in support of all necessary action. The United Nations Charter allows for regional security arrangements—and the nations of this Hemisphere decided long ago against the military presence of outside powers. Our other allies around the world have also been alerted.

Sixth: Under the Charter of the United Nations, we are asking tonight that an emergency meeting of the Security Council be convoked without delay to take action against this latest Soviet threat to world peace. Our resolution will call for the prompt dismantling and withdrawal of all offensive weapons in Cuba, under the supervision of United Nations observers, before the quarantine can be lifted.

Seventh and finally: I call upon Chairman Khrushchev to halt and eliminate this clandestine, reckless, and provocative threat to world peace and to stable relations between our two nations. I call upon him further to abandon this course of world domination and to join in an historic effort to end the perilous arms race and transform the history of man. He has an opportunity now to move the world back from the abyss of destruction—by returning to his Government's own words that it had no need to station missiles outside its own territory, and withdrawing these weapons from Cuba—by refraining from any action which will widen or deepen the present crisis—and then by participating in a search for peaceful and permanent solutions.

This nation is prepared to present its case against the Soviet threat to peace, and our own proposals for a peaceful world, at any time and in any forum in the Organization of American States, in the United Nations, or in any other meeting that could be useful—without limiting our freedom of action.

We have in the past made strenuous efforts to limit the spread of nuclear weapons. We have proposed the elimination of all arms and military bases in a fair and effective disarmament treaty. We are prepared to discuss new proposals for the removal of tensions on both sides—including the possibilities of a genuinely independent Cuba, free to determine its own destiny. We have no wish to war with the Soviet Union, for we are a peaceful people who desire to live in peace with all other peoples.

But it is difficult to settle or even discuss these problems in an atmosphere of intimidation. That is why this latest Soviet threat—or any other threat which is made either independently or in response to our actions this week—must and will be met with determination. Any hostile move anywhere in the world against the safety and freedom of peoples to whom we are committed—including in particular the brave people of West Berlin—will be met by whatever action is needed.

Finally, I want to say a few words to the captive people of Cuba, to whom this speech is being directly carried by special radio facilities. I speak to you as a friend, as one who knows of your deep attachment to your fatherland, as one who shares your aspirations for liberty and justice for all. And I have watched and the American people have watched with deep sorrow how your nationalist revolution was betrayed and how your fatherland fell under foreign domination. Now your leaders are no longer Cuban leaders inspired by Cuban ideals. They are puppets and agents of an international conspiracy which has turned Cuba against your friends and neighbors in the Americas—and turned it into the first Latin American country to become a target for nuclear war, the first Latin American country to have these weapons on its soil.

These new weapons are not in your interest. They contribute nothing to your peace and well being. They can only undermine it. But this country has no wish to cause you to suffer or to impose any system upon you. We know that your lives and land are being used as pawns by those who deny you freedom.

Many times in the past Cuban people have risen to throw out tyrants who destroyed their liberty. And I have no doubt that most Cubans today look forward to the time when they will be truly free —free from foreign domination, free to choose their own leaders, free to select their own system, free to own their own land, free to speak and write and worship without fear or degradation. And then shall Cuba be welcomed back to the society of free nations and to the associations of this Hemisphere.

My fellow citizens, let no one doubt that this is a difficult and dangerous effort on which we have set out. No one can foresee precisely what course it will take or what costs or casualties will be incurred. Many months of sacrifice and self-discipline lie ahead—months in which both our patience and our will will be tested, months in which many threats and denunciations will keep us aware of our dangers. But the greatest danger of all would be to do nothing.

The path we have chosen for the present is full of hazards, as all paths are; but it is the one most consistent with our character and courage as a nation and our commitments around the world. The cost of freedom is always high—but Americans have always paid it. And one path we shall never choose, and that is the path of surrender or submission.

Our goal is not the victory of might but the vindication of right—not peace at the expense of freedom, but both peace and freedom, here in this Hemisphere and, we hope, around the world. God willing, that goal will be achieved.

patrick henry

LIBERTY OR DEATH

MR. PRESIDENT: No man thinks more highly than I do of the patriotism, as well as abilities, of the very worthy gentlemen who have just addressed the house. But different men often see the same subject in different lights; and, therefore, I hope it will not be thought disrespectful to those gentlemen, if, entertaining as I do opinions of a character very opposite to theirs, I shall speak forth my sentiments freely and without reserve. This is no time for ceremony. The question before the house is one of awful moment to this country. For my own part, I consider it as nothing less than a question of freedom or slavery; and in proportion to the magnitude of the subject ought to be the freedom of the debate. It is only in this way that we can hope to arrive at truth, and fulfil the great responsibility which we hold to God and our country. Should I keep back my opinions at such a time, through fear of giving offense, I should consider myself as guilty of treason towards my country, and of an act of disloyalty toward the Majesty of Heaven, which I revere above all earthly kings.

Mr. President, it is natural to man to indulge in the illusions of hope. We are apt to shut our eyes against a painful truth, and listen to the song of that siren, till she transforms us into beasts.

The text is taken from an account in William Wirt's biography, *The Life and Character of Patrick Henry* (1817). According to Wirt, the account was taken from the accounts of those present (March 1775).

Is this the part of wise men, engaged in a great and arduous struggle for liberty? Are we disposed to be of the number of those, who, having eyes, see not, and having ears, hear not, the things which so nearly concern their temporal salvation? For my part, whatever anguish of spirit it may cost, I am willing to know the whole truth; to know the worst, and to provide for it.

I have but one lamp by which my feet are guided, and that is the lamp of experience. I know of no way of judging of the future but by the past. And judging by the past, I wish to know what there has been in the conduct of the British ministry for the last ten years to justify those hopes with which gentlemen have been pleased to solace themselves and the house. Is it that insidious smile with which our petition has been lately received? Trust it not, sir; it will prove a snare to your feet. Suffer not yourselves to be betrayed with a kiss. Ask yourselves how this gracious reception of our petition comports with those war-like preparations which cover our waters and darken our land. Are fleets and armies necessary to a work of love and reconciliation? Have we shown ourselves so unwilling to be reconciled, that force must be called in to win back our love? Let us not deceive ourselves, sir. These are the implements of war and subjugation; the last arguments to which kings resort. I ask gentlemen, sir, What means this martial array, if its purpose be not to force us to submission? Can gentlemen assign any other possible motive for it? Has Great Britain any enemy, in this quarter of the world, to call for all this accumulation of navies and armies? No, sir, she has none. They are meant for us: they can be meant for no other. They are sent over to bind and rivet upon us those chains which the British ministry have been so long forging. And what have we to oppose to them? Shall we try argument? Sir, we have been trying that for the last ten years. Have we anything new to offer upon the subject? Nothing. We have held the subject up in every light of which it is capable; but it has been all in vain. Shall we resort to entreaty and humble supplication? What terms shall we find, which have not been already exhausted? Let us not, I beseech you, sir, deceive ourselves longer. Sir, we have done everything that could be done, to avert the storm which is now coming on. We have petitioned; we have remonstrated; we have supplicated; we have prostrated ourselves before the throne, and have implored its interposition to arrest the tyrannical hands of the ministry and Parliament. Our petitions have been slighted; our remonstrances have produced additional violence and insult; our supplications have been disregarded; and we have been spurned, with contempt, from the foot of the throne! In vain, after these things, may we indulge the fond hope of peace and reconciliation. There is no longer any room for hope of peace and reconciliation. There is no longer any room for hope. If we wish to be free—if we mean to preserve inviolate those inestimable privileges for which we have been so long contending—if we mean not basely to abandon the noble struggle in which we have been so long engaged, and which we have pledged ourselves never to abandon, until the glorious object of our contest shall be obtained—we must fight! I repeat it, sir, we must fight! An appeal to arms and to the God of Hosts is all that is left us!

They tell us, sir, that we are weak; unable to cope with so formidable an adversary. But when shall we be stronger? Will it be the next week, or the next year? Will it be when we are totally disarmed, and when a British guard shall be stationed in every house? Shall we gather strength by irresolution and inaction? Shall we acquire the means of effectual resistance by lying supinely on our backs and hugging the delusive phantom of hope, until our enemies shall have bound us hand and foot? Sir, we are not weak, if we make a proper use of those means which the God of nature hath placed in our power. Three millions of people, armed in the holy cause of liberty, and in such a country as that which we possess, are invincible by any force which our enemy can send against us. Besides, sir, we shall not fight our battles alone. There is a just God who presides over the destinies of nations, and who will raise up friends to fight our battles for us. The battle, sir, is not to the strong alone; it is to the vigilant, the active, the brave. Besides, sir, we have no election. If we were base enough to desire it, it is now too late to retire from the contest. There is no retreat, but in submission and slavery! Our chains are forged! Their clanking may be heard on the plains of Boston! The war is inevitable—and let it come! I repeat it, sir, let it come.

It is in vain, sir, to extenuate the matter. Gentlemen may cry, Peace, Peace—but there is no peace. The war is actually begun! The next gale that sweeps from the north will bring to our ears the clash of resounding arms! Our brethren are already in the field! Why stand we here idle? What is it that gentlemen wish? What would they have? Is life so dear, or peace so sweet, as to be purchased at the price of chains and slavery? Forbid it, Almighty God! I know not what course others may take; but as for me, give me liberty or give me death!

richard m. nixon

VETO MESSAGE

My fellow Americans, I would like to share with you tonight a decision that is one of the most difficult decisions I have made since I assumed the office of the presidency a year ago. I have here on my desk a bill, a bill which has been passed by the Congress and sent to me for signature. For the first time I am exercising tonight the constitutional power of the President to veto a bill and send it back to the Congress for further consideration. This decision is particularly difficult because this bill provides funds for the Department of Health, Education and Welfare.

Now let us clearly understand the issues. The issue is not whether some of us are for education and health and others are against it. There are no goals which I consider more important for this nation than to improve education and to provide better health care for the American people. The question is how much can a federal government afford to spend on these programs this year?

In April, I asked the Congress to appropriate more for the Department of Health, Education and Welfare than it has ever appropriated before. This means that this year the federal government will spend 13 per cent more on programs for health, education and welfare than it spent last year. For federal programs that affect education we will spend over ten billion dollars. Now in this bill

This text was taken directly from a tape of the speech delivered on January 26, 1970. It is printed with the permission of The White House.

that I have before me the Congress has increased the amount that I recommended by a billion, 260 million dollars. Over one billion dollars of this increase is in the field of education.

Now why in an election year particularly would a President hesitate for one moment to sign a bill providing for such politically popular causes as this one? Well, the reason is this. The President of the United States has an obligation to consider all the worthy causes that come before him and he's to consider them having in mind only one principle—what is best for all the people of the United States. I believe that the increase over the amount that I recommended, the increase which is contained in this bill passed by the Congress, is not in the best interests of all the American people because it is in the wrong amount for the wrong purpose and at the wrong time.

Let me address myself first to the questions of the amount of spending power. This nation faces a crisis which directly affects every family in America, the continuing rise in the cost of living. From 1960 to 1970 the cost of living went up 25 per cent in this country. Now for the average family of four in America that meant an increase of 2400 dollars a year in the items that go into your cost of living, your grocery bill, your housing, your transportation, your medical costs.

A major reason for this increase in the cost of living is that in that same ten year period from 1960 to 1970 the federal government spend 57 billion dollars more than it took in in taxes. I think this was wrong. That is why as your President I intend to do everything I can to see that the federal government spends less in Washington so that you can have more to spend at home.

If we are to stop a rise in the cost of living which is putting such a strain on the family budgets of millions of Americans we have to cut the federal budget. That's why I ordered cuts of 7 billion dollars in federal spending in 1970. That is why, for example, the budget I will submit to Congress for 1971 will call for a smaller percentage of federal spending for defense than in any year since 1950. For the first time in 20 years the budget will provide more funds for human resources than for defense.

Now, if I approved the increased spending contained in this bill I would win the approval of many fine people who are demanding more spending by the federal government for education and health, but I would be surrendering in the battle to stop the rise in the cost of living, a battle we must fight and win for the benefit of every family in this nation.

The second reason I am vetoing this bill is that I believe that it increases spending for the wrong purposes. The increase that has been ordered by the Congress, for the most part, simply provides more dollars for the same old program without making the urgent new reforms that are needed if we are to improve the quality of education and health care in America. I believe that when we consider how much we are putting into education in the United States we are entitled to get more out in terms of better quality of education. That is why in my education message, which I will shortly be submitting to the Congress, I will propose a new and searching look at our American school system. In this examination we will look at such basic questions as to why millions of our children in school are unable to read adequately. We will put emphasis on improving the quality of education for every child in America.

An example of the unfairness of this bill is the impacted aid program which is supposed to help areas which need assistance because of the presence of federal installations. The bill provides 6 million dollars for the one-half million people who live in the richest county in the United States, and only 3 million dollars for the 3 million people living in the one hundred poorest counties in the United States. President Eisenhower, President Kennedy, President Johnson, all criticized this program as being unfair, and yet the Congress in this bill not only perpetuates this unfair program, it adds money to it.

The third reason I am vetoing this bill is because it requires the money to be spent at the wrong time. We're now nearly three-quarters of the way through the school year. This bill forces us to spend the money it appropriates, and we would have to spend it all before June 30. When money is spent in a hurry a great deal is wasted. There is no good time to waste the taxpayers money, but there is no worse time to waste it than today.

The Congress will determine on Wednesday whether it will sustain or override my veto of this legislation. If the veto is sustained I will immediately seek appropriations which will assure the funds necessary to provide for the needs of the nation in education and health.

You can be sure that no school will need to be closed, no school child will be denied an education as a result of the action I take tonight. I will work with the Congress in developing a law that will ease the transition to education reforms and do so without inflation.

I realize that a number of Congressmen and Senators as well

as many of the members of what is called "the education lobby" disagree with the views I have expressed tonight. I respect their point of view. I deeply share the concerns of those who want more funds for education and for health and for other worthy causes in this country, but it is my duty to act on behalf of the millions of Americans including teachers and students as well as patients in our hospitals who will pay far more in the rise in the cost of living than they will receive from the increased spending provided for in this bill.

We spend more for health and education than any nation in the world, we are able to do this, and I hope we can continue to do so in the future because we have the great good fortune to be the richest nation by far in the whole history of the world. But, we can spend ourselves poor. That is why no matter how popular a spending program is, if I determined that its enactment will have the effect of raising your prices or raising your taxes, I will not approve that program. Now, for these reasons for the first time tonight instead of signing a bill which has been sent to me by the Congress I am signing this veto message.

My fellow Americans, I believe this action is in the long-range interests of better education and improved health care but, most important, I believe that this action that I have taken is in the vital interests of all Americans in stopping the rise in the cost of living. Thank you and Goodnight.

senator edmund s. muskie

A WHOLE SOCIETY

One hundred and eighty-three years ago, a small group of men gathered in this city in an effort to bring order out of chaos. They met in the shadow of failure. America had won her independence but was now in danger of breaking up into small and quarrelsome states. Their objective was to build "a more perfect union."

We have met in this city to help build a *whole society*—for we have seen the birthright of a free nation damaged by exploitation, spoiled by neglect, choked by its own success, and torn by hatred and suspicion.

The Founding Fathers did build "a more perfect union." They created a nation where there was none, and they built a framework for a democratic society which has been remarkable for its successes. We are now concerned with its failures.

We have learned that their creation was not infallible, and that our society is not indestructible.

We have learned that our natural resources are limited and that, unless those limitations are respected, life itself may be in danger.

We have also learned that, unless we respect each other, the very foundations of freedom may be in danger.

And yet we act as though a luxurious future and a fertile land

The text of this speech, delivered April 22, 1970, in Philadelphia, was supplied by Senator Muskie's office. It is reprinted with his permission.

will continue to forgive us all the bad habits which have led us to abuse our physical and our social environment.

If we are to build a whole society—and if we are to insure the achievement of a life worth living—we must realize that our shrinking margins of natural resources are near the bottom of the barrel.

There are no replacements, no spare stocks with which we can replenish our supplies.

There is no space command center, ready to give us precise instruction and alternate solutions for survival on our spaceship earth.

Our nation—and our world—hang together by tenuous bonds which are strained as they have never been strained before—and as they must never be strained again.

We cannot survive an undeclared war on our future.

We must lay down our weapons of self-destruction and pick up the tools of social and environmental reconstruction.

These are the dimensions of the crisis we face:

No major American river is clean anymore, and some are fire hazards.

No American lake is free of pollution, and some are dying.

No American city can boast of clean air, and New Yorkers inhale the equivalent of a pack and a half of cigarettes every day—without smoking.

No American community is free of debris and solid waste, and we are turning to the open spaces and the ocean depths to cast off the products of our affluent society.

We are horrified by the cumulative impact of our waste, but we are told to expect the use of more than 280 billion non-returnable bottles in the decade of the seventies.

Man has burst upon the environment like an invader—destroying rather than using, discarding rather than saving, and giving the environment little chance to adapt.

We have depleted our resources and cluttered our environment—and only recently have we been shocked by the enormity of our errors.

As long as Americans could escape the confines of the soot and clutter of our cities, the voices of those who were trapped and the warnings of those who understood were never really heard.

Pollution was isolated by the size and openness of America. A river here, a forest there, a few industrialized cities—these examples of environmental destruction seemed a small price to pay for prosperity.

This was the frontier ethic: America pushing ahead and getting ahead. We had an unlimited future under "manifest destiny."

Now we find that we have over-reached ourselves. The frontier ethic helped us build the strongest nation in the world. But it also led us to believe that our natural and human resources were endless, that our rivers could absorb as much sewage as we could pour into them, that there was automatic, equal opportunity for everyone, that our air would always be clean, and that hunger and poverty were always a temporary condition in America.

Early in the life of our country, we were absorbed in harnessing the energy of a people and the resources of the land and water.

But we are finding today—hopefully in time—that we have done much more than harness our resources: we have conquered them and we are on the verge of destroying them in the process.

We moved and changed and grew so fast that tomorrow came yesterday.

Man has always tended to use up his resources, but never have so many used up so much. We have behaved as if another Creation were just around the corner, as if we could somehow manufacture more land, more air, and more water when we have destroyed what we have.

We have reached the boundaries of the land, and the tide of our civilization has now washed back into our cities.

Today's frontier is internal and personal. We now face—collectively and individually—a moral frontier.

That frontier is the point at which we are willing to cut back selfish exploitation in favor of selfless conservation.

That frontier is marked by the extent of our concern for future generations. They deserve to inherit their natural share of this earth—but we could pass on to them a physical and moral wasteland.

We have reached a point where (1) man, (2) his environment, and (3) his industrial technology intersect. They intersect in America, in Russia and in every other industrial society in the world. They intersect in every country which is trying to achieve industrial development.

On this day, dedicated to the preservation of man's earth, we confront our deteriorated environment, our devouring technology, and our fellow man. Relative harmony has become the victim of a three-cornered war—a war where everyone loses.

Our technology has reached a point where it is producing more kinds of things than we really want, more kinds of things than we really need, and more kinds of things than we can really live with.

We have to choose, to say no, and to give up some luxuries. And these kinds of decisions will be the acid test of our commitment to a healthy environment.

It means choosing cleaner cars rather than faster cars, more parks instead of more highways, and more houses and more schools instead of more weapons and more wars.

The whole society that we seek is one in which all men live in brotherhood with each other and with their environment. It is a society where each member of it knows that he has an opportunity to fulfill his greatest potential.

It is a society that will not tolerate slums for some and decent houses for others, rats for some and playgrounds for others, clean air for some and filth for others.

It is the only kind of society that has a chance. It is the only kind of society that has a future.

To achieve a whole society—a healthy total environment—we need change, planning more effective and just laws and more money better spent.

Achieving that whole society will cost heavily—in foregone luxuries, in restricted choices, in higher prices for certain goods and services, in taxes, and in hard decisions about our national priorities. It will require a new sense of balance in our national commitments.

Consider the national budget for 1971. That "balanced budget" represents unbalanced priorities.

That budget "balances" $275 million for the SST against $106 million for air pollution control.

That budget "balances" $3.4 billion for the space program against $1.4 billion for housing. And that budget balances $7.3 billion for arms research and development against $1.4 billion for higher education.

It does not make sense to say we cannot afford to protect our environment—just yet.

It does not make sense to say that we cannot afford to win the fight against hunger and poverty—just yet.

It does not make sense to say we cannot afford to provide decent housing and needed medical care—just yet.

We can afford to do these things, if we admit that there are luxuries we can forego, false security we can do without, and prices we are willing to pay.

I believe that those of you who have gathered here to save the earth are willing to pay the price to save our environment.

I hope, however, that your view of the environment will not be a narrow one.

The environmental conscience which has been awakened in our nation holds great promise for reclaiming our air, our water and our land. But man's environment includes more than these natural resources. It includes the shape of the communities in which he lives: his home, his schools, his places of work, and those who share this planet and this land.

If the environmental conscience which has brought us together this day is to have any lasting meaning for America, it must be the instrument to turn the nation around. If we use our awareness that the total environment determines the quality of life, we can make those decisions which can save our nation from becoming a class-ridden and strife-torn wasteland.

The study of ecology—man's relationship with his environment—should teach us that our relationships with each other are just as intricate and just as delicate as those with our natural environment. We cannot afford to correct our history of abusing nature and neglect the continuing abuse of our fellow-man.

We should have learned by now that a whole nation must be a nation at peace with itself.

We should have learned by now that we can have that peace only by assuring that all Americans have equal access to a healthy total environment.

That can mean nothing less than equal access to good schools, to meaningful job opportunities, to adequate health services, and to decent and attractive housing.

For the past ten years we have been groping toward the realization that the total environment is at stake.

We have seen the destructiveness of poverty, and declared a war on it.

We have seen the ravages of hunger, and declared a war on it.

We have seen the costs of crime, and declared a war on it.

And now we have awakened to the pollution of our environment, and we have declared another war.

We have fought too many losing battles in these wars to continue this piece-meal approach to creating a whole society.

The only strategy that makes sense is a total strategy to protect the total [environment].

The only way to achieve that total strategy is through an Environmental Revolution—a commitment to a whole society.

The Environmental Revolution must be one of laws, not men; one of values, not ideology; and one of achievement, not unfulfilled promises.

We are not powerless to accomplish this change, but we are powerless as a people if we wait for someone else to do it for us.

We can use the power of the people to turn the nation around —to move toward a whole society.

The power of the people is in the ballot box—and we can elect men who commit themselves to a whole society and work to meet that commitment.

The power of the people is in the cash register—and we can resolve to purchase only from those companies that clean themselves up.

The power of the people is in the stock certificate—and we can use our proxies to make industries socially and environmentally responsible.

The power of the people is in the courts—and through them we can require polluters to obey the law.

The power of the people is in public hearings—where we can decide on the quality of the air and the water we want.

And the power of the people is in peaceful assembly—where we can demand redress of grievances—as we are doing here today and all across the land.

Martin Luther King once said that "Through our scientific and technological genius we have made of this world a neighborhood. Now through our moral and spiritual genius we must make of it a brotherhood."

For Martin Luther King, every day was an Earth Day—a day to work toward his commitment to a whole society. It is that commitment we must keep.

archibald macleish

TRUSTEE OF THE CULTURE

There was a time, not longer ago than an assistant professor can remember, when the innovation of a college was a routine occurrence to be recorded, if at all, on page eighteen or twenty of the *Times* back among the retrospective exhibitions and the amateur performances of the B Minor Mass. Colleges provided education. Education was a good thing. And good things weren't news.

They still aren't but the rest of the equation is out of date. Universal agreement that education is a good thing ended with the invention of the Silent Majority. Nothing, according to those who have been able to penetrate that enormous apathy, distresses the Silent Majority as much as a college unless it be a college student. And as for college students, there are even some of them who share the Silent Majority view. The best college, in the opinion of certain outraged gentlemen at Columbia a few years back, was a closed college—preferably burned.

That kind of intellectual reorientation alters even a newspaper's notion of news. Whatever the opening of a college may have been back in the cheerful days of the Great Depression or the two

This speech was delivered at Hampshire College in the Fall of 1970. It is reprinted with Mr. MacLeish's permission. The text follows the text that appears in the Hampshire College Program of the Convocation. An adaptation appeared in *Saturday Review*.

world wars, it must now be regarded as a major event: not merely news but drama and even melodrama—another fleet of costly buildings, another cargo of irreplaceable books, another crew of hopeful teachers and ambitious students and courageous administrators launching themselves into the eye of the hurricane on a voyage as daring as Magellan's with the wild sea ahead already strewn with wreckage and haunted by confused, faint cries.

I have no idea, of course, what the Editors of the *Times* will think of the college opening we witness here today or on what page they will report it but I know very well what *our* emotions ought to be. We should see ourselves as gathered, not on the comfort of folding chairs under an autumn tent in a quiet inland valley, but on a promontory steep as the Butt of Lewis from which we peer into the driving sleet for a last glimpse of brave departing sails.

I persist in my metaphor not for the metaphor's sake but for the truth's. What is new, and newly exciting, about this occasion is precisely the sense of departure, of adventure, of voyage. We are now in the sixth or seventh year of what, following the mellifluous Irish, we might well call The Troubles—meaning, of course, The Troubles in the University. And the opening of Hampshire College is the first action I can think of seriously aimed at doing something about them.

Down to this time, universities and colleges have acted defensively if at all. They have treated The Troubles as private, or at least internal, ructions between their students and themselves, and have attempted only to gird themselves for each Putsch as it came along. Parietal Rules have been modified not to say abolished. Administrative procedures, meaning disciplinary procedures, have been altered. Relations with the community have been reconsidered and frequently improved. A few changes of a public-relations, rather than a scholarly, significance have been offered in the curricula. But no important, positive efforts have been made by those best equipped to make them, which is to say by university and college faculties, to determine what these famous Troubles actually are or how they affect—should affect—the University's undertaking to educate the young.

We have been hearing, in the last few days, about the development of new police methods for academic use, including body guards for presidents and the F.B.I. on twenty-four hour alert. We have seen a good bit of faculty linen, not all of it well washed, hung out to dry. We have learned that there are still courageous Chancellors prepared to battle not so courageous Regents to the verge of coronary and beyond. But the only confident educational pronouncements of this troubled time have issued, not from the colleges or universities, but from Mr. Spiro Agnew. And all Mr. Spiro Agnew has had to tell us is that the whole thing is the doing of wicked boys and girls egged on by "the disgusting and permissive attitude of the people in command of the . . . campuses." By which Mr. Agnew means that the Troubles would go away if only the troublemakers were eradicated. . . .

This, unfortunately, is a conclusion which fails to satisfy. Those who know most about these wicked boys and girls—the men and women who teach them—are pretty well agreed that, far from being a generation of criminal delinquents, this new generation of the young constitutes the hope of the world—such hope, that is, as this raddled, soiled, abused, exploited world still has. The contemporary young have their faults, obviously. They include in their number the usual shoddy elements familiar to every undergraduate generation: the campus politician, the adolescent marching and shouting association and the plain bad actor—together with a new phenomenon, a certain scattering of young exploiters of the idealism of the young for whom there is no adequate epithet. But by and large the contemporary young are nevertheless, and have been for some years back, the most deeply concerned, the most humanly committed, generation we have seen in this century with the single exception of the returning veterans of the Second War.

But though it is fairly clear to those who face these facts that Mr. Agnew's simple explanation explains nothing but Mr. Agnew, it is still true that no other explanation has been forthcoming. No one—no one at least in a position to do anything about it—seems to have asked the next, the crucial, question . . . until Hampshire. If Mr. Agnew is wrong—if The Troubles cannot be blamed on some sudden, mysterious plague of viciousness affecting an entire generation of the young—where then shall the blame be put? How are we to explain the restlessness, rebellion, indignation, violence in college after college, university after university, from one coast of this country to the other and in Europe as well as the Americas, Asia as well as Europe?

This would seem to be the one inescapable question of the time, and particularly for the teachers of the time, for the scholars, for the faculties in all of their disciplines. If The Troubles are not "student troubles" in the simple-minded Agnew sense they must be something other than "student troubles." They must afflict the universities and colleges, not because the university, the college, has a particular relation to the young, but because it has a particular relation to something else. But *what* else?

The established faculties have not told us, but Hampshire College, struggling to draw first breath, has faced at least the question and has hazarded an answer of its own. It sees "the something else" with which the university, the college, has to do, as something existing not within the academic pale but outside it in the time, in what we used to call the world. The Troubles, that is to say, are not disciplinary troubles whatever the politicians, the hard hats and the middle-aged generally may say about them. Neither are they, as the more romantic of the young believe, "revolutionary"— meaning political—troubles. They are troubles at the heart of human life, troubles in the culture itself, in the civilization, in the state of the civilization—troubles which cannot be cured by ranting at the government, however misguided or misdirected government may be, or by sending in the national guard, whatever the provocation, but only by restoring the culture to wholeness and to health— which means, by restoring the precarious balance between the society and the self which defines the culture at any given place or time. And that restoration, Hampshire College believes, is the business of the college, of the university.

I may not be summarizing the College's beliefs precisely, for the crucial word, culture, means more to me, I must confess, than it seems to mean to the learned men quoted in Hampshire's working papers. But on the essential question, the question of the responsibility of the college, of the university, I am not, I think, far wrong. Hampshire proposes—explicitly proposes—to accept for itself a responsibility for the restoration, for the maintenance, of the difficult balance between society and self. And in that acceptance it seems to me not only courageous but entirely right. That balance is the business of the universities and colleges.

Individuals—thinkers, organizations of thinkers, philosophers— can help. A true statesman, another Jefferson, even another Wilson, would be a Godsend. But it is the university, the college, which must bear the brunt of the responsibility because it is the university, the college, which is the trustee of the culture, the trustee of the state of the civilization, the trustee of the means by which the civilization descends from the always disappearing past into that eternal becoming which we call the present.

And it is as trustee of the culture that the university has failed in these years in which the culture has lost its human values and deteriorated into a mere technology which exploits knowledge as it exploits everything else, using even science itself not as a means for the advancement of civilization and the enrichment of life but as a ground for gadgetry and invention regardless of the human value of the thing invented, so that the triumphs of the epoch make no distinction between the glories of modern medicine and the horrors of modern war. When a civilization can declare tacitly and even explicitly that whatever *can* be concocted *must* be concocted regardless of the human consequences, we are already far into that disastrous epoch for which Yeats provided the image and the name:

> *Turning and turning in the widening gyre*
> *The falcon cannot hear the falconer,*
> *Things fall apart, the center cannot hold . . .*

Hampshire College, to its eternal credit, has dared to face Yeats' vision and the reading of history which underlies that vision. It has accepted as the critical contemporary fact the failure of the balance between society and self and has found the reason for that failure in the dehumanizing of the culture on one side and the dehumanizing of the self upon the other: the conversion of a once diverse and fruitful human culture into a crassly technological semi-culture, and the withdrawal of the withered self toward the uttermost wilderness of the self—toward that desert of solipsism in which some ghostly modern selves already wander. Moreover, having accepted the failure of the balance as the underlying ill, Hampshire has gone on to make the restoration of the balance its explicit undertaking: it has committed itself "to a view of liberal education" (I am quoting) "as a vehicle for the realization of self *in* society"—and it underlines the *in*.

It is a measure of the decline of the human in this sorry age that, far from resounding as a declaration of the obvious these words ring like trumpets—like the first courageous trumpets we have heard since The Troubles began. What would once have been a platitude becomes a call to arms. It is only, of course, *in* society that a self can *ever* be realized—in what John Keats called the arable field of events. But what would have been self-evident to the Father of the University of Virginia comes as a shock of blinding revelation to the generation of the depraved Los Angeles murders and the cold-blooded tortures in Connecticut and the brutal killings in Ohio and Mississippi. We suddenly *see*, as we reflect upon those words, what the self which has turned its back on society can become, and what society can be without the sense of self.

Our generation is the first in American history to understand what Daniel Webster meant when he cried, in those dark decades before the Civil War, "Liberty and Union, one and inseparable, now and forever." Even Emerson misread him. Emerson rejected "Union" in that context as the young today reject what they have christened, the Establishment. Liberty was all that mattered—human decency—the freedom of the slaves. But when the Civil War finally came Lincoln took his stand where Webster had taken his—upon the preservation of the Union. For without the Union there could be no Liberty. And this, as always with Lincoln, was no such shrewd political calculation as we know so well today. It was human truth. Yeats's truth. Without a center that can hold, "things fall apart . . . The falcon cannot hear the falconer." Without a center that can hold, human liberty becomes an inhuman liberty to mutilate and murder. Without a center that can hold, freedom becomes the opposite of freedom.

Only when freedom is as human as humanity is free can a nation of free men exist. Only when the balance between society and self is both harmonious and whole can there truly be a self or truly a society. Hampshire has been founded on that proposition.

I do not know, ladies and gentlemen, how it is with you, but as I think for myself of this all but impossible commitment, and as I look around at the faces of the men and women who have made it, I feel a surge of excited hope. In a time like ours, it is only the impossible commitments which are believable, for only the impossible commitments are now worth making. If the probabilities of the future overwhelm us there will be no future which men, as we have known men in the past, will wish to live. It is precisely the probabilities—even the certainties—that must change. And only education can perform that miracle.

I think we may be present at a greater moment than we know.

INDEX